The Ideal of Kingsh‌[...] of Charles Williams, C‌[...] and J.R.R Tolkien

CW01083255

Divine Kingship is Reflected in Middle-Earth

Christopher Scarf

In this distinctive work, Christopher Scarf explores the writings of the three most prominent Oxford 'Inklings' – Charles Williams (1886–1945), C.S. Lewis (1898–1963), and J.R.R. Tolkien (1892–1973) – to reveal and contrast their conceptions of the ideal of 'Kingship': divine, human, and mythological.

As practising Christians, the faith of all three writers was central to their literary and personal visions of Kingship, society, love, beauty, justice and power. Scarf investigates their belief in God as Creator and Heavenly King, opinions on the nature of His very being, and the way in which all believed the Creator to be unique rather than one among many. The relation between the earthly and heavenly King is considered, as well as the extent to which the writers contend that earthly kings are God's vice-regents, act with His authority, and are duty-bound to establish and sustain just and joyous societies. Examining the writings of all three men in detail, Scarf also highlights the covert evidence of their lives and personalities which may be discovered in their texts.

Dr Christopher Scarf studied Music at Wadham College, Oxford. He took a D.Phil. in English Literature at the University of Sussex. Once Assistant Organist at Ely Cathedral, he now lives in Devon, where he is Master of the Music at St Marychurch Parish Church.

©

for more information and to see our other titles, visit:
www.jamesclarke.co

Order Form

(Please use capital letters while filling in this form)

Name ....

Address ....

....

....

.... Postcode ....

Country ....

Tel. .... Email ....

Qty	Title		Special Flyer Price $	Running Total
......	*The Ideal of Kingship*	~~25.00~~	*22.50*	....

*Postage: Subtotal. ....

UK standard delivery: £4 for the first book and £2 thereafter.   P&P* ....

Europe & USA: £6.50 for the first book and £3 thereafter.   **Total** ....

Rest of the world: £11 for the first book and £5 thereafter. For orders of 5 or more copies, please contact us to arrange terms.

Payment Method:

Pro-Forma Invoice for payment before despatch of goods. ❑

Cheque for £.. made payable to Lutterworth Press.

Cash with Order: Please make sure that notes are sent by registered mail.

Card: Visa / MasterCard / Maestro

Card No.: ....

Start Date: .... Expiry Date: ....

Security Code: ....

Cardholder Details (if different than above)

Name ....

Address ....

....

....

Postcode ....

Country ....

Any Special Offer is only valid when presenting this leaflet.

Your Data: We would like to send you information on new books in your subject area by post or E-mail. If you wish to receive this information, please tick the box ❑

Conditions of Sale: Returns will be credited only if the items are received in perfect condition, and within 14 days of receipt.

Please return to: **James Clarke & Co**, PO Box 60, Cambridge, CB1 2NT, UK
Tel +44 (0)1223 350865 / Fax +44 (0)1223 366951 / orders@jamesclarke.co.uk

The Ideal of Kingship in the Writings of
Charles Williams, C.S. Lewis and J.R.R. Tolkien

Dedicated to the memory of Stephen Medcalf,
a great Christian, a great scholar,
a great man.

The Ideal of Kingship
in the Writings of Charles Williams,
C.S. Lewis and J.R.R. Tolkien

Divine Kingship is Reflected in Middle-Earth

Christopher Scarf

James Clarke & Co

James Clarke and Co
P.O. Box 60
Cambridge
CB1 2NT
United Kingdom

www.jamesclarke.co
publishing@jamesclarke.co

ISBN: 978 0 227 17401 2

British Library Cataloguing in Publication Data
A record is available from the British Library

Copyright © Christopher Scarf, 2013

First Published, 2013

All rights reserved. No part of this edition may be reproduced, stored electronically
or in any retrieval system, or transmitted in any form or by any means, electronic,
mechanical, photocopying, recording, or otherwise, without prior written
permission from the Publisher (permissions@jamesclarke.co).

Contents

The world was fair, the mountains tall,
In Elder Days before the fall
Of mighty kings in Nargothrond
and Gondolin. Who now beyond
The Eastern Seas have passed away . . .
J.R.R Tolkien, The Fellowship of the Ring, Book II, p. 330.

Preface

I have a vivid memory of being part of the excited crowd when King George VI and Queen Elizabeth the Queen Mother were visiting Birmingham in 1950. I was at the time a late teenager. The experience that stays with me the most poignantly is while looking at the royal visitors standing graciously on the steps of the Council House, a fine Victorian building in the city centre, I became suddenly aware of a feeling of 'Presence'. Like C.S. Lewis's character Jane Studdock in *That Hideous Strength*, I "*tasted* the word *king*". I was conscious of almost hearing words in my mind, thinking to myself, "He is not just an 'important man', not just an 'authority-figure' nor yet even a President: he is a . . . a King!"

What, indeed, did this powerfully evocative word convey? It was fortuitously around this time that I encountered C.S. Lewis at a Sixth-Formers' conference in Jesus College, Oxford. He told the dozen or so there virtually what he was later to have published as *Surprised by Joy*. His main impact on me was not even his actual route to conversion to Christianity; but rather the very depth of him *as a man*. Much more recently, and a little mysteriously, while sitting in the garden at home in glorious sunshine, in a somewhat reflective mood, I spontaneously became aware of the whole sentence that has long since become the sub-title of this book: "Divine Kingship is Reflected in Middle-earth". It was indeed a seedling – the germ of an idea that was later to develop into what I found compelled to embark on – an enquiry into the 'Mystique' of Kingship as expressed by the Inklings, Williams, Lewis and Tolkien.

Acknowledgements

I would like to thank Professor William Tamblyn for suggesting that I undertake research after supervising my M.A. I thank Professor Tom Shippey for suggesting that I write about *all three* of the *central* Inklings; to Professor R.E. Clements for encouragement and the gift of a copy of the "Proceedings of the Oxford Old Testament Seminar"; to Dr Paul Joyce for discussions on ancient Israel; to Dr Brian Horne for putting me in touch with the Emeritus Reader in English at Sussex, the late Stephen Medcalf, who supervised my doctorate, and to Professor Norman Vance, who supervised me after Stephen Medcalf's retirement. I thank the Tolkien Society for their invitation to lay a wreath at Tolkien's tomb at an 'Oxonmoot'. I thank the British Library and the Bodleian Library for access to manuscripts. I thank Dr Judith Priestman for illuminating discussion on the Inklings. I thank Roland Spahr at S. Fischer Verlag in Frankfurt-am-Main for information on Thomas Mann in connection with parallels in Lewis. I thank Dr Christopher Mitchell at Wheaton College in Illinois for encouragement and information. My thanks also go to Professor Grevel Lindop for access to one of Williams's unpublished letters; to Walter Hooper for the gift of an unpublished article of Lewis, and to Christopher Tolkien for generously affording me his opinions on his father's work. I thank Dr Veronica Groom for her support in the venture. I thank Adrian Brink at James Clarke & Co. Ltd, and especially my copy-editor, Bethany Churchard, for patience, insightful suggestions and for her kindly encouragement. Finally, I would like to thank my wife Margaret and my son Peter for their constant support and encouragement.

Christopher Scarf

Prologue

Who is he, the King of Glory?
The Lord Almighty –
He is the King of Glory.

Psalm 24:10.

The Inklings' Ideals of Kingship

I hope to explore the writings of the three central Inklings, the Oxford writers, Charles Williams (1886-1945), C.S. Lewis (1898-1963) and J.R.R. Tolkien (1892-1973), to discover and compare their concepts and ideals of 'Kingship', divine, human and mythological. This will involve investigating their beliefs as Christian writers in God as Creator and heavenly King, the nature of His very 'Being' and whether He is believed to be unique, rather than one among many. The relation between the earthly and the heavenly King will be considered, as will the extent to which the writers contend that earthly kings are God's vicegerents, act with His authority, and are duty-bound to establish and sustain just and joyous societies.

All three Inklings were Christians, Williams and Lewis as sacramental high Anglicans and Tolkien as a Roman Catholic. They all believed both in God and in His Creation. They saw God not only as Creator, but also as sustaining and ruling His creation as Creator-King. Their ideal of monarchy stemmed from this vision of God *as* King. This conceptual understanding has vital connections with their beliefs concerning love, justice and power, on earth as in heaven. An understanding of their individual but overlapping views of the essential meaning of kingship enhances an appreciation of their mental pictures of the world. To further our understanding of the 'world' that Williams, Lewis and Tolkien would have seen around them, the actual development of the historical notions of kingship will be referred to in order to contextualise the authors' writings.

I would suggest that all three writers ratify Christian ideals of kingship, running counter to the prevalent beliefs of their day (at least in intellectual circles) albeit we shall find different emphases when comparing and contrasting their distinctive views. These very emphases were themselves not *in toto* original, but show their authors' sympathies with extant concepts of sacral kingship. What, then, *are* these extant concepts and from whence do they originate? Was, for instance, the king's office always regarded as in some way sacred? Let us look at the Inklings' own emphases in *their* concepts of sacral kingship.

Tolkien, both in his writing of 'Story' and the 'Primary' (or 'real' world), saw a divine Creator with a benign purpose that derives from His essential nature. Tolkien presents us with a paradigm – an iconic picture – of the Judaeo-Christian divine King, whose primary quality is love of 'the Other', and the selfless love (*agape*) for others that is the prime mover in His act of Creation itself.[1] The same quality is 'reflected' in the 'Secondary World' of Middle-earth, as His creatures are made in His image. The kings are God's vicegerents, whose essential role is to create and defend their societies, and who should be able to live in what I call 'Collegiate Joy'. By this, I mean that this 'Joy' is contingent upon reciprocity of love to each other.

Lewis showed profound belief in God whom he saw as Heavenly King. Lewis was convinced of the truth concerning God's Son, whom he believed to be both redeemer and King. To Lewis, God was primarily immanent, that is to say, 'close to us', though with his deep sense of awe, of wonder, he also saw a transcendent God, that is to say, a God far above us, in whom he glimpsed a 'Glory' that afforded him what he called 'stabs of joy'. Due to his Ulster Protestant background, Lewis may have been more keenly royalist than he might otherwise have been, his loyalty to the United Kingdom being given to the monarch rather than the Westminster government.

Williams goes daringly further theologically than most previous writers. In *The Image of the City* (edn. 1958), he says he is willing to accept Creation as good in itself. He also accepts making creatures to share God's joy as "credible", and even allows the increasing of that joy by giving them the power of free will, leaving them free to choose whether or not to look for joy in Him. He endorses God's 'maintaining and sustaining' the universe in what he calls a state of "infinite distress", only because God is "fundamentally responsible" for the "finite choice" that resulted in it, and was willing to share it.[2] In his sonnets in *The Silver Stair* (1917), Williams creates a picture of the crucified king, crowned with a "jewelled circlet or with thorn".[3] Renunciation is allied with Christ's sacrifice of His Incarnation. The thorn is here equated with the King of Love, the jewelled crown suggesting the King of Glory.

In the context of the Inklings' belief in God as divine King, the use of the image of *King* for God will be recurrent in this study. The image occasions a complex problem that can conveniently be divided into two classes, *viz.* 'contextual' and 'inherent'.[4] Some writers, contemporary with the Inklings, have objected to their beliefs, questioning their truth. For example, at the first meeting of the Socratic Club in Oxford, Dr R.E. Havard said he had "deserted Christianity in the face of the advance of science". Dr Stephenson said, "Man's ideas of religion . . . were a direct gratification of his aspirations. . . . He created a God".[5]

There is also the problem inherent in the very use of the ancient image of *King* for God. Its very truth is challenged, asking if such use is actually valid. One must show, as Lewis says, *that* a belief is wrong before showing *why*.[6] The validity of using this image needs to be either upheld or opposed by reason. Is what is implied by the use of the image of *King* for God actually applicable? The reasons for the Inklings' beliefs, and the associated problem, provoke the underlying question, How does one *understand* their beliefs when one tries to imagine what it would be like if they were not true? To approach their shared and their individual tenets like this allows us to see more clearly what they actually were, why they held them and how they defended them.

Such a method is based on a supposition, one that is not only a hypothesis put forward to cast the Inklings' beliefs into stronger relief, but is pertinent in view of the times in which the authors lived, and the ideologies then in vogue, political, theological and philosophical. To understand better the Inklings' notions of the Ideal of Kingship, we need to explore them in the light of this problem, *inter alia*. To do this, we have first to discover what actually caused the problem raised by using the royal image for God. The contextual reasons were on several fronts: the theological element was itself multi-faceted. For example, Lewis referred to the "barricades" built "across the high road" of the "wayfaring Christian", by the modernistic writings of "the 'de-mythologisers'", in particular the theologians Rudolf Bultmann and Dr John Robinson, a former Bishop of Woolwich.[7] Bultmann's writing de-mythologized the New Testament to remove the need to believe what Lewis called "repellent" doctrines. For example, Lewis firmly believed in miracles, and, difficult as this may be to understand, disapproved of trying to give an historical event like the Resurrection, a seemingly more rational explanation, an explanation that derives belief in the miraculous. Such an explanation obviated the need for Bultman to believe in what Lewis thought Bultman saw as a "repellent" doctrine.

It was, as Lewis's secretary Hooper says, by "thinking them through" to the absolute end "that he [Lewis] arrived at his orthodox position".[8] Robinson had written, "In place of a God who is literally or physically 'up there' we have accepted, as part of our mental furniture, a God who is spiritually or metaphysically 'out there'". The bishop argued against belief in a transcendent God. "If God is 'above it all' he cannot really be involved". He also argued against the anthropomorphic image of "an old man in the sky", preferring Tillich's "ground of all being",[9] even if he (Robinson) *was* wary of ideas of either height or depth for God. In *Letters to Malcolm*, Lewis spoke of "the ground of the matter that surrounds me".

Of anthropomorphism, Lewis said, "Never . . . let us think that while anthropomorphic images are a concession to our weakness, the abstractions are the literal truth. Both are equally concessions", which he united dialectically in his idea of God.[10] He took, perhaps, a 'This also is Thou: Neither is this Thou' approach. The lion-King in Lewis's *Narnia* stories presents both a physical and an 'abstract' image as the Son of the Emperor-over-sea – allegorically God.

Controversially, Lewis contended in the revised version of *Miracles* (1960), that Naturalism gives us a "democratic" picture of reality and Supernaturalism a "monarchical" picture.

> In a real monarchy, the king has sovereignty and the people have not . . . in a democracy, all citizens are equal . . . for the Naturalist one thing or event is as good as another . . . The Supernaturalist, on the other hand, believes that the one original or self-existing thing is on a different level from, and more important than, all other things.

Lewis defined Naturalism as "the doctrine that only Nature – the whole interlocked system – exists". What the Naturalist believes "is that the ultimate Fact, the thing you can't go behind, is a vast process in space and time which is *going on of its own accord*".[11] In Lewis's *original* version of *Miracles* in 1947, he maintained that Supernaturalism may be suspected of rising "from reading into the universe the structure of monarchical societies". By contrast, "it may with equal reason be suspected that Naturalism has arisen from reading into it the structures of modern democracies". In chapter three, 'The Self-Contradiction of the Naturalist', he refutes the claims of Naturalism to explain the "'the whole show'" when he speaks of Naturalism's "irrational causes".[12] In the *later* version of *Miracles*, where he now entitles chapter three 'The Cardinal Difficulty of Naturalism', Lewis says, "Every event in Nature must be connected with previous events in the Cause and Effect relation. But our acts of thinking are events. Therefore the true answer to 'Why do you think this? ' must begin with the Cause-Effect *because*".[13]

At the Socratic Club in Oxford in 1948, the philosophy don, Elizabeth Anscombe, asserted that Lewis's contention that Naturalism was "self-refuting" was mistaken. Anscombe argued against the contention that "naturalism" is "self-refuting because it is inconsistent with a belief in the validity of reason", asking, "What sorts of thing would one normally call "irrational causes" for human thoughts?" Even Marxists and the Freudians claim to expose causes for various traditional beliefs. A Roman Catholic, she felt it unnecessary to go into his claim that one must either believe it (Naturalism) or be a Supernaturalist", that is, "believe in God".[14] It is notable that Lewis felt constrained to re-write chapter three of *Miracles* in view of the debate.

Linked with Supernaturalism and its association with Lewis's monarchic picture of reality is the question of Theism and valid reasons for belief in God. Lewis suggests that to the Naturalist everything "would still be 'the whole show' which was the basic Fact, and such a God would merely be one of the things . . . which the basic Fact contained".[15] Thus, to Lewis, it erroneously makes God appear to be 'one among many other things'. The choice tends to imply that God could not be both transcendent *and* immanent. Robinson had asserted that belief in a transcendent God suggested that He could not 'really be involved'.

With Theism and its attendant problems, if the image of *King* for God is to be even feasible, the idea of God *qua* God first needs to be feasible also. At the Socratic Club, Professor H.H. Price spoke of "the present phase of Western Civilisation". Price was debating the question: "Is Theism important?" Amongst other things, he said that he "would almost venture to suggest that no one can be a genuine Theist unless he has some sympathy with Polytheism, and some sympathy with still more primitive attitudes, such as Animism and Polydaemonism".[16] He said one needs to "pass through" such phases to "reach something better". Lewis "welcomed most cordially his sympathy with the Polytheists".

> We must admit that Faith, as we know it, does not flow from philosophical argument alone; nor from experience of the Numinous alone; but from historical events which at once fulfil and transcend the moral category, which link themselves with the numinous elements in Paganism, and which (as it seems to us) demand as their pre-supposition of a Being who is more, but not less, than the God whom many reputable philosophers think they can establish.[17]

Lewis said this (above), which indicates that, in this respect, he held similar beliefs to Williams. Williams affirmed his belief in the Incarnation, in an immanent God who, by definition, "permanently pervades the universe",[18] demonstrating in *The Image of the City* belief, unlike Robinson, in God's willing 'involvement'. Williams quotes Joseph Conrad: "Charity is divine and universal Love, the divine virtue, the sole manifestation of the Almighty which may in some manner justify the act of creation".[19]

Williams believes in God's justice. He states, "This then is the creation that 'needs' . . . justifying. The Cross justifies it to this extent . . . just as He submitted us to His inexorable will . . . He consented to be Himself subject to it . . . He deigned to endure the justice He decreed". [20] The 'decreed' justice is *partially* parallel with that of Lewis's Emperor-over-sea in the *Narnia* chronicles, where the lion-King frees Narnia through His self-sacrifice. The atonement through Substitution had, indeed, been 'decreed', but *not* actually caused, by the Emperor.

The lion-King, Aslan, is relevant only as taking part in an allegory of one version of the Atonement, in the form that Williams paradoxically, and perhaps surprisingly, seems to avoid, a simple, unconditional and straight Substitution. In fact, Substitution with certain provisos is not only a central thread of Christianity, but also one of Williams's central tenets. Neither in *The Lion, the Witch and the Wardrobe* (1950) nor in *The Magician's Nephew* (1955) does Lewis acknowledge Williams's difficulty that God actually accepts responsibility for our pain and injustice because He upholds the universe. In *The Image of the City*, Williams says the Cross "does enable us to use the word 'justice' without shame, which otherwise we could not. God therefore becomes tolerable as well as credible."[21]

Williams's view of Christ to whom he refers in 'The Redeemed City' in *The Image of the City* as "Christ the King"[22] is also found in *The Silver Stair* where, *as* Love, Christ the King of Love makes an act of Substitution for us. In 'A Dialogue on Hierarchy' in *The Image of the City*, Williams talks about the relevance to Society of "equality" and "degree". He speaks of almost a 'contention' between the "Hierarchy" and the "Republic", feeling that "both imaginations are necessary". His hierarchy is 'movable' from person to person, a movement he calls "Equality", his angelic and "heavenly occasions of movement". Society must also see these changes.

There are "stable hierarchies", but "in the organization of society . . . they are rather of honourable function than of individual merit. . . . The ancient monarchy of the English is one such. The anointed figure of the King does not 'deserve' to be royal . . . The hierarchies of function remain fixed". Williams sees in the King and his people a co-inherence (i.e., living in, and for, each other): "Each exists and is understood in the other, and their fruit in them".[23] 'Co-inherence' is an important idea in Williams's thought. In 'The Image of the City in English Verse' in *The Image of the City*, Williams upholds the unique position of 'the King', saying of hierarchy and the City, and alluding to Agincourt in *Henry V*, "'We few, we *happy* few, we band of brothers'. Falstaff has not, and could not have, *brothers*: the King is universal".[24]

Of Justice, Williams quotes *Measure for Measure*: "'If we lose this justice', Angelo says, 'the form of the State will break down'". Of the one thing necessary, living together in the 'City', in *Coriolanus* (1605-8), Williams tells us:

> The nobles cannot bear to live in poverty; Coriolanus will not allow of freedom, and the tribunes will not allow of obedience. It is not easily possible to find words for these opposed persons outside the play; they are made up of details, they are all of them right and yet all of them wrong in their rightness . . . The only way out would be for someone to accept the apparently impossible.[25]

Williams is interested in this kind of situation, implying that such 'Impossibility' is normal in human experience. He coined the term "the Impossibility" for what he saw as apparently contradictory, even "a contradiction in terms".[26]

A second facet of the contextual reasons for a problem in using the image of *King* for God is seen in the somewhat atheistic *Zeitgeist* of the mid-twentieth century. The forties were inclined to be secularist and the following decades were increasingly so, apart from the fifties. The 'death of God' and the Nihilism of Nietzsche, the Existentialism of Sartre and the atheistic Communism of Karl Marx, who said, "Religion . . . is the opium of the people",[27] were influential. There were also the atheistic psychoanalyst's claims of Freud. Humanist ethics is known by the way it makes the purpose of moral action the welfare of humanity rather than doing the will of God. The drift of the twentieth century was, therefore, 'anti-monarchical', with ideas like 'gods are deified rulers' being rife.

However, a classic twentieth century defence of monarchy is to be found in Harold Nicolson's *King George V: His Life and Reign* (1952). Nicolson said, "The influence which any British King or Queen is able to exercise is derived, not merely from the personal qualities of an individual Sovereign, but also from the respect and affection with which the Monarchy, as an institution, is generally regarded".[28] Nicolson was, in fact, an Atheist, who did not validate monarchy *via* the idea of a divine King. Defending it for different reasons, Walter Bagehot says in *The English Constitution* (1867), that "the best reason why monarchy is a strong government is, that it is an intelligible government". He said the King "was the Lord's Anointed", and the Monarchy "was a divine institution", and "the place of a constitutional king has greater temptations than almost any other", also that "A Republic has insinuated itself beneath the folds of a Monarchy". He said of royalty, "Its mystery is its life. We must not let daylight in upon magic".[29] Charles Williams was later in *James I* (1934) to describe the King as "Mystery",[30] though here Williams was *not* referring to a 'constitutional monarch'.

Some aspects of the problem of using the image of *King* for God are not purely from the philosophical ideas 'in vogue', but are actually inherent in the very notion of such imagery. The problem stems from questioning the reasonableness of using *any* image at all for God, as it would be bound to be inadequate, limiting the unlimited, indeed irrationally anthropomorphic. Portraying God as King, some would say, makes Him simply not credible. Even the idea of a '*good* king' is to some minds impossible. They do not (so they say) exist, thus seeming to invalidate the image. The greater the power of the king, (even in Tolkien's mythology) the greater is the risk of corruption. Some would argue that the foundation for using a royal image is based on impossibility.

However, Williams, Lewis and Tolkien took the converse view, saying what, as vicegerents, the earthly king *ought* to be in the light of the divine King's own attributes. Tolkien actually appears to have believed in the rightness of an absolute monarch in council. In a draft letter of c.1963, he described his ideal king as "*monarch*, with the power of unquestioned decision in debate",[31] advocating subservience, reminiscent of King Richard II's idea of "the subject's obligation of obedience to the king".[32]

Williams and Lewis, on the other hand, tend to stress the *symbolic* 'functions' of a monarch. The problem of the royal image relates to the need to underpin earthly monarchy with devolution from a supernatural being, king or otherwise. The Atheists would say that the ideal monarchy *could* not, therefore, be founded on the Creator-king since one does not exist. The Inklings suggested mythologically their image of *King* for God.

In the essay 'Myth Became Fact' (1944), Lewis suggested that "in the enjoyment of a great myth we come nearest to experiencing as a concrete what can otherwise be understood only as an abstraction".[33] Alluding to the myth of Eurydice's vanishing when Orpheus looked back at her too soon, Lewis is "trying to understand something very abstract indeed – the fading, vanishing of tasted reality as we try to grasp it with the discursive reason". The Inklings would look for 'reality' rather than 'truth', as Lewis says: "Truth is always *about* something, but reality is that *about which* truth is". Lewis maintains that:

> the heart of Christianity is a myth which is also a fact. The old myth of the Dying God, *without ceasing to be a myth*, comes down from the heaven of legend and imagination to the earth of history . . . By becoming fact it does not cease to be myth: that is the miracle.[34]

I would suggest that the Inklings see kingship applied to God in a mythical way of imagining Him. Tolkien said, regarding imagination, that "The mental power of image-making is one thing, or aspect; and it should be called Imagination".[35] It is difficult, however, to imagine God, not as an abstract 'truth' – even though He may well be that too – but as an existential reality.

To study the connection between Tolkien's idea of 'Imagination' and his creation myth helps our understanding of his underlying beliefs about God and divine Kingship. There were, indeed, gradual changes and philosophical developments in his view of 'Imagination'. However, was Tolkien actually deliberately and interminably ambiguous about different meanings of the idea of 'invention' or 'discovery' of what he calls 'Fantasy', or were there really gradual and definite 'changes' in his beliefs, especially regarding creation? Tom Shippey suggests that Tolkien's "conviction is that fantasy is not entirely made up", and that because he did not actually *say* this "in so many words", he "continually equivocated with words like 'invention' and 'no idle fancy'"[36]

Tolkien's definition of 'fantasy' was born "with a long haggle over the inadequacies of the *O.E.D.* [on which he once worked] and S.T. Coleridge", both as a "sub-creative Art" in itself, and also "a quality of strangeness and wonder in the Expression, derived from the image", thus implying that the 'Image' was there before anyone derived any expression from it at all. Tolkien "insists" that Elves "form an image, a true image, of the 'Elvish' craft of fantasy itself.[37] The 'gradual change' in Tolkien's outlook makes us question Shippey's assertion that Tolkien "*continually* equivocated" over the idea of 'invention'.[38] What, we ask, *had* Tolkien said 'in so many words' apropos of fantasy not being 'entirely made up'?

In a letter of "probably" 1951 to Milton Waldman, Tolkien said, "I had the sense of recording what was already 'there', somewhere: not of 'inventing'."[39] This was a clear retrospective account of his actual *experience*, including a decisive affirmation of his original philosophical attitude to the divinely-created world. The "Primary World" was, he said, "entirely the act of God".[40] Nevertheless, what do the Inklings say of God's existential reality?

As Lewis said, "Indeed, it is a speculative question as long as it is a question at all. But once it has been answered in the affirmative, you get quite a new situation. To believe that God – at least *this* God – exists is to believe that you now stand in the presence of God as a Person".[41]

In *Letters to Malcolm: Chiefly on Prayer*, Lewis discusses the experience of placing himself "in the presence of God". He remembers two 'representations', 'God' and 'me', which Lewis said he had created. He must, he says, "break the idol". He can, after this, "'place [himself] in the presence of God'". The "momentary confrontation . . . is certainly occurring". He stresses that "there is no question of a God 'up there' or 'out there'; rather, the present operation of God 'in here', as the ground of my being, and God 'in there' as the matter that surrounds me".[42]

This image is recurrent, we recall Tillich's – 'the ground of my being'. Lewis continues. "Thus and not otherwise, the creation of matter and the creation of mind meet one another and the circuit is closed. He is earnest when he adds, "May it be the real I who speak. May it be the real Thou that I speak to". God, he says, "must constantly work as the iconoclast. Every idea of Him we form, He must in mercy shatter",[43] which, of course, eventually must include the image of King.

Criticism has been levelled at the Inklings for a patriarchal view of monarchy. Tolkien and Lewis were for the greater part of the time "dogmatic patriarchalists", unless Lewis altered his usual view in *Till We Have Faces*, where he creates a convincing picture of a 'good' queen, in spite of her earlier exploitation of her servants. She is depicted in sharp contrast to her tyrannical and brutal father.[44] Lewis's heroine here stands out in what is otherwise a male-orientated world.

I hope to discover the meaning of Tolkien's Ideal of Kingship through exploring his mythological 'Story' found in the various versions of his Creation Myth, *inter alia*, and in the *History of Middle-Earth*, edited by Christopher Tolkien, who has graciously afforded me some valuable insights into his father's work. The Creator-King's creative thought and action, and the significance of the part given to the Angels – the Valar – in Creation will be sought. Tolkien's profound ideas were communicated through what he termed 'Story' rather than through discursive philosophical discussion, except, of course, in his letters. It was, indeed, in 'Story' that Tolkien told us what he had, as he put it, 'discovered' of the Creation of his Secondary World by a mythological divine Creator. We shall look also at the ultimate purposes of the Creator-King; and Tolkien's concept of an 'Ideal King', in whom he depicts a 'type' of Christ, who will establish, sustain and maintain justice, and create a joyous society. I hope to show how the Inklings believe that Creative writers play a part in revealing truth; and how divine kingship is 'reflected' in creating Collegiate Joy in Middle-earth.

PART ONE

Monarchy and Republic

Chapter One
Williams and the Historical Notion of Kingship

The single bliss and sole felicity
The sweet fruition of an earthly crown
    Charles Williams, *Shadows of Ecstasy* (1931), p. 61.

An Inkling

Williams's (1886-1945) ideal king is modelled on Christ the King. Williams's ideal kingly 'type' is, then, a 'mirror' of Christ. Through His sacrifice on the Cross, the suffering servant is the king who "reigned from the tree".[1] Williams's kingly characters 'reflect' Christ's sacrificial Love, *agape*, and also radiates the 'Glory' with which Yahweh "was entering the sanctuary".[2] The Ancient Hebrews had two words and two ideas for 'Glory', the first a shining light, as from a lamp at night, the second a more profound quality that evokes awe.[3] Williams's King leads and protects his people, bringing about conditions conducive to the creation of a peaceful, just and prosperous society. Like Tolkien, Williams's ideal king emulates the Anglo-Saxon *Rex Pacificus* who had "the same responsibility" (as his predecessor, the pagan priest-king) "for bringing 'peace and plenty' to his realm", as achieved by Alfred the Great.[4]

Charles Williams had been born in London and was an Englishman, an Anglican and, albeit with sympathies for republican ideals, a royalist. Alice Mary Hadfield, who worked with him "in the Oxford University Press at Amen House, London, . . . for six years", tells us in *An Introduction to Charles Williams* (1959), that it was in an area that though not "working class" was "drab and dominated by the massive bridge of the railway . . . His father was, like himself later, an ordinary rank-and-file member of a business firm in the City with a taste for literature".

Walter, Charles's father, Hadfield describes as having "always had a sense of helplessness before the economic and social world", in a time when Victorian industry "was suffering the second slump in ten years". This is significant because Walter had lost both his job and the greater part of his sight. The family moved to St. Albans in 1894, where his mother, Mary, took a shop. Williams went of his own volition to the Abbey every week, and he chose to read a great deal of Dickens. He won a Junior County Scholarship to St. Albans Grammar School in 1888. In 1901, he obtained a County Scholarship to University College, Gower Street, London, and started there in 1902. His time at University College lasted a mere two years, simply because his parents could not afford to keep him there any longer. He obtained a job "at the Bookroom, in Holborn, in 1904". Hadfield tells us that Williams "had another instinct" that though hidden, showed there was "another world and a deeper struggle". He became aware of his mother's "struggles with money", an awareness that created in him a "sense of guilt".[5] In view of Williams's early life, and the attendant serious stresses caused to his family by ever-present problems over money, it is small wonder that, although he was at heart an Anglican and a royalist, he was eager to see a society that was just, caring and egalitarian, in the way he truly believed was inherent in the ideal of a republic.

Williams and the Historical Notion of Kingship

As Williams's model is *Christus Rex*, it is not surprising that Williams regarded the office of the earthly king as sacred, in fact, as a 'spiritual' monarchy. In this, Williams mirrored the Anglo-Saxon idea that as the Old English term *giftstol* means both "king's throne and God's altar", the "person of the ruler . . . was sacred *ex officio*". In the Christian use of the image of the *giftstol*, the "sacred is described . . . in terms of the royal throne instead of the throne in terms of the sacred", the throne of the sacral monarch.[6]

Williams regarded the earthly king as the heavenly king's vicegerent, reflecting another idea of the Anglo-Saxons whose king, like St. Edward the Confessor is "king by the grace of God, *dei vicarius*", and as vicar of God, *ipso facto*, His vicegerent.[7] The ancient Hebrews believed that the king was "the Messiah of Yahweh", the 'anointed one', His vicegerent.[8] Kingship itself "came down from heaven".[9] Williams describes the coronation ceremonies, emphasising in his 'Arthuriad', in the collection of poems, *Arthurian Poets* (ed.1991), the importance of being anointed. The Archbishop anoints King Arthur with oil as Samuel anointed King David. Arthur's kingship is 'willed' by God. In *one* view of the establishment of the kingship among the Ancient Hebrews, in the 'Saul Tradition', the King was "specially commissioned for this high office".[10]

Williams sees a king who, somewhat like the Homeric king, "was at once the chief priest, the chief judge and the supreme war-lord of his people.[11] In his portrayal of King Arthur Williams presents a king who, if not actually chief priest, is the Pendragon, the Chief, the war-leader, who will bring justice and peace to the mythical land of Logres, which is to become the Britain that we know. Williams's ideal king is ready (though not without misgivings) to lead his people in war, even risking his own life for them, to promote peace and prosperity. In the *Arthuriad*, King Arthur is a *dux bellorum*, a war-leader like the Homeric king, a royal function long expected of the "earliest" of kings.[12]

An inherent part of King Arthur's 'justice' is his freeing of Logres from the tyrant, King Cradlemas, by force, the use of which makes Williams ambivalent. It could be argued that Williams would have preferred a Platonic republic to a despotic monarchy. Williams, to this extent like the Romans, had an abomination of tyrants, of unjust despots. Arthur's kingship is 'willed' by God. In Williams's *James I*, the King saw *his* kingship as 'willed' by God. He would have abhorred the tyrannical King Tarquin the Proud, the last King of Rome, who was both "ambitious and domineering", and had shown himself guilty of "high-handed tyranny".[13] Aristotle defined tyrants as "men who . . . seized kingship, and perverted it for their own benefit",[14] while the Romans "had a horror of monarchy", because "the word *Rex*" suggested "myths of tyranny and enslavement".[15] The Greek word *týrannos* had once meant 'king' or 'sovereign'; but came to have the connotation of tyrant.

Sophocles' *Œdipus Rex* translates the Greek 'Œdipus' as '*týrannos*'. Not originally meant in a 'pejorative' sense, it was "properly used of revolutionary despots". It would have been applicable to Cromwell, Napoleon, Stalin, or Idi Amin, but not to even the most blood-thirsty of hereditary kings".[16] Williams shows a profound desire to create the vision of a kingdom that engenders a truly just society. His envisaged king, whose office is holy, will earnestly strive to create a society that evinces the egalitarian qualities of a Republic. He is not even averse to an actual republic, although he remains at heart a royalist. The king, reflecting Christ, is there to serve his people, rather than to be served by them. This inclusive attitude in Williams calls to mind observations about sixteenth and seventeenth-century "royalist writers, whether in France or England", who had "no quarrel with other forms of government, when once established, whether elective monarchies or republics".[17]

Williams's magnanimous overarching perspective concerning right governance is echoed in John Buchan's *The Path of the King* (1921). Having eulogised the late President Lincoln, Buchan's Mr Lovell said as the coffin passed him: "There goes the first American", to which Mr Hamilton replied, "I dare say you are right, Professor, but I think it is also the last of the Kings".[18] Buchan, having seen a king-like quality in a republican President, said conversely in *The King's Grace* (1910-35), "Majesty and Grace are in the royal office. Monarchy in some form is universal". Speaking of King George V, Buchan said, "The King has led his people [as Buchan felt true of President Lincoln], for he has evoked what is best in them".[19]

Questing for an ideal society, Williams presents Logres as a kingdom which owed allegiance to the mythical Emperor of Byzantium. This Emperor, Lewis posits, symbolises God. Imperial authority, Dante insisted, emanates directly from God Himself. Nevertheless, Williams said in *The Descent of the Dove* (1939), "It is at least arguable that the Christian Church will have to return to a pre-Constantine state before she can properly recover the ground she too quickly won".[20]

Williams, with enthusiasm for the egalitarian qualities of a republic, makes it clear that the king has both to be just himself, not to use his kingdom for his own ends but also, as judge, to dispense justice. Williams reflects a Platonic ideal, that justice must be seen to be good *per se*, and this simply because it is morally right. His idea of royal justice stems from God's Justice, from Yahweh, who is just and dispenses justice. "Justice was of God and it seemed therefore best delivered by those most familiar with the holy sphere. . . . The king is the supreme judge".[21] The Hebrew King, God's Vicegerent, was responsible for the "administration of justice within his realm".[22] Williams is wary of the possession of royal power which, if used in extreme self-interest, is highly dangerous. Power is really safe only in God's hands, those of the Divine King, who overcame the "Chaos Powers".[23] Christ, the King of Love, used His royal power selflessly, and thus, very differently "from those who in days of old had been symbolically anointed".[24] Williams exemplified in his work the danger of misuse of royal power when King James I believed his Prerogative should not even be *discussed*.

James's exigency is only too reminiscent of Richard II's unshakeable belief in Divine Right, and *his* preoccupying "emphasis on the prerogative".[25] There is something of Emperor Augustus' 'restoration of peace' in Williams's ambition to have an 'ordered' society, the antithesis of a land without the 'form' of a Republic. Williams exhorted right use of royal Power, making it inherent in the symbolic bond between King Arthur's kingdom and the mythical Emperor of Byzantium – symbolising God. Developing classical ideals, where individuals should 'function' *pro bono publico*, Williams advocates the Christian principle that will achieve the Order he looks for in society. It will, he believes, be brought about by what he calls 'Co-inherence' when people, from the King down, live as "members one of another",[26] a Pauline doctrine arguably more profound than even equality.

Williams regarded a Christian kingdom as the kind of society where each member carries out their peculiar 'function' for the good of all. Williams saw a paradigm in Plato's ideal Republic, where justice is believed to be morally right. He prefers a freely made compact to a legally enforced contract. The king (or president) exercises his authority for the benefit of all, an idea encouraged by Socrates. The previously un-tamed land of Logres is established as a Christian kingdom when King Arthur has been anointed and crowned. Williams believed that once crowned, the King is Majesty, as he felt that King James I assumed. Williams saw 'Mystery' in contemporary monarchs, seeing a parallel between the spiritual monarchy of King George VI and the mythical Pendragon, King Arthur.

The King's Sacral Office and the Matter of Britain

Williams's most profound view of kingship is found in his treatment of the 'figure of Arthur' in two sequences of poems, *Taliessin through Logres* (1938) and *The Region of the Summer Stars* (1944). Williams convincingly portrays an organic fusion of apparently contradictory concepts, Sacral Monarchy and the Republic. He had made a real contribution to the expression of his concept of kingship in his early poetry, where the emphasis was on the divine king. He saw a direct connection between romantic love and the experience of that love which itself actually *is* God; and in Christ's kingship a coherence of both His love and His glory. *The Silver Stair* in particular illuminates Williams's ideal of divine kingship. However, the main focus will be on the *Arthuriad*.

Williams's *archetypal* king is Christ, the essential idea of whose kingship is twofold, a unity of self-sacrificial Love and kingly Glory. He saw in the Godhead a co-inhering trinity of persons who live in eternal reciprocity of love, who live *in* and *for* each other and who are, at the same time, *one* God. In the earthly king, especially in Britain, Williams finds a spiritual, in fact a Christian king, whose task is to enable the people to be a cohesive and just society. The king is the 'mirrored image', or perhaps the vicegerent, of the heavenly King, who will lead and protect his people, engendering peace and justice. Williams, drawing a distinction between the monarch *qua* monarch and as a private person, saw mystery in the monarch, whose office is holy: its fulfilment is his function as a private person.

Williams looked for equality in society. This indicates an egalitarian outlook that extends even to the king who, as a type of Christ, is there to serve his people, rather than the converse. He expected to find in a Christian monarchy the same quality he saw in his idea of a republic, where all co-inhere as equals. Williams's distinctive ideals are encapsulated in the *Arthuriad*, in which King Arthur the Pendragon, the leader or chief, is himself a pattern of sacral monarchy. Williams was not only recounting the Arthurian myths in a manner congenial to him, exploring the early British monarchy, but to obtain deeper understanding of its meaning in his own day, especially the reign of King George VI. That is to say, Williams saw in Arthur the epitome of a just, heroic king, faithful to his people, who maintains their well-being, a father to the nation, a generous, patient and temperate monarch, and a Christian withal. Williams's writing is still pertinent to the 'Matter of Britain' in the twenty-first century, enhancing greater awareness of the essentially spiritual nature of the monarchy of Queen Elizabeth II.

The twentieth century was an era somewhat atheistic and anti-monarchic, especially in intellectual circles, with regard to religious and political matters. The exceptions were, perhaps, during the reign of the genuinely devout King George VI, and especially during the war, when the people 'turned to God'. To an extent in opposition to the beliefs of his day, or to the lack of them, Williams creates in King Arthur an image, or type, of an earthly monarch who mirrors or reflects the heavenly King. He is God's vicegerent on earth, the very God in whom Arthur and Williams believe. In this spiritual monarchy, he portrays the creation of a potentially ideal society (the Christian kingdom of Logres before it became merely

Britain). He sees this kingdom as being just one part, the head, as of a body, and therefore the mind, of the much larger Byzantium. The independent, loving relationships between the different parts of the Empire, for instance Logres and Byzantium, are modelled on the Trinity.

Williams made a detailed study of the legends from as early as 1908. He made careful notes on the Arthurian theme in his *Commonplace Book*. In 1908, a significant year for Williams, he both fell in love with Florence Conway, who he married in 1917, and also became convinced of the inherent truths and the scope for poetry to be found in the Arthurian legends and Grail myths.[27] Since then, he had written poems on the legends in *Heroes and Kings*, published privately in 1930 and *Three Plays* in 1931.

Williams attaches considerable importance to the figure of the king in the actual history behind the legends, being eager to give his poetic treatment 'depth' and verisimilitude. He looks to the sixth-century historian and monk Gildas for the history of the Britons since the coming of the Romans, and to the ninth-century Welsh monk Nennius, whom he quotes: "Arthur fought with the Saxons, alongside the kings of the Britons, but was himself the leader in the battles".[28] Williams based his own version of the Arthurian myths on that of Sir Thomas Malory's *Morte D'Arthur*, printed by Caxton in 1485. This was itself based on various French and English versions of the legends, including four by Chrétien de Troyes (written in the second half of the 12th century), the *Roman de Brut* (1155), the *Vulgate Cycle* (1225-56) and *Morte Arthure* (early fifteenth century) among others. Williams was considerably influenced by some of the Victorian poets, in particular Tennyson, Swinburne, William Morris and Hawker of Morwenstow. A source, perhaps Williams's earliest, is the Victorian novelist, poet and essayist Thomas L. Peacock and his *The Misfortunes of Elphin* – the Elphin who found Taliessin in a "leathern bag".[29] The writing of the Taliessin poems began with "certain things in Malory".[30] Williams expresses a "vague disappointment" with the way in which "Tennyson treated the Hallows of the grail in Balin and Balan". Williams is not attacking Tennyson as a poet, but feels that "in this particular respect his treatment of the Sacred Lance as a jumping-pole left a good deal to be desired." Williams defends his position when he pleads that he is not claiming to be better than Tennyson", and also that the "great and awful myth of the Grail had not been treated adequately in English verse".[31] Williams believed that "the only English poets who have spoken almost worthily" of "Merlin" are Tennyson and Swinburne, and of the two Swinburne is for once the greater".[32]

Williams considers that the matter of Britain begins with the "freeing of Logres (or Britain) from the pagans and tyrants", which leads to the coronation of the king. What ought not to happen, "and what in Malory and Tennyson is already an almost minor episode, is his war against the Emperor . . . All that Tennyson says is that Arthur strove with Rome". Williams pointed out that the Grail had been an episode, but could no longer be accidentally so. Tennyson thought the Grail was "only for certain people, and he modified the legend accordingly". Williams felt that "Tennyson, in that sense, was right; he meant to make the Grail an episode, and he did". But "it is not, as in Tennyson, only for the elect; it is for all".[33] Tennyson's *Idylls of the King* (1856-85) and Williams's *Arthuriad* were similarly written without an overall narrative, and were related in episodes. Williams saw relevance for the times of King George VI in his recounting of the tales.

Tennyson went further and not only dedicated his *Idylls* to the memory of the Prince Consort, Prince Albert, and presented them to Queen Victoria, but he also explicitly said she would find there "some image of himself", that is, he saw King Arthur in the Prince Consort. When Tennyson presented this poem to his Queen, Victoria was ruler over the world's greatest empire. "There is implicit in the poem a warning that even the perfect King and the perfect Kingdom cannot survive the loss of faith".[34] Williams believed that "Tennyson was really writing (and very properly) a modern moral story, as he said he was. He could not – he did not even try to – get the Myth . . . The poet who, in an occasional touch, gets nearest to the tone of the Myth is Swinburne".[35]

In creating his kingly type, the great importance Williams attaches to the actual figure, or office of the king is seen in emphatic statements in "The Coming of the Grail" in *The Figure of Arthur*:

> It is to the French poets and romancers that we owe the bringing of this high myth into relation with Arthur, King of Britain or Logres, as it is to Geoffrey of Monmouth that we owe the development of the figure of Arthur the king out of the doubtful records of the Captain-General of Britain; and as we owe to Sir Thomas Malory the most complete version of the whole in the English language . . . It is perhaps worthwhile to reshape the whole tale here once more.[36]

In an unpublished letter of 9 November 1916 to Alice Meynell, Williams wrote, "If *you* say that Tennyson is final, I will drop the idea at once. But perhaps . . . Why were Tennyson and Patmore both so monarchical and Tory – not so much in direct politics as in idea? It seems strange that they were neither moved by the great drama of the Republic".[37] Lewis remembered Williams describing the growth of the legend in his mind and its form in his poems, and was to have in his "unwritten poems",[38] those he *intended* to write but never did. With the republicanism Williams expressed to Meynell, it is notable that in *The Figure of Arthur* (1945) he wrote, "But we cannot go behind the royalty invented. No one can ever uncrown Arthur. The king may have – indeed must have – the qualities of the Captain-General, but he must be the king".[39] In *The Calling of Taliessin* (1944), Williams looks back to the Old Welsh poem, the *Mabinogion*, and describes the land called Logres as disordered, with its kings at war. Taliessin finds a land without 'form': it has no 'public thing', no *res publica*. It is not a republic, an ordered State. For Williams, a president or a king may rule it, as long as its society is just, for as Rousseau says, "All legitimate government is republican".[40]

Co-inherence in the Kingdom: the Republic

Williams regards a Christian kingdom as a society where all fulfil their 'function' for the general good as a 'republic', and where everyone is an integral part of the body politic. This ideal of Society, the *res publica* is Platonic. In the *Republic*, justice is seen to be good for its own sake. To avoid wrong or injury, Plato says, "It will pay to make a compact with each other by which they forgo both",[41] a statement that anticipates the Social Contract of the seventeenth and eighteenth centuries.

Williams, like Plato, draws a continual analogy between the State and the human person, and in Williams's case, perhaps with the nature of the universe as well. Williams says, "a man is a small replica of the universe . . . 'a little world'".[42] Sympathetic to Plato's ideal, Williams exhorts each member of society to fulfil his or her 'function' for the good of all; and encapsulates this decree in a quotation from his book *The Figure of Beatrice: A Study of Dante* (1943) – "The proper operation (working or function) is not in existence for the sake of the being, but for the sake of the operation".[43]

Williams places this same quotation at the beginning of the two cycles of Arthurian poems, which is significant. Dante's injunction applies as much to the king as to everyone else, perhaps especially to the king and his 'function' on account of his great power. Williams sees in fulfilling one's 'function' the Pauline notion of living as "members one of another". He calls it 'Co-inherence' – living in-and-for each other. Co-inherence applies both to the people *and* to the king, from whom it spreads out like a vine. He people will endeavour to emulate the Christ-like inter-personal love that Williams sees existing between the Persons of the Holy Trinity.[44] Williams is aware of two types of society, that is, with and without co-inherence. In *The Calling of Taliessin* we are shown a land where it does not *yet* operate, a land where there is still a great deal of the in-fighting so graphically expressed by the sixth-century *historic* Taliesin (who before Tennyson had no second 's'),[45] in his elegy to Owain, the son of King Urien of Rheged. It displays a harsh atmosphere, including a sinister play on the word 'sleep'.

<blockquote>
When Owain killed Ffamddwyn
it was no more
to him
than to sleep.
The great host of Lloegr
sleep with a glaze in their eyes.[46]
</blockquote>

Williams shows a society, if indeed it is as yet a 'society', in which Man lived. Thomas Hobbes (1588-1679) would have dismissed it simply as "a state of nature, before there is any government". Bertrand Russell (1872-1970) points out that Hobbes's view is that "every man desires to preserve his own liberty, but to acquire dominion over others; both these desires are dictated by the impulse to self-preservation". From continual conflict arises a state of war against all, which makes life, in Hobbes's brief description, "nasty, brutish and short". To escape from such "evils", Hobbes suggests gathering each subject into a central authority by means of a "social contract". The people would come together and choose a "sovereign, or a sovereign body". Russell says that "Hobbes prefers monarchy, but all his abstract arguments are equally applicable to all forms of government in which there is one supreme authority not limited by the legal rights of other bodies".[47] Such is one view of the causes of Taliessin's 'wild land'. Williams, though, saw vicious, self-seeking aggression as the result of the historic Fall of Man, his Primal Curse. For Williams, there was only one satisfactory answer to the tragedy of Man, he must be reconciled to his Creator.

Williams saw reconciliation being made available through the Holy Eucharist, through the Body and Blood of Christ, which he symbolised as the Holy Grail. Williams said later in "The Cross" in *The Image of the City* (1943) that, on the Cross, Christ had

> substituted Himself for us. He submitted in our stead to the full results of the Law which is He . . . By that central substitution, which was the thing added by the Cross to the Incarnation. He became everywhere the centre of, and everywhere He energised and reaffirmed, all our substitutions and exchanges.[48]

Williams emphasises the vital actions of Christ, whose self-sacrificial love necessarily preceded the return of His glory. In "The Redeemed City" in *The Image of the City*, Williams said that after His substitution of Himself for Man, He asked the disciples whether Christ "*ought* not to have suffered these things" before entering into His glory? He then celebrated for them the great exchange of the Eucharist – "and vanished". Very pertinently he added, "It was by an act of substitution that He renewed the City; this He had commanded as the order in both nature and grace".[49]

It is hardly surprising, then, that Williams was keen not only to recount the legend of King Arthur as Malory told it, but also to give due attention to the Grail element. It is through Christ that Williams sees the ultimate redemption and *renewal* not only of 'the City', his figure for all society, but of Logres and the country of Britain it would become.

Chapter Two
Williams and the Vicegerent

The Ideal of Monarchy as God's Will

Logres and, by extension, Britain's founding on a king was, Williams indicates, in accordance with God's will. In *The Calling of Taliessin*, Merlin tells Taliessin that he and his sister Brisen were sent by their mother Nimue "to build, as is willed, Logres, and in Logres a throne / like that other of Carbonek, of King Pelles in Broceliande".[1] "As is willed" implies a *providential* 'will' or 'purpose'. Although Williams sees the establishment of a kingdom in Britain as 'willed', he did not always insist that a Christian country *must* have a king. There is a significant conversation in *Shadows of Ecstasy* (1931). Sir Bernard asks " . . . Why is royalty so impressive?" "It's the concentration of political energy in a person", Caithness said thoughtfully, "the making visible of hierarchical freedom, a presented moment of obedience and rule" "I think I prefer the Republic", Sir Bernard said, "It's the more abstract dream".[2]

Williams sometimes sympathises with republicanism in his early poetry. Despite this, he remains a monarchist. However, in an early poem called 'Conformity' in *Poems of Conformity* (1917), he spoke eloquently in favour of the French Revolution and the establishment of a Republic, after the destruction of the monarchy of King Louis XVI. Williams gives unequivocal approbation to "An England praised of Milton joins / The France that learned Rousseau".[3] One may conjecture that Williams's position is, perhaps, attributable to constitutional monarchy after 1688 under William and Mary. Lewis points out in *A Preface to Paradise Lost* (1942), dedicated to Williams, that while Milton *did* indeed uphold the "monarchy of God", he would not countenance the idea of the rule of "one man over other men".[4] Milton was no monarchist, but a Republican. Still upholding the ideals of the republic, Williams, welcoming the French Revolution, wrote in 'The Wars' in *Poems of Conformity*, "Lo, the Republic comes!" Fourteen lines later he says of the French Republic, "France, taught of Rousseau and Voltaire . . . struggling to be free / from tyrants, their fraternity".

Williams is driven by his profound respect for freedom. Attacking the outright tyranny caused by unlimited acts of extreme self-interest, Williams welcomes the Russian Revolution, in the "falling stones of Petrograd", and exchanges the "King" for "brotherhood".[5] Here, Williams, like Milton, suggests that only God rules over all. Williams referred to the French Revolution and those who provoked it. When he speaks of France being "taught" of Rousseau, it is Rousseau's actual ideas to which he refers. Rousseau's maxim in Chapter I of *The Social Contract* (1762, tr. 1782) reads, "Man was born free, and he is everywhere in chains".[6] This statement has, from the French Revolution's terror to the Directorship of the proletariat, been used as a basis for revolution. Rousseau's statement that a man "shall be forced to be free" has echoes of totalitarianism, and insinuates the making of yet another tyrant.

However, Williams still lauds the idea of founding a Christian monarchy in Logres and Britain. The matter of the Grail and the founding of a Christian society on a king are essentially inseparable. Williams ideal of the divine king and His will based on love, are literally and figuratively 'crucial' rightly to understand his type of earthly king as God's Vicegerent. Williams shows in the *Taliessin* poems, the interchange, the love for others at its very origin, and his distant vision of the co-inhering Trinity – "each in turn the Holder and the Held".[7] In 'The Way of Exchange' (1941) in *The Image of the City* (edn. 1958) he said:

> The later definitions of the inspired Church . . . declared that the Father and the Son existed co-equally, but that they existed co-inherently – that is, that the Son existed *in* the Father and that the Father existed *in* the Son. The exact meaning of the preposition there may be obscure. But no other word could satisfy the intellect of the Church.[8]

Williams makes an almost miraculous leap from the spiritual world of the co-inhering Trinity to the physical world in which we live. He is not describing a mutually exclusive situation but one where both worlds co-inhere in an 'impossible' *union*, a union he sees in the Person of the divine Son, the Incarnate Christ. Williams said we are not divided from God or each other, for Christ's nature is not divided.[9] Williams believed that the highest level of Christian dogma is that of "Exchange between men and God in the single person, who is, by virtue again of that Manhood, itself the City, the foundation and the enclosure".[10] That is, the coexistence of God and Man as one body.

Williams's ideal king will be based, then, on Christ. Williams creates a picture of the way this exchange takes place through Christ's love. God 'wills', or we might say 'longs for', out of His infinite love, our greatest good. The wondrous patience which anthropomorphically I have called 'longing', is an intrinsic part of what God, in Himself essentially *is* – Love. This longing implies some element of willing suffering, as does the word 'patience' itself, its practice born of self-sacrificial love and renunciation.

The 'Vicegerent's' Model: Christ the King of Love

Williams gave us his overall picture of Christ the King in an early sequence of poems, *The Silver Stair* (1912), where several key concepts concerning His kingship are expressed. In discovering these concepts we see the model for God's vicegerent. The eighty-four sonnets in *The Silver Stair* were written ostensibly as love poems for Florence Conway. They portray some of Williams's earliest ideas on kingship, especially Christ's. The love content and the ideal of kingship are closely connected. For example, the love of Florence is equated with the love for God. Williams even personifies the abstractions life and love, using images like "Love's palaces", though images pertaining to 'the City' predominate.[11] Reflecting on what Williams expressed later on the question of love and kingship, we find that in *He came down from Heaven* (1938), he sheds light on a further connection between romantic love and kingship in Dante's experience of love for Beatrice. His 'falling in love' – "the pre-eminent moment" is comparable to one of Wordsworth's 'spots of time' and was "like a state of adoration".

Dante's "experience" of the sight of the beloved girl gave him a "sense of intense insignificance", namely that "an explanation of the whole universe [was] being offered".[12] Dante's experience widened into a theophany as he saw, as it were, divine "light" and "glory" disseminated from Beatrice, the light and glory of Christ. He saw her as a "visibly miraculous . . . means" of assisting our faith in Him. Williams saw this as "the Dantean equivalent of the first coming of the kingdom," by which he means Christ Himself. Dante's first experience of Beatrice, when she greeted him in the city, had filled him with "beatitude, a state of bliss". Later, she "snubs him, and she dies". The "loss of [his] beatitude" takes away his "exultation". Initially, Dante had found "self-forgetfulness", which had made room for "adoration", for the "vision of the divine glory". It had been an actual "means of salvation".[13] Dante imagined he saw another young woman called Giovanna who, allegorically, is followed by Beatrice, as was St. John by Christ. Beatrice radiates "divine light", and "is the Mother of grace, and even of the occult God,"[14] who is made miraculously visible. She is the means of Dante having the 'Impossible' experience, as it were, of seeing God in Beatrice.

Williams regarded this as "a result of the Incarnation". After her death, Dante imagined finding his way to a mountain, where he went through the purging of his sins, especially of envy, jealousy and pride. He sees Beatrice and "paradisally recovers the perfect knowledge of the good". He sees her facing the "two-natured Gryphon of Christ" and the "reflection" of those natures. "Romantic Love is seen to mirror the Humanity and the Deity of the Redeemer".[15] In Paradise, Dante sees more clearly what he first saw when Beatrice greeted him in the city.

Williams connected the experience of falling in love with the "Incarnation of the kingdom". In parallel, Beatrice's death does *not* in Williams's eyes mean her "non-existence". Her glory, like Christ's, is real, whose "disappearance has not been supposed to invalidate" His fact and authority. Williams believed that "to be in love must be followed by the will to *be* love", to the beloved, to all and to be, like Christ, perfect. The experience of "communicated humility and goodwill" is that of the kingdom", the kingdom which "came down from heaven and was incarnate". The kingdom is seen through a "carnality of joy. Love's "divine nature" is "united with our 'undivine' nature. That, by definition, is "the nature of the kingdom". Williams sums up Dante's resurrection from his 'loss of beatitude' with Beatrice's death, saying that "to love is to die and live again; to live from a new root".[16] In the Incarnation he sees the King who is the pattern for earthly monarchy.

Twenty years earlier, in *The Silver Stair*, we can see Williams's emerging concept of kingship. Newly in love, he describes "the woman loved" as the "Regent from the immovable throne of God" in the sonnet *That the Love of a Woman is the Vicegerent of God*. We find the "direct experience of God in loving her". The lover "sees the Passion of Incarnate Love",[17] with its two meanings – physical erotic ardour and that piety associated with suffering. Already linked with sacrifice inherent in Incarnation, Williams poetically if not practically gives God a "throne", implying the image of *King* for God. His poetic "Regent" is not only the 'woman loved', but also Christ, the image underlined by the expression "Incarnate Love".

Williams emphasises renunciation involved in the very making of that sacrifice. He writes: "Choose now thy present for the king . . . when thou com'st to die". Evidence of Christ's nature is shown by the poet's choice – "fashioned in work of silver or of gold",[18] silver symbolising the sacrifice of renunciation, even used in the title of the poems. Silver may suggest youth and gold maturity or silver may, indeed, mean virgin, the "virgin loves" of another poem.[19] Williams tells us that *The Silver Stair* "was meant as a study in and songs of virginal love".[20] He pursues the link between renunciation and sacrifice when, again, he writes: "The silver and the golden stairs are His / the altar His",[21] the word 'altar' suggesting sacrifice. This is evidenced by the way in which Williams deals with the themes of 'Affirmation of Images' and the way of 'Negation of Images'. He seeks the profound mysteries shown only to those who follow the latter way. He refers to the 'ascetic Way' of the rejection of images[22] when he writes: "They builded palaces of silver stand . . . That they may follow thy virginity".[23]

Renunciation and virginity become even stronger when Williams speaks of the 'self-emptying love' of God in Christ, which we call *Kenosis*. He asks: "In sight of stretched hands and tormented brows / How shall I dare to venture or to win / Love?" Williams says, if Love is crucified, nevertheless, it *is* Love, "His it is, not another's",[24] the altar clearly referring to the Cross.

Williams writes in 1943 in 'The Cross' in *The Image of the City*, that Christ's "central substitution . . . was the thing added by the Cross to the Incarnation".[25] He is true to orthodox Christian doctrine where *kenosis* is concerned, in that Christ 'empties Himself', as St. Paul said, *by* 'taking on the form of a servant'. It shows the depth to which renunciation had led Christ.[26]

The Vicegerent's Hope: the King of Glory

Williams believes that, because of the Fall, King Arthur cannot emulate Christ *as* king. Through the benefits of the passion remembered in the Eucharist, *anamnesis*, the king is able to be reconciled to God, and redeemed from the failure that the Fall inevitably brought about and enter, like Christ, into his royal Glory. Christ is portrayed as redeemer as Williams shows the 'impossible' union between God as King and Judge before whom we come after death and, ironically, God who *as* Love must *be* judged. Williams writes in another sonnet, "Love [The king] . . . must go / Unto the Pavement . . . abjure His love deifical, set aside His comeliness", thus renouncing 'on oath' His timeless sharing in divine love and glory. Addressed as "Heir of kingdoms . . . these are the laws whereto thyself shall swear", Christ is again seen having 'deigned to endure the justice He decreed'. Williams said in another poem, that Christ either took up His "majesty, His pride, / Leaving a memory of God crucified" or that He dwells "apart in His disdain, / hearing the worlds cry out in vain".[27] The crucial expression here is "God crucified".

Williams asks: "With what shall we "crown our lord", offering the choice of a "jewelled circlet" for a king's crowning, or a painful symbol of criminality, "with thorn"? The figure of rejection gives way to that of affirmation: "Let Him . . . to His throne be borne . . . God is He: Hearken"![28]

Williams's use of intentional ambiguity between glory and sacrifice instances his expression 'The Impossibility'. In 1943, in the 'Introduction' to *The Letters of Evelyn Underhill*, Williams "coins the phrase 'the Impossibility'" for a situation when Underhill had to live "out a contradiction in terms". Cavaliero says, "The paradox is borne out by the fact that the Impossibility is both the experience of, and the summons to, the Cross."[29] Williams combines the 'Impossible' options – the 'jewelled circlet' and the 'thorns' in the king *and* victim of the 'decreed justice'. He tells how the "Heir of kingdoms . . . assume(s) possession of His dignities", taking up His royal power, having kept His own laws.[30] Williams addresses the King's followers with a direct communication from God after the Resurrection as a voice suddenly and commandingly says: "Why seek ye still the living with the dead? He goes before you into Galilee". Williams again speaks about the followers. "Love called us . . . for three years we followed after Him", as the disciples followed Christ, living in co-inherence with the King.[31] The poet says to the lovers, "Draw near: Himself Love gives you in His feast".[32] The King invites the lovers to share in the Eucharist: the words "Draw near" traditionally symbolise sacrifice. Williams speaks of the "mysterious cup", anticipating the place taken by the Grail in the *Arthuriad*.

In *The Silver Stair* we have a glimpse of the heavenly City that is to be the pattern for the earthly capitals, in Byzantium and in London-Logres. In a brief vision of heaven, Williams takes the lovers "out of the gate of

Time's regality", where Time has sway, bringing them "to the borders of his realm . . . herein is joy".[33] He shows the lovers a vision of eternity, beyond time, a vision of the City of the King, His capital, like Sarras, the heavenly city of the old Arthurian romances.

Taliessin the King's Poet: Order

Logres lay
without the form of a republic, without letters or law,
a storm of violent kings at war – smoke
poured from a burning village in the mid-east,
transport had ceased, and all exchange stilled.[34]

In *The Calling of Taliesin*, it was to this essentially untamed land that King Arthur was to come. Taliessin the king's poet whose "true region is the summer stars", with implications of Sarras, says, "Every king shall call me Taliessin",[35] recalling the prophecy in the *Mabinogion*, where, in "Taliesin [with one 's'] the poet answered the king, who had asked him "what he was", that "At length every king will call me Taliesin".[36] He "heard a word of the empire", of Byzantium, magic, the "former spells" of Adam and thus of the Fall, and of hope through "The Second Emperor at operative Byzantium". Logres is to be built 'as is willed', fulfilling God's 'will'. This involves a sense of vocation. In *The Calling of Taliessin*, Taliessin follows *his* vocation as he "sought the sea and the City".

Taliessin is being drawn to the City for a purpose. As warrior poet, the bard of Old Welsh poetry, he took his 'covered harp' and "a sword of Rome",[37] both of which are symbols of civilisation and defence. Williams's symbol of 'order' is 'the City'. Order, that is to say 'Order' in society, though not in any sense hierarchical, signified perfection, order frequently symbolised by the 'straight hazel stick', whether used for the harsh discipline of a slave or for exact measurement. He sees in the concept of order a significant pattern for kingship in that it enables co-inherence. Order is inherent in the Imperial City of Byzantium, the order that should persist not only in Byzantium itself but also throughout the Empire.

Lewis says Williams's "whole conception of Arthur's kingdom", and therefore of any Christian monarchy, "and the offered grace of the Grail are attributed to the Emperor. From this point of view, the Emperor symbolises God". The Empire is symbolised "as an organic body, a human body." Lewis stresses the need to "see with our imaginations why God should be so envisaged", suggesting that Williams saw in Byzantium and the Emperor one who actually creates a beautiful and splendid sense of order in what "he often referred to simply as the city", that is, as society. Williams's awareness of order reminds us of the policeman whose "hand held them up" in his novel *The Greater Trumps* (1932), which had made Henry think of the divinely, or at least papally accredited Emperor Charlemagne "or one like him [who] stretched out his sword over the tribes of Europe . . . order and law were there".[38] However, the Emperor's *and* the policeman's authority both rest on the potential use of force, of which Williams is both aware and uncomfortable. The same military force was necessary to establish Charlemagne's empire and, as found in Williams's *Mount Badon* (1958) and the 'extra poems' published by David Dodds, Arthur's kingdom.

There is, however, another side to Williams's concepts of 'Law and Order'. Does this other side suggest anything untoward in Williams's delitescent view of monarchy? With repeated references to 'straight hazel rods', there is some tension between his "loving-kindness" and a "certain sadism", which weakness of his nature could be reconciled within himself and "turned to good".[39] The underlying question is whether he really advocates totalitarianism, a concept far from unknown in the twentieth century. Perhaps Williams cannot easily reconcile his co-inherence with the guilt-inducing use of force, even to achieve good ends.

Is Williams really Totalitarian?

Robert Conquest, to some extent anticipating the theses of Michel Foucault in 1957 in his article 'The Art of the Enemy', interprets Charles Williams's writings in terms of the party struggle of the twentieth century. Poet, historian and critic, he believes "the effects of totalitarian thought on art" have been explored by several writers, and that Williams exemplifies those who fully accept a "closed and monopolistic system of ideas and feelings", and that he did so with the "libidinal component scarcely disguised", thus ruining his "admirable talent". Conquest regards Williams's ideological "straightjacket" as religious. Williams is accused of omitting the "Christian virtues proper", failing to mention humility and pity except as "orthodox trappings". Conquest asserts that Williams may not justifiably seek a defence in Dante, whose ideas *were* acceptable in the Middle Ages, though they would *not* be so today.

Conquest regarded Williams's 'Arthuriad' as his "masterpiece", a view shared by Lewis in his analysis of the poems. Conquest thought that Lewis expressed the same ideas more coarsely and crudely. Conquest also said that Williams's symbolism is generally "too elaborate and complicated for poetry", for instance that Byzantium represents God seen as hierarchy.[1] Lewis is quoted: "Order envisaged . . . as beauty and splendour".[2] This, the literary scholar Stephen Medcalf suggests, is totally misleading; the ellipsis covers up words that quite alter the case. What Lewis actually said was, "Such is Byzantium – Order envisaged not as restraint nor even as a convenience but as a beauty and splendour". This is a more abrupt definition than Williams's own – "Byzantium is rather the whole concentration of body and mind than any special member. The Lady Julian I found last night says that the City is built at the meeting place of Substance and Sensuality."[3] Lewis saw 'order' not as something limiting or constraining, but as something beautiful, like getting the steps of a minuet right, and finding joy in it, whereas Williams tended to emphasise the serious effort made by the whole individual to conform, also suggested in his own poem, *Conformity*.

In Conquest's view the Arthurian cycle is a very complicated series of episodes. When everything is "worked in", the "self-reflexive symbolic pattern is too much for poetry". The hierarchical Byzantine attitude is reflected in Williams's style, though much of his verse Conquest admits is of a "high quality" with, for example, effective use of the "recurrent image", such as in *The Calling of Taliessin*, where "the summer stars" is very effectively repeated several times. Nevertheless, there is, Conquest claims, overall "failure", due to "a central error". Williams and Lewis sneer at those who do not accept that the whole truth is available, lesser creeds deserving the "unattainable whip" or the "labour camp".

In a questionable attack, Conquest suggests there is a marked "tendency to terrorism", and "pleasure in and justification of corporal punishment". The notion that "force" should be used to bring in "unbelievers" is present throughout. The scar of the "whip" or "sword" on the slave-girl's back is seen as an aesthetic pleasure for Taliessin, though her flogging with the hazel stick was simply a part of Logres at its height. The barbarian is made a slave, "compelled to come in", and whipped. This is deemed entirely desirable, a harsh idea of discipline central to Williams's whole position. Williams's symbol of order and discipline is, then, the hazel rod, an appropriate implement both for exact measurement and for beating a slave. Totalitarianism's appeal is directly linked in Conquest's view with the "impulse to power and cruelty", crude in Hitlerism, but subtler in Stalinism, especially in the way it was presented to intellectuals: Williams and Lewis apparently belong to the "refined type".[4]

Conquest unjustifiably exemplified the 'refined type' of totalitarianism, perhaps a little sarcastically, the suggestions that the lost may be treated cruelly, and justifiably at that. Conquest is unjust in accusing Williams or Lewis as 'totalitarian' – though some sadism appears in Williams's work. Lewis makes the claim, (as, in fact, does Williams in the *Prayers of the Pope*, 1941) that "We confess and declare our coinherence in them while they deny their coinherence in us". Pity and regret are at times shown to "higher class" sinners, like Lancelot. What is wrong about sadism, Conquest claimed, is not so much the personal element, but rather its use to justify an authoritarian intellectual system, the source of some of the "greatest evils".[5] Conquest accuses Williams, in his verse, of identifying with order, religion and art, using words like "precision" and "accurate" of order, and their opposites to describe "chaos", insinuating that the uses of the hazel rod for measurement and for punishment are virtually identical.

Some totalitarian regimes give a seemingly 'objective' basis for using force and cruelty, for example the Pharisees said that it was *right* that one man *should* die for the people, though Williams usually uses this imagery of precision reasonably discreetly, except when it is ruined by being associated with metaphysical self-justification. Conquest said that Williams uses words like style and tincture, but these words can lead into a heavy 'imperial' vocabulary – words like "porphyry" and "glory". In Williams's poetry the "hierarchical attitude" is, so Conquest claims, essential to his position, and it is no accident that in Logres society is based on slaves, who are not all barbarians, incidentally.

The hierarchical society, Conquest maintains, starts from the slaves at the bottom to the Lords, and on to King Arthur. Position in society is not based on virtue. Slaves are put in the stocks for brawling, except when Sir Kay finds that a slave is a friend of one of the Lords.[6] On the other hand, Arthur, Guinevere, Lancelot, Morgause and Mordred are much more sinful. Conquest says that the cynical reason the leaders are on top is simply that it happens to be "the will of God". Arthur thinks he is only fornicating: he is actually committing incest; and Balin kills his brother Balan without actually knowing who he *is*. Conquest, being unable to see the need for slavery and hierarchy to the context of the legend, accuses Williams and Lewis of manipulating their system of intellectual abstractions, and of trying to force on others a total acceptance of their ideology. This is the opposite of "Lewis's enemy Keats", as Conquest describes him, who saw as the essential for a poet "negative capability". Keats "noted" it is "a weakness of the mind and not a strength to feel that one must have settled opinions about everything".

Conquest, in a politicised and over-deterministic reading influenced his historical context, writing in the 1950s with the onset of the Cold War, denounces *Williams* for "surrendering" his talent for his system, a system of totalitarian thought, hierarchy and sadism. It should be emphasized that Williams's 'sadism' is, in fact, of a personally despotic, rather than of a political nature. Conquest would have been more sympathetic to Williams's work if he had not misunderstood this aspect of his character. As for the policeman in *The Greater Trumps*, Lewis said, "The modern world . . . has poets not a few; but they rarely see beauty in policemen". "No, indeed," replied Conquest.[7] The Order seen in the policeman, the "metropolitan copper" is, as Pitt discerningly remarks in a critique of Conquest, "not imposed but discovered". Pitt instances how Taliessin's eye caught "each smallest insect dance pattern in the air". He is not drawn to the slave girl "because she is a slave, but because of the grace of her movement".

In *The Sister of Percivale*, in part one of Williams's *Arthurian Poets*, 'Taliessin through Logres' (p.11), the slave girl's "bodily movement" is "fused" with the heralding of Blanchefleur as "A trumpet sound from the gate leapt level with the arm". Taliessin saw in the girl "the awareness of his journey through the Empire". A woman's body is made an image of the Empire and its symbol because, in the perception of the lover or the poet, the human body reveals that *"unity in difference"* that is at the "heart of order."[8] Williams's central theme is surely the primary Christian virtue of Love, self-sacrificial and romantic, of 'Exchange', 'Substitution' and of life lived in 'Co-inherence'. While we should not see Williams as actually totalitarian, we must concede there is a decidedly violent atmosphere in *Mount Badon*, Arthur's battle for the taking of Camelot. Arthur is to this extent like Charlemagne, who killed a number of people to establish his empire. Lewis had said that kings exist "for the sake of kingdoms: not *vice versa*. And Arthur is already wrong about this". We see that what destroys the kingdom "is not the king's incest, but the king's totalitarianism",[9] his egotistic subjugation of the kingdom.

Williams said the result of the 'Dolorous Blow' has to "work itself out through the King". Arthur and his two sisters, Morgause and Morgan, are:

man loving himself and hating himself. This, and not mere incest, is the reason that Mordred is born of Arthur and Morgause. And Mordred is entire egotism, Arthur's self-attention carried to the final degree. This is why it is he [Mordred] who wrecks the Round Table.[10]

Chapter Three
Williams and Life in the Kingdom

The King's Coins: Exchange

In *Bors to Elayne: on the King's Coins* (1938), there is an attempt to make the kingdom "serve" the "aristocracy of Logres", in fact "to make the machinery of power autonomous".[11] Far from promulgating totalitarianism, Williams warns about the serious dangers to society if the king chooses "the kingdom made for the king".[12] That is, if he sets up a monetary system that has the potential to become not *a* useful medium of exchange for the people, but *the* new medium with its own "autonomous" life. This autonomy is like the way we speak of money giving us independence, whereby we start to forget the other kind of exchange, the exchange of services, as when Elayne and her women bake the flour sown and harvested by the men. Williams evinces the potential both for tyranny and for good when Kay says that "Money is *the* medium of exchange" and twenty-five lines later, the Archbishop says, "Dying each other's life, and living each other's death, / Money is *a* medium of exchange", as the people live and die for *each other*.[13] Sir Kay is full of praise for the new coins and for "controlling the world" more effectively than "the swords of lords or the orisons of nuns", and also for creating a "common medium of exchange between London and Omsk". Williams is here clearly promoting the Christian idea of exchange, rather than Sir Kay's worldly idea of monetary exchange.

The poet Taliessin discerns the dangers of the symbolic power of the coins, sensing that the symbolism may result in perilous views. "When the means are autonomous, they are deadly . . . " Money *can*, indeed, make exchange easier; but it can also cause members of a society to become oblivious of the fact that in the city "we all live in and on each other".[14] The early part of the poem considers the type of exchange manifested in love, shown through work, such as baking bread, both to sustain physical life, and also for the spiritual life through the Sacrament.

Williams, with a mathematical metaphor, says, "The hall is raised to the power of exchange of all / by the small spread organisms of your hands" – the organisms of loving exchange. In the King's coins, however, we see in Arthur's "creaturely brood" that assumes autonomy, and breeds "small crowns", units of money that symbolise "sovereign rule" and "dragons" that symbolise "power".[15] A competitive spirit replaces one of "exchange", and the new-found "individualism replaces co-inherence".[16] Arthur no longer controls the medium of exchange, but is being controlled by it. The situation will arise when "the poor have choice of purchase, the rich of rents",[17] and "the many will pay" prohibitive prices, and "the few will earn".[18] In the kingdom, Man yearns for "gold" like "Midas"; and "without order" – "Compact is becoming Contract; man only earns and pays".[19] Elayne "still affirms compact [covenant] over contract"[20] – compact is a freely made agreement; contract is enforceable by law. Bors asks, "What can be saved without order . . . What without coinage or with coinage can be saved"?[21] He speaks of Williams's order of Civilisation where "security lies",[22] that is discovered in those, like Bors and Elayne, who co-inhere in love.

Did Williams actually advocate Conquest's "force and cruelty", displaying "scarcely disguised" libidinal tendencies, in view of the hazel rod and the "scar on a slave?" Was there an "impulse to power and to cruelty"? Surely not. Williams is not speaking of "slavery as a social institution, nor about abuses of secular power". He is merely creating "an image that describes the fallen human condition as it has existed since the Fall",[23] that is, having a tendency to sin.

Lewis believes that to Williams "the Fall was an alteration in knowledge". God always knew "both good and evil". Man, "limited by experience . . . at first knew only good". Adam and Eve unwisely wished "to know as gods" both good and evil. God "knew evil as a contingency". Man could, then, experience "good *as* evil".[24] However, Taliessin sees in the scars on the slave girl's back a 'good' picture of salvation, "a half-circle to be completed in the face of Blanchefleur". The "scarred body" stands for all flesh, fallen but "subject to redemption". The slave girl, in *The Sister of Percivale*, "passed" after filling "her bucket", suggesting she had thus "died to self", indeed a previously sometimes rebellious self. The slave girl *and* Blanchefleur had in their own ways "experienced slavery", the one as a literal slave, and the other as having known the "dark night of the soul".[25]

Williams sees, then, 'good', not *as* evil, but as coming *out of* evil. Anne Ridler suggests that "only poetry" can make us accept seeing "evil as good".[26] Freedom from slavery requires discipline. Not to be equated with cruelty of sadism, or Conquest's "hierarchical attitude", such an interpretation is sometimes applicable to Williams's imagery. He has been thought "to be very unwise in pushing his physical symbolism to the point Conquest describes". The slave-girl's discipline is "physical and not sexual".[27] Physical violence is part of the way barbarians were brought into the City, with the hope that they would "by their will" stay there. Blanchefleur and the slave-girl are two sides of the same coin of Exchange. Taliessin sees both. The idea of substitution is integral, as it "shows its heavenly face in heaven can show little more than its scarred back in this world".[28]

Is it, then, inconsistent to use brute force to bring the slave-girl, or anyone else, into the Empire, Williams's ordered City? The unity of the Empire exists by the free consent of all its members. In *The Vision of the Empire* (copyright 1938), we read that "the organic body sang together", as Taliessin discovered that "the Empire and a human body symbolise each other".[29] In *The Founding of the Company* (copyright 1944), the mutual functions of the members and their vocations emanate from "the fact that they have taken into their hearts the doctrine of Exchange".[30] It does not, then, seem consistent with Williams's ideal of co-inherence and discomfort induced by 'necessary' violence, to regard being beaten into submission to enter the "confines of the City" as in any way 'good'. It is, perhaps, more basic. Williams knew that this painful *entrée* into the city was quite plainly what sometimes actually *happened*, notwithstanding Taliessin's aesthetic pleasure. It would be entirely *because* of the parlous state of Man, because of the Primal Curse – the Fall – that it was *at that time* seen as necessary for "barbarian souls" *to* be whipped to be brought into the City and, as Lewis said, "by their will, remain there".[31] Williams struggled with the question of the use of force, let alone actual brutality, and experienced considerable tension when trying to resolve the use of force even to remove a tyrant. He expressed Taliessin's "blood-guilt" over it in *The Taking of Camelot* when Arthur fought with King Cradlemas to lay claim to Logres.[32]

By contrast, and at a higher level, we see a case in point in the situation of "a certain unskilled assistant" in Williams's novel *Descent into Hell* (1937), a workman whose "name no one troubled to know", and who was made unceremoniously redundant. Williams says of him, "The Republic, of which he knew nothing, had betrayed him . . . The Republic had decided that it was better one man . . . should perish . . . his salvation was not something he himself had planned". Even his return was decided through means of "the Omnipotence". By the moment of Margaret Anstruther's death, God had allowed her to bring about the workman's salvation. The workman was, as Williams described it, in the world where everyone "carried someone else's grief".[33] His world, with all its pain, was an 'un-ideal' world, whereas Logres was an 'ideal' world.

The parallel is that through the unsought pain of the workman and the slave-girl they found salvation – in her case, by entering the city. Spacks, in another response to Robert Conquest's attack, suggests that in this novel Williams "is concerned . . . with the nature of the progress to salvation". He does not wish to "treat other human beings badly; he merely recognises that they *are* treated badly". Spacks reminds us that "C.S. Lewis reports of Williams, 'He was ready to accept as a revealed doctrine the proposition that existence is good'".[34] "The whole universe is to be known as good", as Anne Ridler quoted.[35] Williams is conscious of the problem of inherent injustice, since it raises the juxtaposition of God's justice and the suffering of extreme pain, a difficulty aggravated by the sadism which Williams recognises in himself. He not only tells us what happened, even when it is brutal, but he also shows the place that this takes in a person's eventual salvation, and how the evil, itself to be abhorred, is transformed by divine grace into something good. Perhaps something of the ultimate good is found in *The Throne and Councils of Arthur* (1938, edn. 1991), as Dodds entitled it. King Arthur is arrayed in his "new glory", crowned with the significant rituals that Williams regards as vital – the "sacred oil" was used to anoint him; the king was duly "censed"; he had been given the "privy letters"; the "gold had come to Camelot".[36] In *The Calling of Taliessin*, there are even hints of a potential "mature treatment of the Dolorous Blow", with all the implications for the wounding and salvation of the Fisher-King, (itself reminiscent of the wounding of King Bran in the *Mabinogion*). Merlin tells Taliessin that there shall be "in Logres a throne / like that other of Carbonek, of King Pelles in Broceliande, / the holder of the Hallows".[37] Williams suggests that the Grail will prove efficacious in reconciling King Arthur in Logres, as was King Pelles in the sacred Carbonek. Williams had said the Dolorous Blow, itself caused by the Fall, "must work itself out through the king".

"Between One World and Another"

In the light of the problems that Williams experienced over the use of force, he knew that taming the land to clear it of pagans inevitably involved warfare and the suffering it brought. How, then, does he deal with the significant transition from an earth-bound world to the ideal world of Logres, where the Eucharist will be available? One has, we discover, to go through the legendary Broceliande. The 'Grail Castle' and the Hallows, the Spear of Longinus with which Christ was wounded, the nails used in the Crucifixion and, above all, the Grail itself are all, in fact, found at Carbonek.

Where, then, is Broceliande? Broceliande is actually in Brittany but, in a letter to C.S. Lewis, Williams said it is a mysterious forest-cum-sea, "West of Logres, off Cornwall".[38] This imaginative idea was beautifully taken up by Lewis in "The Wood between the Worlds" in *The Magician's Nephew* (1955). Broceliande has echoes of the recurrent image and setting of the forest in Icelandic mythology, *Myrkvið* (Mirkwood), of *The Poetic Edda*. Ursula Dronke, the editor of the *Edda*, says it is "the archetypal Black Forest . . . In Norse poetic tradition, 'crossing Myrkvið' comes to signify penetrating the barriers not merely between one land and another, but between one world and another".[39] In *The Sister of Percivale*, there is a transition to another world, when the three following poems describe the nature and effect of Divine Grace as it becomes known in the life of Galahad, who is a type of Christ.[40] In both cases, we move to the sacred.

The image of a forest, says Williams, is common enough in English verse, particularly in the Pastoral tradition. He refers to episodes of poetry about lovers, dukes and their followers, a poet listening to a nightingale and to other inhabitants belonging to the wood – "dryads, fairies, an enchanters' rout". He says, "The whole earth seems to become this one enormous forest . . . The forest itself has different names in different tongues – Westermain, Arden, Birnam, Broceliande",[41] and the Old Norse *Myrkvið*. It has a good deal in common with Tolkien's Mirkwood in *The Hobbit* and *The Lord of the Rings*.

Beyond the forest, "(at least beyond a certain part of it)" is Carbonek (the castle of the holy things, the dwelling place of King Pelles the Wounded King, the guardian of the Grail), Williams told Lewis, "then the open sea, then Sarras. A place of making, home of Nimue . . . and all this is felt in the beloved". Sarras, the heavenly city, is the "land of the Trinity".[42] This change, this crossing from land to land, we find as Taliessin comes to Broceliande.

Between the anarchy of yet unmade Logres
and the darkness of secret-swayed Broceliande
Taliessin took his way.[43]

In *Bors to Elayne: The Fish of Broceliande*, Bors tells Elayne, "In the great hall's glow / Taliessin sang of the sea-rooted western wood . . . a forest of the creatures". Williams had said then that "all this", including Broceliande, "is felt in the beloved". Bors "plucked a fish from a stream that flowed to the sea".[44] Bors "has found love in Broceliande" in Elayne's presence, though he does not actually say "love". Bors feels that Elayne "*is*" Broceliande. He offers her the fish – itself a Christian "cryptogram".[45] Bors and Elayne think perhaps you have to be "a twy-nature" to bring the fish from the pool, suggesting that when two lovers become one, they will symbolise Christ, the grand "Twy-Nature", the hypostatic union of Christ as God and Man in one Person, He who Himself *is* Love. More humbly, the lovers feel the unity, the Co-inherence, of spirit and body. Bors and Elayne know now that under "all possible Camelots",[46] where the "king sits on the throne", the "wood in the wild west . . . probes everywhere". Bors rejoices in seeing Elayne's glory when he says to her, "Everywhere the light through the great leaves is blown on your substantial flesh, and everywhere your glory frames".[47] Williams showed again (as with his 'Silver Stair' poems, where he ostensibly was writing about his beloved, and was aligning her with his love of Christ) a correlation between Bors' beloved, Elayne, and the holiness of Brocliande, ruled by a king. Williams equates their love with the union of Christ as God and man. Elayne manifests glory, the glory that emanates both from Christ – the King – and thus from God. This parallel between the lovers and the divine underlines Williams's belief in the sacred nature of Christian kingship.

The Bodily Kingdom of God

Williams, who used the image of a woman's body as a symbol of the Empire and its co-inhering parts, said that "man is a small replica of the universe". The Sacred Body "is the plan upon which physical human creation was built, for it is in the centre of physical human creation". Williams believed that, even without the Fall, "Christ would have become incarnate". For "in His union and conjunction with Body, God finds His final perfection and felicity".[48] Anne Ridler suggests that Williams is perhaps the Christian writer of all who has "restored the body to its proper place of honour", notwithstanding his "sense of revolt against the flesh".[49] Williams's thought about the "symbolism of the body" owed a great deal to the diagram of the Sephirotic Tree laid out on the figure of a man, in the frontispiece of A.E. Waite's *The Secret Doctrine of Israel* (1913).[50] Anne Ridler explains that in spite of Williams's restorations of the proper place of honour of the human body, he sometimes felt "repelled" by the human needs of some of the greatest poets, and also when considering his own needs. Ridler says that "the sense of a deep division in his own nature had made Charles Williams's expression of some final possibility of union so convincing."[51]

Williams said, quoting Dante, in *The Commonplace Book* that he saw a very wonderful vision. He hoped to write concerning Beatrice that his spirit "should go hence to behold the *glory* of its lady" (my italics).[52] Williams himself would have mentioned Coventry Patmore's *The Rod, the Root and the Flower* (1890) and *The Unknown Eros* (1877) in connection with the body, as he would with regard to romantic love and the Incarnation.[53]

According to Cavaliero, Williams is drawing on theology where "the Incarnation forms the central reality", and deriving from Mary's motherhood is "representative of, human love". Williams's "belief that lovers may justifiably behold in their own amorous rites a manifestation of the divine" is seen in *The Unknown Eros*, where the "answer is to be found in the knowledge of sexual love itself".[54] Williams says in the *Prelude* to *The Region of the Summer Stars* (1944), "The young Church breakfasted on glory; handfasted, / her elect functioned in the light".

They caught the glow of Christ's transfigured bodily glory in their own flesh, especially in young love and in a sense of wonder at the marvel of the nature of the earth.[55] In *Bors to Elayne: The Fish of Broceliande*, Elayne becomes the transferred "holy and glorious flesh" (quoting Dante's *Paradiso*, XIV, 43), a passage loved by Williams, where Elayne is likened to Beatrice. This glory gives both Bors and Elayne a foretaste of the salvation they both share, "a mystery". The "uprightness of the multitude" confirmed in Elayne's body becomes a diagram of the archetypal body.[56] The unknown can be "inferred" from the known, the greater sensed in the pattern of the lesser, the "archetypal Holy Body in the human body".[57] The place of women, like the Virgin Mary, as *Theotokos*, God bearer, in the world's base is a recurring theme in *The Region of the Summer Stars*.

In *Taliessin in the Rose-Garden* (1941), the Rose-Garden itself is "a symbol of Caucasia" and of the human body. Williams says that women in their periodical menstruation "shared with the Sacrifice the victimization of blood". It stands for the blood "that drops from Pelles's wound" and "archytypally, the timed and falling blood of Christ".[58] Williams argues that falling in love is the "most universal of experiences". In *The Coming of Palomides* (1938), we hear of the unique experience of falling in love. Palomides says, "for till today no eyes have seen".[59] Of the significance of

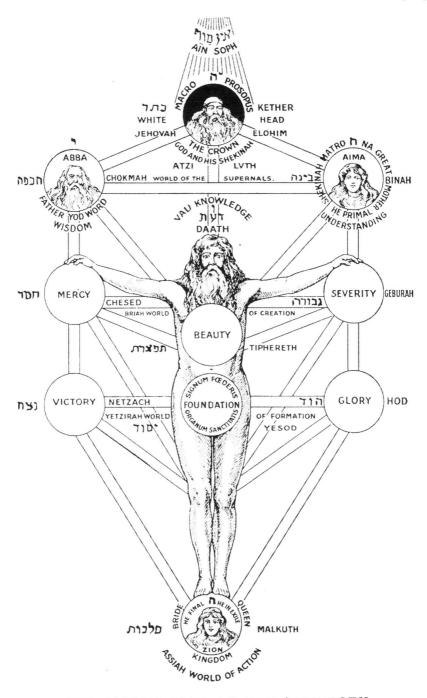

THE SACRED TREE OF THE SEPHIROTH

The frontispiece to A.E. Waite's *The Secret Doctrine of Israel* (1913)

this experience, Williams says in 'The Index of the City' in *The Image of the City* (1958), "We experience, physically, in its proper mode, the Kingdom of God".[60] Williams said, "Let the queen's majesty . . . deign to exhibit the glory to the women of Logres".[61] He sees, then, in the "pattern" of the "archetypal Holy Body in the human body"[62] and the inherent glory and transfiguration they share. Williams's whole thought, including his concept of monarchy, centres on that glory and transfiguration, neither merely poetic nor even theological, but felt as actual experience, felt and perceived in a woman's body. It was, we remember, in Williams's own first experience of falling in love that he equated his beloved with the "Regent from the throne of God".[63] Influenced, to an extent, by Dante, Williams made it clear that his doctrine emanated from his own experience.[64] Love in the City, the Household and the Body were developed in *The Silver Stair*.[65]

It is not, then, a great leap from the experience of Christ in his beloved – reminiscent of Dante and Beatrice – to his conviction that the model for a Christian king is Christ Himself, so that the king and his people may co-inhere with each other and with God. Williams shows that the establishment of Logres, the country that is to become the Britain we know, is a specific part of the divine will. Merlin in his priestly role added to the political dimension a sense of spiritual authority in the coming coronation. Williams underlines the role of the Archbishop of Canterbury, who crowns the monarch even to this day, and imbues the ceremony with the authority of the Church.

Sir Humphrey Milford, Williams's employer and the London publisher at the Oxford University Press at Amen House, was a man of astute literary judgement and sharp intelligence, and with his combination of authority and great kindness, "he helped to give life to Williams's conception of the ideal ruler".[66] Milford became the image of King Arthur, and Williams the King's poet, Taliessin.[67]

He shows us a microcosm of his view of a just society. The life of the company in Taliessin's Household was extended into the life of the company of Logres. Lewis asserts that in *The Founding of the Company* "their goodness in each vocation springs from the fact that they have taken into their hearts the doctrine of Exchange".[68] Each member of the company has his own function, whether as King or King's Poet. In *The Calling of Taliessin*, the King's Poet discovers *his* vocation, a prophetic and oblique way of saying that Logres will be a Christian kingdom, where he will be the king's man and a soldier, with his "harp" and "sword". Thus creating an image of both military strength and poetry, seemingly reconciling the images (occurring earlier) of order and control, with lyrical harmony.

Though still untamed, Williams says that Logres will be sacred like Carbonek and the Grail castle. In *The Calling of Taliessin*, the poet meets the wizard Merlin and his twin sister, Brisen, "alongside our marches", sent, "as is willed", to build Logres, implying God's will. Merlin, in an angelic role, ambiguously tells Taliessin that Logres will be in Byzantium, "which shall" cryptically "be by Thames", that is, in London. [69]

Williams suggests with rhetorical techniques that he is not only writing about sixth century kingship, but more relevantly about modern Britain. Every age is 'modern'. King Arthur would have seen *himself* as a modern. Williams subtly implies that he is calling attention to King Arthur and King George VI at the same time. David Jones, perhaps mistakenly, felt that a sense of the contemporary is lacking in Williams's work, whereas Dorothy Sayers had said, "Williams never forgot that every age is modern to itself, and that this fact, or illusion, links it with our own".[70] Williams has no need to labour the point: to 'suggest', as Mallarmé the French Symbolist poet said, is sufficient.

Perhaps Williams's most effective suggestion regarding the contemporary relevance of his poetry is the use in a later poem, *The Son of Lancelot*, of an avowedly modern image – that of "lorries". The word 'lorry' was used as early as 1838 to refer to a "long, flat wagon . . . a word of unknown origin . . . The current meaning in British English of a large truck for transporting goods appeared in the early 1900's."[71]

It was night still when the army began to move,
Embarking, disembarking, before dawn Asia
Awoke to hear the songs, the shouts, the wheels
of the furnished lorries rolling on the roads to the east.[72]

The graphic image here could be the British Army setting out on an offensive mission in Afghanistan, or a battle in the Second World War. Cavaliero believes that Williams was an unusual poet, in that he was inspired both in having an acute sense of historical epoch, and also in having a keen awareness "of a timeless world . . . only Eliot and David Jones surpass him in this respect".

"The co-inherence of time and eternity is the essence of his poetic vision"; and the discovery of the implications underlies his theological explorations. The poet and the theological "disciplines are complementary".[73] Williams is talking about his own times as those of King Arthur by using language and images that are both archaic and anachronistic. His theological explorations inform him that the type of king he envisages for Logres and Britain must be a reflection or mirror of Christ, King of Love and King of Glory.

Chapter Four

Williams and the Ideal of Kingship

King of Love / King of Glory

Williams emphasises another aspect of the divine King – His glory. Through Love, Christ reconciled Man to God, in order that Man could share his Glory. The timeless sharing of divine Glory that Christ had with the father was restored to Him. Williams had hinted at this *veiled* glory in *The Silver Stair*. He had asked, "Wherewith? With jewelled circlet or with thorn". The answer indicates both. "Let him . . . be with honour or reproach adored". The word "adored" is telling. Again, we read, "The silver and the golden stairs are His",[1] images both of Rejection and Affirmation. The gold speaks of all that is associated with the glory of kingship, like the gift of one of the Magi. The romantic love that Williams equates with God's love is joyful, full of light and filled with the bride's glory. The Bride of Christ, the Church, reflects His glory, the glory of the Bride in the New Jerusalem, itself like the heavenly Sarras. The suffering and the Passion of the glory of Romantic Love co-inhere, a union of apparent 'Impossibilities'.

This union is also found in Williams's ideal king, reflecting God's glory, the king who will co-inhere with the Emperor who, in Charles Williams's mind is, somewhat mysteriously, not only the ruler in Byzantium, but who also, Lewis says, "symbolises God".[2] Symbols contain what they symbolise. God acts in and through the Emperor, whose empire is "the earthly type of the Holy City, Sarras".[3]

In stark contrast is P'o-Lu, set in the East, where we encounter the Headless Emperor, the very antithesis of the Emperor in Byzantium. He walks backwards as Lewis reminds us. "Heaven-sweeping tentacles stretch, dragging octopus bodies over the level". One's "consciousness in P'o-Lu consists only of 'rudiments or relics . . . the turmoil of the mind of sensation'. It is on the very fringe of Hell".[4] In Williams's play *The House of the Octopus* (1945), he says the danger of P'o-Lu "is rather a spiritual threat than a mortal dominion". This remark distinguishes P'o-Lu from Japan, as by the time the play was completed this would have been a natural "identification".[5]

The Emperor at Byzantium, Williams says, is not God, but literally the historical figure. However, figuratively he is an image of the earthly king, God-in-operation, God-as-known-by-man".[6] The Emperor, like the king, symbolises God and acts through him, as His vicegerent. He is a focus for the people who see in him God's glory reflected, if imperfectly. God purposes to share His Glory, Love, Joy and Peace with His people eternally. Williams believes that divine glory is inherent in the person of the monarch. He demonstrates this in the coming of Arthur, in some of our historic kings, and expects it in contemporary monarchs. It need not be in any way merited: it is, after all, a 'reflection' of *God's* glory. Williams, conscious that monarchs are capable of using their power in a self-centred way, sees the Grail as vital in reconciling the king and the kingdom with God, restoring their joy and the hope of sharing His glory.

Glory in Historic Monarchs

Williams saw glory belonging to the monarch *qua* monarch rather than as a private person. The tenor of his historical biographies, *Bacon* (1933), *James I* (1934), *Rochester* (1935) and *Henry VII* (1937), shows that Williams was sensitive to the greatness of great men. He recognised a divine glory and also the glory peculiar to each individual person,[7] calling to mind Thomas Carlyle's lectures on the glamour of great men, *On Heroes, Hero-Worship and the Heroic in History* (1841). Williams said that "To Matthew Arnold . . . 'conduct was three-fourths of life' . . . to Tennyson and Carlyle . . . it was almost the whole".[8] He says of James I, "He was the forfeit that his house paid to existence for their romantic glory", ironically adding, "being the one member of it to whom the word could, in no sense whatever, be applied".[9]

Williams deftly caught the flavour of the glory in which James revelled. In *James I*, having described the "glory of the blood" of the Earl of Lennox, he says of James, "More magnificent still – for himself – than all such benevolence and beneficence was the kingly display in which James indulged".[10] The height of James's glorying in his power is seen in Williams's ingenious metaphor, "Each of them who desired pardon must come and kneel and entreat. The King found himself loving those moments – the feel of power, the paw of the good-tempered leopard touching the prey".[11]

Williams suggests an aura of personal glory surrounded the first Tudor king. In *Henry VII*, the royal party reached St. Paul's. The standards of the Pretender were put on the High Altar. There were the arms of Edward III with the Tudor Roses, the Cross of St. George, the Red Dragon of the old Welsh kings, and a flag bearing a dun cow on a yellow field. Around it, thanksgivings were offered. The *Te Deum* was sung. "The dun cow put on its glory", not just its apparel, its crown or its sword; but its "*glory*". Williams adds:

> Instead of a wife he [Henry] gave himself a bodyguard . . . It served for safety, for splendour, for the more awful aloofness of his person . . . He became royal in his dress and surroundings, beginning that habit of gorgeousness which . . . he continued to maintain.

Henry VII was "always the king without a face". Subtly describing Henry's glory, Williams quotes a certain "Miss Temperley, who had studied the King". It is not for nothing", he quotes, "that the word 'Majesty' first appears in this reign". Williams tellingly adds, "The King multiplied his majesty", instancing the establishment of the King's Justice, "his own special" Court of Law.[12]

Referring to Henry's intention of being a tyrant, and the possible erosion of his Glory, Williams tells us, in a masterpiece of understatement, this time quoting W. Busch's *England under the Tudors* (1895), "Whoever raised himself above what was, in Henry's opinion, his proper sphere was at once energetically suppressed", that is to say, the king's glory was *not* to be outshone.[13]

Williams endorses royal glory in *Thomas Cranmer of Canterbury* (1936). The Archbishop says of King Henry VIII, "O that the King, O that God's glory's gust from heaven would drive the dust from the land".[14] King Henry says as God's Vicegerent, "The will of the king is as the will of God". Cranmer supports him: "The King is masked with his majesty". The Skeleton, acting as the Chorus or Narrator, speaks of "the webbed light of the glory wherein is the angle of creation".[15] The Skeleton reminded the Commons that they "saw and handled aboriginal glory, sown from spirit, seeding in flesh" (an instance of Wordsworth's 'feeling intellect' and the co-inherence of the spiritual and the physical) and asked if they had forgotten the King's glory. "O bright fish caught in the bright light's mesh"? Williams here uses the same image – the fish – that he later used in *Bors to Elayne*. The Skeleton says to Cranmer, "O master and doctor, have you forgotten when the woman [Joan's] . . . face was moulded of heavenly fire? Or how you . . . saw King Henry God's spoken splendour? Shall I the splendour and the glory tire?" The Skeleton shows the Commons, and Cranmer, the intertwined ideas of the consecration of the bread and the wine, "spirit, seeding in flesh", and the wondrous thing that Cranmer will do "with the flesh of that hand", when he retracts his heresies, symbolic of repentance. He refers to the vision of the beloved, "the woman Joan", and how Cranmer sees the King *as* King.

Williams underlines royal glory as the Skeleton says to the Commons, "Have you forgotten, O my people . . . when the glory is doubled by the sweet derision . . . "?[16] The Skeleton is here mocking his beloved, as Christ reminded the disciples of the prophesy of scripture on the road to Emmaus. Independent of the individual king or queen's merit, neither King Henry nor Queen Mary appears to have acquired their royal glory through their intrinsic virtue.

Cranmer is condemned to burning at the stake for apostasy in the eyes of the Roman Catholic Queen Mary Tudor. The Skeleton warns, "Something happens . . . when the King commands something against the kingship". Cranmer observes, "When the Queen came riding yesterday into the town; she had no head, over her shoulders the Crown threw a golden light", a visible sign of glory. She denounces Cranmer for his attitude to adoration in the Mass. Too late, he says that the sacrament "was given for communion and not for adoration". He addresses the Court and, in spite of her injustice, says, "Good people, give not your minds to this glozing world, nor murmur against the glory of the Queen".[17]

Williams attributes the mark of glory to the ritual power of the coronation, which he sees as both a civic and a spiritual function. In *The Crowning of Arthur* (1938), glory attends the new king. "The king stood crowned", and "the kingdom and the glory chimed", a picture of the new "glory of Logres".[18] Williams intends the concepts that apply to Arthur's imminent coronation and kingdom to apply also to King George VI.

He demonstrates his view of the complexities of Christian monarchy in *Henry VII*, where he relates a historically accurate account of Henry's having become king by defeating King Richard III at the Battle of Bosworth in 1485. Having little right to the crown by inheritance, he was, as Williams puts it, "on both sides, almost a bastard". Henry, the Pretender, clearly, says Williams, "had one immediate business – to make it clear to everyone that he was already the King. He must not be King by descent . . . by any cause . . . The fact must be accepted merely as a fact." However, his new glory was tinged with a bad omen – "the sweating Sickness".[19]

The King obtained from the Pope a Bull that "proclaimed all rebels against Henry *ipso facto* excommunicate. Henry was pontifically declared King (i) by victory (ii) by succession, (iii) by choice and vote of the entire realm and of the three estates. He was King in every way and on every ground".[20] Williams saw Henry VII as a man who preferred "the glory of gold instead of the less reliable gold of glory",[21] reminiscent of the gradual change from compact to contract in *Bors to Elayne: On the King's Coins*. Williams, not looking for moral perfection, but for reconciliation, is still creating a portrait of the essentially Christian king. Henry's religious observance combined with policy was seen when "the King went to the great shrine of Our Lady of Walsingham as an act of devotion, and caused the Papal Bull in his favour to be read publicly.[22]

James I saw his kingship as being 'his' by Divine Right, demonstrating at least the King's belief in the sixteenth and seventeenth-century theory of kingship. In 1681, moreover, the address to King Charles II expressed a continued belief that the King derived his title "from God", and not from the people.[23] Sir Winston Churchill (1620-1688), father of the first Duke of Marlborough, in his *Diva Britannici* (1675), addresses the King, "To His Most Sacred Majesty Charles II by the Grace of God King", showing both his tacit approval for the idea that the King's Majesty is "Sacred", and that his Kingship was appointed by God.[24] Williams tells us in *James I* that the young prince was coercively separated from his parents, Mary Queen of Scots and Lord Henry Stuart, Earl of Darnley, and "sent to Stirling Castle". On "his third birthday" he was told that "now he was a man, and Christian, and king", King James VI of Scotland. James would be "the King by divine right . . . It would be God's work; that it would also be his own did not diminish his glory".[25] James, Williams says somewhat ironically, was right in thinking that "it surprised him to discover how right he always was" – that "even the coronation oath was taken to God, not to the people, and the people must not therefore invoke its clauses for their own protection. They ought not to have discussed the Prerogative; it is Mystery", referring to Harold Nicolson's "mystiques of Royalty".[26] James was mystery – and King. "His body from its birth had been royal . . . He half identified royalty with his material flesh". It had often been held, Williams tells us, "that kings were made royal by their crowning and anointing, not by their mere birth".[27]

James had been crowned and anointed by the Scottish lords. What if they had chosen *not* to crown him? Perhaps their assent was not *sine qua non* to his being made king. James thought otherwise. Williams believes "the King is king in himself, and by no assent of his subjects". He repeats the phrase: "It is Mystery", adding "sacerdotal in its office . . . The King is the Law".[28] He is, in effect, then, a priest-king. Williams says, James "desired that all men should live peaceably under the rule of the King". James's *and* Williams's "idea of monarchy postulated the bestowal of such power by God on certain chosen souls". Williams said that James "dared not trifle with . . . the sacred Justice of the King, the supernatural and awful quality of Majesty".[29]

Williams says that in the *Basilikon Doron* (1599, published anonymously) King James says, "Let it be your chiefest earthly glory, to excel in your own craft", and that James believed he "would have behaved [himself] as became so great a king, and so infinitely loving a master". If he saw himself as a "loving master", he nevertheless believed that he had the "majesty of the mortal god".[30] He recognised his own function. James's attitude to his function is more readily reflected in the (more recently so-called) Tory prayer for the monarch in Cranmer's 1549 King Edward VI Prayer Book than in the contrasting Whig prayer.[31] The Whigs were generally less monarchically-minded than the Tories, and were associated with Republicanism. The Tories, on the other hand, were explicitly Monarchist. The Tory version prays, "Rule the heart of thy chosen seruaunt Edward the Sixt our kyng" and asks that "we his subiectes (duly consydering whose auctoritie he hath) maye faithfully serue, honour, and humbly obeye him. . . . " By contrast, and more in keeping with Williams's egalitarian beliefs, the Whig prayer says, "that the hearts of Kyngs are in thy rule and gouernaunce", and asks "that, in all his thoughtes, wordes, and workes, he maye euer seke thy honour and glory, and study to preserue thy people committed to his charge, in wealth, peace, and godlynes".[32] King James would have seen himself as "chosen", and to be obeyed. James I is a historic king who came to the throne through direct succession, and who was capable of choosing 'the kingdom for the king', seeing kingship as his by Divine Right. Williams depicts a Christian king who wished to rule a just and, as James believed, a "fortunate" society. James I believed that by right he *could* have had anything he wished, but seeing himself as a good king, "he had demanded no such tribute".[33]

By contrast, in many ways Queen Elizabeth I epitomises for Williams his very Englishness, his Anglicanism and his loyalty to the royalist cause. In Williams's biography of Queen Elizabeth I he makes "a symbolic figure of

the Queen, a living embodiment of the Impossibility". Unlike King James
I, Queen Elizabeth I was "undogmatic", and did *not* think she was always
right. Her temperament appealed to Williams, whose biographies tell us as
much "about their author as they do about his subjects".[34]

Williams said, emphasising royal glory, "National, or at least dynastic, glory
obtruded itself upon universal glories". Behind any attempt in "arrogance of
femininity", Elizabeth had the benefit of the "power of England" to protect
her, though she demonstrated an English trait in "becoming an incarnate
variation of compromise". Reminiscent of Arthur, she liked, when seeing
herself in the mirror, to see "Elizabeth crowned", that is "the crowned Queen
of England", and this "because she liked the English".[35] The English Church,
of which she was Supreme Governor (*not* Head), was helped to recover a
quality of "freedom, tolerance, comprehensiveness, which made it not less
after the mind of Christ than any other". Elizabeth was, Williams asserts, "at
once monarch and person".[36]

Williams was a ritualist, a term coined by the theologian Brian Horne,
meaning one who sees society as taking part in a ritual, a game.[37] In
Witchcraft (1941), Williams maintained that in the Church, and among
Sorcerers whose rites the Church denounced, through rituals results were
made first in the imagination, then "received" in the "body, at least in its
emotions. Williams likens such a result to when, in the *Arabian Nights*,
Marcarius restored a woman who magically had been made to appear in
the "form of a mare". He took "water and blessed it and threw it over her,"
akin to the Asperges in the Mass. Williams believes the human body *does*,
indeed, have meaning, and that it is "packed with significance". He asserts
that phenomena are not always "what phenomena seem", that sometimes
the associated sensations are due to "the Mercy of God". Ritual, that is,
ordered movements of the body, he sees as "natural to men", and that it
actually maintains and increases the natural sense of the "significance" of
that very movement. The notion of ritual necessarily includes the formulae
of "words", as in the Liturgy, sacramentally effecting what it symbolises. The
formula of the bread and wine is, then, "effective": the "Words controlled
the God", in the ritual to which He "had submitted Himself". Another
formula, coronation, Williams believed could "make and unmake kings".[38]

Queen Elizabeth I, who believed in both rituals, had vowed to be
"dedicated to the motherhood of her people". She felt guilt for the execution
of her first cousin Mary Queen of Scots, "anointed and royal", reminding us
of Taliessin's "blood-guilt" over King Cradlemas. Nevertheless, Williams said
with great approval, "Few sovereigns have loved the common people better
than Elizabeth", and being loved *by* them, he adds, she saw the "glory of
[her] crown".[39] In her love of the English, her distaste of "extreme" doctrine
and the "spectacular Majesty" of her royalty, Elizabeth showed "a spirit, a
quality of mind, which may be called scepticism or realism or toleration
or cynicism or wisdom". Making allowances for her "femininity, perversity,
obstinacy, and fear, it might be called Elizabethan".[40]

Williams's Christ-like King: Inkamasi

Williams stresses the importance he attaches to the glory he sees inherent in royalty, and the unity of God and the Crown in *Shadows of Ecstasy* (1931). He states ironically, "The National Anthem implored Deity on behalf of royalty, and dismissed many incredulous of both". Of Inkamasi, "the chieftain and the king", Rosamond said, "I hate him to look like that", that is, showing signs of his glory. She and her sister Isabel, recognised in him that same certainty of his own "dark alien royalty" – as had King James I of *his* kingship – "the Zulu chieftain's own strength and conviction".

They "felt a shadow" of their "wide reading" about "The King's Most Excellent Majesty", redolent of Williams's awe for Majesty. They were on edge at having an African in the house "overwhelming" them with himself,[41] readily evoking scenes in Rider Haggard and the Indian and African empires generally. Isabel recalled part of a poem:

> The single bliss and sole felicity,
> The sweet fruition of an earthly crown.

To Williams, and the sisters, these lines not only "described" but actually "invoked kingship", growing into the "enormous royalty" that the Zulu had worn. Rosamond felt as though the Zulu represented what she "most detested"; that the world was not simply her oyster but it was "a great deal more like an octopus".

In *Shadows of Ecstasy*, Williams tells us that the "crisis was not separate from Inkamasi; it *was* Inkamasi",[42] a crisis centred on the person of the king. However, Williams rejects the ideas of the morally ambiguous Nigel Considine, who attempts to defy physical death permanently, and to involve the king in his occult schemes. Williams shows his faith in the healing power of the Eucharist for Inkamasi, as he did with King Arthur and the Grail. Inkamasi said to Considine resolutely, "I must do what I choose", though Considine had "persuaded" him to an extent. The priest Caithness said, "Last night he [the king] said he was a Christian" When Considine had the king in a controlled sleep – "the king was comatose" – Caithness attempted to wake him by invoking the "Body of Christ", but as yet to limited avail. Williams's belief in the power of the Blessed Sacrament, the "Mystery", to reconcile and to *restore* this and *any* king, is seen in the Mass at Lambeth. The Archbishop of Canterbury celebrated, and "the king received the Mystery, setting him "free from a power" that had held him since he was a boy.[43]

Williams embodies in Inkamasi his 'type' of Christ, his self-sacrificial ideal. In Considine's final choice to Inkamasi we shall find a reflection of Williams's King in *The Silver Stair* who, like Christ, "must go unto the Pavement".[44] In Africa, Considine tells him, "they know neither the Crown nor the Republic . . . If I must choose I will choose the king and not the State, for the king is flesh and yet undying, and is a symbol of that we seek",[45] that is to say, earthly immortality. Williams shows not only the value he sets on kingship, but also the price that *may* need to be paid for it.

Considine actually offers King Inkamasi a choice; that he may either be given "a house and servants and money, all that he needs, and he may live contented with his knowledge of his own inheritance" or he "will give the king a royal death". Inkamasi says, "I know there is no place for me upon earth . . . Royalty is a shade and Equality not yet born". Williams showing here the importance of the equality that he sees in the Republic. Considine sets out the choices. He says, "If the king choose to live without his majesty, though the choice is his own, he will choose to live in a dream". Considine's alternatives suggest the king be taken back to Africa in a submarine, and choose firstly whether he will be set among his people, and "try the fates between himself and the man who now rules them, and who inherits royalty if Inkamasi dies", or secondly, sent back as Considine's friend "till peace is signed and he may live as a private man wherever he chooses on the face of the earth". Williams again makes a distinction between the king *qua* monarch, and as a private person, as he did in his biography of Queen Elizabeth I. Considine's third and final choice is that the king "shall go clothed with royalty and death".[46] The King must choose today. Inkamasi knew that his "creed" would not let him kill himself, "yet he had a duty to his kingship". He must accept death.

This compounds Williams's belief that his ideal king must be willing to die sacrificially for his royalty, and thus for his people. He cements the Christ-like image by elaborating a quotation from Christ's Passion. "He set his face to go up to Jerusalem, that the king's crown might be properly received by the unvestmenting hands of Death".[47] Williams encapsulates the essence of his idea that a king is a union of an individual person *and* that same person stamped with the ordaining mark of kingship through coronation. They are, in fact, inseparable, an instance of co-inhering. Williams believes "peace" is found in King Inkamasi, who unites "within himself . . . a more powerful union of opposites" (than the twilight), a real co-inhering, "the day of his own individual being and the mysterious night of his holy and awful office".

Williams consummates the action of his kingly type. Considine says, "I invite you to a sacrifice of death, by virtue of that hope and determination which shall make you masters of death as you are in your degree masters of love".[48] Williams has established a parallel between King Inkamasi and Christ throughout this episode. Considine says, "By no compulsion and no persuasion the King Inkamasi turns to the throne we offer him and awaits immolation there". That is to say, the King is, as was Christ on the Cross, to be destroyed in sacrifice. Considine, in his "insolence", says:

> He is driven by the might of his own royalty which demands of him no lesser conclusion . . . Who knows but this very night the work may be accomplished and there may descend upon one of us that ecstasy which shall drive him into death and in death to resurrection . . . He dies for the sake of his kingship.

Inkamasi says, when asked, that he is "willing to restore [his] kingship through [them]". Considine bids the king farewell, and says to him, "Drink Majesty", and hands him a poisoned chalice. Before the king's body reached the floor, a shot rang out. Considine was dead, an instance of the land of 'a tooth for a tooth' of the Old Testament.[49]

Williams's Ideal King: a Spiritual Monarchy

Williams's ideal king is modelled, then, on Christ, of whom King Inkamasi is a type, in view of his ultimate self-sacrifice, made though love for his people. Inkamasi preserved the glory of kingship, reconciled by the Eucharist which, Williams said is not "only for the elect; it is for all".[50] Christ sacrificially renounced His glory in the Incarnation and restored Man through the Cross by enduring "the justice He decreed".[51] An ideal society, like the company at Amen House, maintains peace through continual acts of Exchange, acts applying to the king and the commons. Williams sees equality as inherent in the Republic, royal or presidential. The members make compacts rather than contracts. In Co-inherence, each member's function benefits all. Williams describes the potentially ideal and just society of Logres that becomes Britain, where Pauline interdependence pertains. Order is essential for good kingship, actually enabling co-inherence, and reflecting the heavenly kingdom. Williams portrays Christ as a window onto God, who reveals His kingship, as God Himself is symbolised by the Emperor at Byzantium. He co-inheres with the King, reflecting God, whose Trinity co-inheres in a continual reciprocity of love.

Williams sees King Arthur as an historic king, or at least as a *dux bellorum*, and also as the mythical King of Logres, the Pendragon, whose kingship was providentially willed. The ideal king, God's vicegerent and type of Christ, is to emulate Him as far as is humanly possible, and choose to see himself as "the King made for the Kingdom".[52] Because of this Impossibility, caused by the Fall, King Arthur, who fails in his choice, is reconciled by the achieving of the Grail by Galahad, also a type of Christ. The achievement of the Grail, Williams asserts, is "to be Christ-conscious instead of self-conscious".[53] Arthur is, then, following his vocation to create a spiritual monarchy, a vocation discovered through Merlin's spiritual guidance.

Williams is aware of the historical efficacy and necessity to use force – actually to fight – to clear the untamed land of Logres from pagan tyrants, and of the ambivalence it causes him, expressed when he says that Taliessin "ought to be understanding what blood-guilt is".[54] However, Williams says that Logres will have a sacred quality. Not only will the Empire and Broceliande "meet in Logres", but as Merlin said in *The Calling of Taliessin*, "The Hallows [the Spear of Longinus, the Nails and the Grail] shall be borne from Carbonek into the sun".[55]

Williams's concept of kingship is illuminated in the rituals at Arthur's coronation, and subsequently in that of King George VI. Williams sees in the crowned monarch the figure of the divine Vicegerent *par excellence*. In *The Crowning of Arthur*, Williams presents the act of his coronation as *fait accompli*. In *The Figure of Arthur*, he says that Arthur was "crowned by Dubricius, Archbishop of the City of the Legions, Caerleon, at the age of fifteen".[56] In *Taliessin's Song of the King's Crowning* (1931), Taliessin said that he saw "the King rise crowned", and that there were "bishops about",[57] making it reasonable to assume that a Coronation Mass was celebrated. At a later celebration of the Mass, in The Star of Percivale, we are told that "More than the voice is the vision, the kingdom than the king",[58] where the Dantean republican maxim about the primacy of "the operation" is emphasised.[59]

Williams sees the king, once crowned, as "Mystery", as he said of King James I, and as chosen by God. Williams says of kings, "all power flows from them". He speaks of "the sacred Justice of the King, the supernatural and awful quality of Majesty".[60] He believes the monarch, like King Inkamasi, combines a "wonderful union of mysterious opposites". The king unites within himself his "own wonderful being and the mysterious night of his holy and awful office",[61] stressing the distinction between King *qua* King, and as a private person. It is the *holiness* at the heart of this office that Williams sees as vital. God, through the Church, gives the king his vicegerency: the king reigns, then, with His authority. "The establishment of the Kingdom", he says, "is the establishment of man".[62]

However, Williams warns against the inherent dangers of the wrong use of Power. In *The Throne and Councils of Arthur*:

the king sat
in a new glory of disciplined ferocity, burnished
golden beauty.[63]

Williams deprecates use, and perhaps the possession of excessive power. As Lord Acton said, "All power tends to corrupt: absolute power corrupts absolutely".[64] Williams abhorred self-interest or excessive self-love to cause a monarch to become tyrannical though abuse of their power.

Misuse of power caused the failure of Logres, not simply actions like incest, immoral in themselves. In *The Star of Percivale*, Arthur was close to this, as "the king in the elevation beheld and loved himself crowned". In *The Thrones and Councils of Arthur*, there is "King Arthur's throne . . . of two dragons twined",[65] the dragons on his banner that symbolise power, "both good and evil", and that personify primeval force, and a supernatural and cosmic power. On the hierarchical ladder, Arthur's station is one of function.[66] Williams emphasises the royal glory seen *after* Arthur has been crowned King. The king is crowned, Mass is sung. In *The Crowning of Arthur*, we hear that Camelot is in a "furnace of jubilee" as torches and fires blaze. God's Vicegerent is fêted. "The kingdom and the power and the glory chimed".[67]

King Arthur has his royal glory and the people enjoy the revelry. Williams described how King Arthur was anointed with chrism and became king of a previously untamed land, pagan and ruled by a tyrant. Now tamed, Logres is established. However, Lewis says, Body and spirit, Broceliande and the Empire, "are not, or not yet, at-oned".[68] Williams believes that this and all other kingdoms can be reconciled through the Grail. He tells of Elayne's significance for the king and the kingdom, in that she will bear a son, Galahad, who will achieve the Grail. He, as a type of Christ, will bring the life of Christ to Man, through the eating of the Bread and the drinking of the Wine.[69] In the *anamnesis* the reconciliation takes place, as the Wounded King, Pelles, and King Arthur come into a relationship of co-inherence and exchange. In both Arthur's and the modern coronation the newly-crowned monarch receives the Holy Communion and the Grail, an acknowledgement of their reliance on the grace of the Blessed Sacrament, which is of vital necessity to the monarch, both as an individual *and* in their sacred office as Sovereign.

Charles Williams was a young man of twenty-five at the time of the coronation of King George V in 1911 and would have read detailed accounts of it. The Coronation ceremony falls into four main sections, each of which possesses historic symbolism. The rituals include the Recognition, Oath, Anointing, and the Homage of the Lords Spiritual and Temporal. King George took the Coronation Oath, the symbolic contract, with his hand on the Bible. As rituals effect what they signify, of paramount importance is the "holy oil" with which the king is anointed and thereby 'set aside' for his special task. Cranmer regarded the legend of the *sainte ampoule*, the cruse for the holy oil or chrism, as "savouring of a superstition". By contrast, the late Archbishop of Canterbury, Dr Geoffrey Fisher, publically stated that he regarded the anointing as the most significant ritual in the whole Coronation ceremony. The Archbishop is, of course, the only one who *can* anoint.[70] After a "short Communion service . . . the ritual was concluded". For King George V, a religious man, this ancient ritual was "an act of dedication".[71] Williams saw the rite of Coronation as bestowing on a 'private person' the indelible 'mark' of Christian kingship, as he did in the coronation of King Arthur in Logres that was to become the Britain that we know.

The historian Sarah Bradford asserts that "The Coronation is the single most significant ceremony of a sovereign's life, transforming him or her from an ordinary mortal to a powerful symbol, half man, and half priest". For King George VI in particular, King George V's second son, whose interest in history was very strong, it was to have an extraordinarily strengthening, confidence-giving effect. For both him and the Queen the religious significance of the ceremony, in which they were to dedicate themselves before God to the service of their people, was very strong".

During the ceremony itself, a religious exaltation came upon the King. He later told the Archbishop of Canterbury "that he felt throughout that Some One Else was with him. Harold Nicolson said, "There is no doubt that they have entered on this task with a real religious sense".[72] The coronations of both King George VI in 1937 and of Queen Elizabeth II in 1953 included a private reception of the Sacrament during the ceremony, after the anointing, crowning and enthronement.

Something of the deep spirituality of King George VI is seen in the letter that Williams, calling himself Serge, wrote to his wife, addressed as Michal, on 7 June 1944, in *To Michal from Serge*: "Did you hear the King? I thought it was magnificent and quite unexpected – all that about the Queen's 'waiting upon God'. It must be generations since an English King has spoken so to the People". This is in keeping with the King's Christmas Day broadcast, when he included Minnie Louise Haskins's words:

> I said to the man who stood at the gate of the year, 'Give me a light that I may tread safely into the unknown'. And he replied, 'Go out into the darkness and put your hand into the hand of God. That shall be to you better than light and safer than a known way'.[73]

The distinction Williams draws between the office of the monarch *qua* monarch and as a private person is most marked in an unpublished letter he wrote to Anne Ridler, who was still Anne Bradby at the time of writing, 18 May 1937. Williams said, "Talking of Ritual, someone ought to tell the King not to smile when he is crowned and robed", thereby confusing his two roles. By contrast, Williams thought the photograph of the King taken in the Abbey was "amazingly good", as the King had "become, like Hadrian VII, a piece of ivory". Williams was alluding to Frederick ('Father') Rolfe's novel *Hadrian the Seventh* (1904). Williams thought the "face under the crown looked carven – a lifted image". However, he felt that the whole effect was about to be "ruined". The 'carven image' suddenly and inappropriately became a private person, in spite of his regalia, because, as Williams said, "he must needs come out on the balcony of the palace in his majesty and smile", showing the crowd a "well-meaning youngish man who had dressed up curiously to please someone else's children".

Howbeit, he acknowledges, "King he is, and the beacons are on the towers and hills". King George VI was "anointed and crowned", Williams said, "much as I could wish otherwise",[74] probably implying that he felt that King Edward VIII ought to have been crowned as the true king, and not abdicated – or as he put it, "throw up his job".[75] Charles Williams – Englishman, Anglican and Royalist saw, then, a direct parallel between King Arthur, his kingly type and the modern British monarchs. Williams saw it as their royal function to lead the nation by example and to be an inspiration. To Williams, the Monarch is a father or mother to the nation, engendering co-inherence in Society, symbolising co-inherence with God. A 'republic' exists, royal justice abounds, law is kept and a Byzantine sense of heavenly Order is rooted in Love.

Williams would rejoice that a Monarch 'reigns' while Parliament 'rules', a constitutional monarchy being the best compromise engendering social cohesion. Part of the royal function, through Parliament, is to protect the Realm and ensure its safety. Williams would be happy that the Monarch still speaks to the nation on Christmas Day. In regard to our current monarch, Elizabeth II, the emphasis has increasingly been upon the monarch's offering of service to the nation and royal duty, which Williams would have strongly approved of. Williams had, in his own day, seen the City, British society, as ideal a society as can be envisaged. British society had remained firm in Co-inherence and Exchange under King George VI and the Prime Minister, Winston Churchill,[76] embodying Williams's 'Impossible' union of a Monarchy and the Republic. Logres is now Britain – London-in-Logres. Williams saw society as the Company at Amen House writ large. Lewis said that the last stanza of *Taliessin at Lancelot's Mass* "returns us strongly and gently to the real world".[77]

Williams sees the king as a war-leader, yet one who engenders a peaceful society. He depicts a king who is like the Anglo-Saxon *Rex Pacificus*, who brings peace and plenty. To Williams, the king's office is sacred, his king is God's Vicegerent and, like King David, anointed. Arthur's kingship is 'willed', like the Hebrew monarch's, by God. He is judge and *dux bellorum*, though not, like the Homeric king, also a priest. Williams abhorred tyranny and would, indeed, have preferred a Republic to a despotic monarchy. He welcomed the inherent egalitarianism of a republic, insisting that the king should be there to serve his people, rather than be served by them. He saw in his monarch a union of Majesty and grace. Moreover, Williams also valued the creation of order, a quality he found in the king's relationship with the Emperor of Byzantium who was mythically the successor to Constantine, and the upholder of the imperium of Rome. The kings of other parts of the Empire were effectively 'vassal-kings', subordinate to the Emperor, on whose image their own kingship should be modelled.

To Williams, his idea of Co-inherence where all live 'in-and-for each other, like St. Paul's teaching that we are all "members of one body" (Romans 12:5), was paramount. Williams, like Nicolson and James I, saw monarchy as Mystery. Williams regarded the king's office as spiritual, in Arthur's day and in that of contemporary monarchs, especially King George VI.

The Development of Williams's Ideal of Kingship.

In Williams's poems in *The Silver Stair* (1912), he refers to "the woman loved" as the "Regent from the immovable throne of God", making a close connection between the experience of love for his future wife, Florence, and his love for God. At the same time, he saw her as God's Vicegerent. Like Dante's Beatrice, he regarded her as a harbinger of grace. From the first, Williams ties in earthly relationships with heavenly counterparts. The word "throne" implies a royal image. In this early sequence of poems, Williams presents Christ, the scriptural 'Regent', as the King whose present is of gold *and* silver, images representing Kingship and Renunciation. Here, Williams symbolises in these gifts Christ's sacrificial Love *and* His royal Glory.

In *Reason and Beauty in the Poetic Mind* (1933), Williams says the patterns of English verse have been too "often" repeated. He believes they "imposed themselves on us as something more personal than any

movement of prose . . . the sonnet is an example".[78] More specifically, in
The English Poetic Mind (1932), Williams says, "Poetry . . . is 'about' human
experience . . . But to whatever particular human experience it alludes, it is
not that experience . . . Love poetry is poetry, not love . . . religious poetry
is poetry, not religion".[79]

Glen Cavaliero opines "The more doctrinal the content, the more clearly
Williams's authentic voice is heard" adding that "The poems really derive
from late Victorian rather than from Georgian verse. Williams drew on the
metaphysical and the devotional traditions. . . . The metaphysical tradition
had its precursors in Coventry Patmore and Francis Thompson". I suggest
that Williams almost magically combined the two traditions, mingling his
love for Florence with his Christian faith. Williams was also influenced by
the Rector of Morwenstow in Cornwall, the poet R.S. Hawker, and his
blank-verse Arthurian poem, *The Quest of the Sangraal* (1864).[80]

In the sonnets in *The Silver Stair*, Williams paints a picture – perhaps more
of an *ikon* – a devotional painting of his model for earthly kingship in his
portrayal of Christ the King, Jaroslav Pelikan's *Christus Rex*, who "reigns
from the tree"[81] Williams makes a connection between the idealised, indeed
the 'iconic', beloved in Renaissance sonnet sequences – Laura, Delia, and
the dark lady – and the iconic figure of Christ the King in his own sequence
where he equates his love for Florence with his love for God. In his poetic
Ikon of *Christus Rex*, Williams reflects his beliefs, creating a theological
picture rather than painting a portrait of the more human aspects of Christ
as found in the Bible. Williams's *Ikon* is in contrast to Peter Abelard's (1079-
1142) writings, which strongly *emphasised* Christ's humanity, an emphasis
that brought him into conflict with the ecclesiastical authorities, who actually
twice accused him of heresy.

Williams's ideas developed in his novel *Shadows of Ecstasy* (1931),
where an African king, Inkamasi, is seen as a type of Christ, as evidenced
in Williams's quotation of Christ's acceptance of his Passion. In focusing
an instance of Christian royalty on an *African* king, Williams is here less
Eurocentric than either Lewis or Tolkien. Williams was, perhaps, influenced
by Frazer's exploration of 'magicians as Kings' especially in East Africa, in
The Golden Bough (1922) and, indeed, by Rider Haggard's *King Solomon's
Mines* (1885). Here, evidence of Haggard's examination of the Zulu culture
is found in his portrait of Umbopa, the dispossessed King of the Kukuana
people. Williams says King Inkamasi "set his face to go up to Jerusalem",[82]
accepting *his* sacrificial death so as to be true to his kingship, death at the
hands of the evil Considine, a latter-day Pilate.

King Inkamasi, an iconic figure of Williams's idea of what a contemporary
king should be, is very much alive, truly human and, at the same time, a
mythological epitome of Williams's 'good king'. Williams tells the story of a
Christian king, Inkamasi, whose every word and every action are in accord
with his own beliefs, and in the glory he sees in his own Majesty, the possession
of which Williams applauds, as he revealed in his biography of James I.

The figure of the king is for Williams the union of a private person and of that same person stamped with the ordaining mark of kingship, an instance of organic co-inherence. Williams felt strongly about this duality, as he demonstrated when writing to Anne Ridler, as he complained about King George VI "smiling when he is crowned and robed",[83] thereby confusing his two roles. Williams develops his ideal further, focusing on the king's *humanity*, showing insight in his description of the Christian King Arthur in the poems of the *Arthuriad* (1938, 1944, edn. 1991). Arthur's task is to create a peaceful, just and prosperous society, in fact, a Christian society, his function like that expected of a Christian Anglo-Saxon king. Since Williams's model for the earthly king is Christ, it is no surprise that he sees Arthur as a sacral ruler, whose monarchy is, therefore, spiritual.

The picture is now far less theological and much more human, depicting a good king, though clearly less than perfect. Williams explores the Arthurian legends and paints a poetic portrait of the Celtic King (the *dux bellorum* or war-leader) Arthur the Pendragon. Manifestly a brave leader and protector of his people, he *does* create a peaceful, just and prosperous society. It is notable that we have here a convergence of Old Testament and Homeric ideas of the Shepherd-King protectively guiding his people. However, the 'all too human' side of his character is discovered when Williams portrays him as an egocentric, adulterous king who, preferring contract to compact, relishes the power derived from 'the King's Coins'. Williams believes that Arthur *cannot* emulate Christ *unless* reconciled by the Grail, that is, by the Eucharist. Nevertheless, Williams sees in Arthur the 'type' of the monarch who, as His vicegerent, actually reflects Him.

Williams intensifies the appeal of the fine qualities he attributes to kings as he confronts the reader with the antithesis of the good king by describing Aristotle's perversion of kingship, which is manifested as the tyrant. Arthur finds it necessary to use military force to remove King Cradlemas, whom Williams rather exaggeratedly describes as a tyrant. He voiced his personal difficulty over the use of force in *The Taking of Camelot*, part II:

Taliessin

Suddenly, with violence, the interior life began;
guilt fell on him; open beneath the skies,
blood-sprinkled, alone, outrageous, he stood.[84]

Williams develops the tyrant image into virtually a 'type' of the Devil. In *The Vision of the Empire*, "beyond P'o-Lu the headless Emperor moves",[85] the antithesis of the Emperor in Byzantium who, as Lewis said, symbolises God. In Williams's play, *The House of the Octopus* (1945), Williams said the danger of P'o-Lu "is rather a spiritual threat than a mortal dominion",[86] to obviate the idea that P'o-Lu might be thought to stand for Japan in view of the date of its completion.

Williams vacillates between an *overstated* description of Cradlemas who, no barbarian, but only the last "sinister representative of the Roman civilisation",[87] as a tyrant, and the *understated* evil he describes in his Headless Emperor in P'o-Lu. Williams said "the whole universe is to be known as good",[88] hence his reticence totally to condemn the Headless Emperor.

Having ousted the so-called tyrant, King Cradlemas, King Arthur was duly installed as king. In *The Calling of Taliessin*, Merlin had told the king's poet, Taliessin, that he and his sister Brisen had been sent "to build, as is willed, Logres, and in Logres a throne".[89] Highly significant, as well as succinctly implying that the founding of Logres (later to become Britain) as a monarchy is 'willed by God', it also underlies the tension created by Williams being so drawn to the Republic.

It is perfectly rational for Williams consciously to try to encapsulate the egalitarian qualities inherent in a republic in a constitutional monarchy. Williams might have been thinking along the same lines as those whom the historian J.N. Figgis had described, when he said that in sixteenth and seventeenth century England, "There is no trace of propagandism in the work of royalist writers", who maintain that some have "no quarrel with other forms of government . . . whether elective monarchies or republics".[90]

However, this study shows that Williams not only succeeds in combining the qualities of a republic with those of a constitutional monarchy in striving to attain one of his so-called 'impossibilities', but that he insightfully anticipated two important concepts of the mid twentieth century, 'Negative Freedom' and 'Positive Freedom'. Williams looks to the freedom inherent in the republic to engender equality, and also to obviate the dangers he fears in the possession of excessive power in a despotic monarchy. I believe that, in spite of his sensitivities over the use of what he regards as violence, he is not, in fact, equivocating when he shows ambivalence over the use of military might to achieve freedom from a tyrant, but is being discerning.

Rousseau said in *The Social Contract* (1762) that "all legitimate government is republican". Rousseau's editor, Maurice Cranston, clarified that Rousseau meant "any government directed by the public will . . . so even a monarchy [could] be a republic." Rousseau asserted that "A man shall be forced to be free". This forcing, as advocated by 'Positive Freedom', almost certainly engenders further tyranny. Cranston says that Rousseau is not, in fact, seeking power, but rather he has need for authority.[91]

'Positive Freedom' requires force to create freedom for people in *general*, whereas 'Negative Freedom', seeking to minimise possession of power, 'negates' the barriers that diminish the *individual's* loss of freedom. The political philosopher, Sir Isaiah Berlin, suggests that 'Negative Freedom' alone is not sufficient: 'Positive Freedom' is also needed.

Berlin said in "Two Concepts of Liberty" in *Four Essays on Liberty* (1958, published 1969), "Perhaps the chief value for liberals of political – 'positive' – rights, of participating in the government, is as a means for protecting what they hold to be an ultimate value, namely individual – 'negative' – liberty".[92]

However, there is an important difference between Williams and Berlin's route to Freedom. Berlin believed that "One belief, more than any other, is responsible for the slaughter of individuals on the altars of the great historical ideals – justice or progress . . . even liberty itself . . . The belief that somewhere . . . in divine revelation . . . there is a final solution".[93] Williams also believes in what we may call a *'Positive Vision'*. This vision is of a Christian kingdom, in which the king, reconciled by the Grail, serves his people. Williams sees a Christian monarchy in modern Britain – London-in-Logres – incorporating the values of Logres after Arthur became its king. Anne Ridler, showing something of Williams's growing idea of a kingly society, said that his employer, Sir Humphrey Milford, with his combination of authority and kindness, "helped to give life to Williams's conception of the ideal ruler".[94] Alice Mary Hadfield, shedding more light on Williams's microcosmic portrait of a just society said that Williams saw Milford *as* King Arthur and himself as Taliessin.[95]

Williams is talking about his own times as much as those of King Arthur. Williams manifests the royal Glory he believes attaches to Arthur and to the later historic monarchs in his biographies. He believes that Glory pertains to his contemporary monarchs, especially to King George VI, who saw the Coronation as transforming him, as Sarah Bradford had said.[96] Williams regards the king, anointed by the Archbishop of Canterbury, as God's Vicegerent *par excellence*, a monarch reconciled, both as the crowned king and as a private person, through the Grail – the Eucharist. It is extremely significant that King George VI's coronation followed soon after the crisis caused by the Abdication of the uncrowned King Edward VIII. It needs must have focused the minds of many on the meaning and significance of Monarchy at the time.

PART TWO

The Monarch and God's Vicegerent

Chapter Five

Lewis and the Historical Notion of Kingship

Once a King or Queen in Narnia,
always a King or Queen in Narnia.
 C.S. Lewis, *The Lion, the Witch and the Wardrobe* (1950), pp.189-90.

An Inkling

C.S. Lewis (1898-1963), was a scholar, and, if sometimes thought to exhibit chauvinist traits, also a gentleman. He was born in Belfast of Welsh and Irish extraction.[1] After his conversion in 1931 he was, like Charles Williams, an Anglican. Belfast was, and still is, a city of grave divisions, between Roman Catholicism and Protestantism; and between Irish Nationalism and Unionism, which might engender exposition of those things that Christians held in common, beliefs Lewis expressed in *Mere Christianity* (1952).

Lewis's early life was very different from that of Charles Williams. Lewis was born in Belfast in 1898 at "a time of economic expansion". His father was "a police court solicitor", his mother "the daughter of the Rector of St. Mark, Dundela . . . The combination of good Christian parents and a loving elder brother ensured Clive [Jack, as he called himself] a very happy childhood". The family moved from a semi-detached house in an inner suburb of Belfast into a larger house on the outskirts, which Albert had specially built for them, a sure sign of prosperity. Jack and his brother Warren were both sent to England to be educated in Public Schools. Jack was subsequently educated privately with a retired headmaster, W.T. Kirkpatrick, in Surrey. He won a scholarship to Oxford, and began to read Classics in 1917.[2]

Lewis's Protestant-Unionist Ulster middle-class and professional home background, with its political conservatism and monarchist sympathies, though not exactly rich was, indeed, more than merely 'comfortable'. It was, indeed, natural for Lewis to be a staunch royalist, and even with a caveat concerning excessive royal power, to uphold the ideal of a Constitutional Monarchy – "the consecration of secular life".[3] Lewis, a royalist, like Williams, believed in Christ the King, *Christus Rex* who "reigned from the tree"[4] (though he rarely sympathises with Williams's dialectic stance over the idea of a Republic).

Lewis and the Historical Notion of Kingship

Lewis finds His self-sacrificial love demonstrated in the sacrifice of the Cross, part of the myth that Lewis said "really happened".[5] There is some similarity between Williams and Lewis's view of the Atonement. Lewis manifests an Anselmian idea of salvation through Substitution. This can be seen most obviously in *The Lion, the Witch and the Wardrobe* (1950), Aslan, who allegorically represents Christ (and whose name actually means *Lion*), is 'substituted' for the traitor, Edmund, to save him from perdition. Lewis says that Williams's idea of Atonement is "summed up" in three propositions. Firstly, there is 'Substitution'. Secondly, we can "'Bear one another's burdens'". Thirdly, Williams speaks of "exchanges". He devoted a whole chapter in *He Came Down from Heaven* (1938) to 'The Practice of Substituted Love'.[6]

Williams saw the Incarnation as an act of renunciation, a sacrifice in itself, whereas Lewis regards it more in the light of a miracle, an "invasion by a Power . . . the God of Nature".[7] Reflecting Williams's idea of 'Exchange' (as a means of salvation of others) Lewis's hero Ransom, in *Perelandra* (1943), is sent to enact Christ. Ransom experienced a 'Presence in the Darkness', who told him that Maleldil (whose Presence it was), allegorically representing Christ, would "save Perelandra not through Himself but through Himself in Ransom".[8]

Therefore Ransom *is* the miracle sent to Perelandra to preserve its innocence. Ransom's actions demonstrate his obedience to his vocation, and are an instance of democratised kingship, of which the French Jesuit, Jean-Pierre de Caussade, said that people can "all surrender themselves to his action . . . and in the end all be participators in his majesty and privileges . . . Every soul can aspire to a crown".[9] Ransom becomes the Fisher-King, the wounded king, like King Pelles, and King Bran in the *Mabinogion*. In the *Arthuriad*, Williams shows how the kingdom of Logres is reconciled to God as Arthur, and Pelles wounded by the 'Blow', come into a relationship of co-inherence and exchange. Williams's earthly and heavenly Kings manifest royal glory. Lewis, indirectly evincing glory, speaks of God as the source of his joy, the joy that, in fact, drew him to God. He tells of His awe-inspiring absolute beauty. In *Out of the Silent Planet* (1938), Lewis rejoices in the sight that Ransom saw from his spacecraft. He saw "planets of unbelievable majesty", and "celestial sapphires, rubies, emeralds and pin-pricks of burning gold",[10] description that suggests both the 'Glory' of the created order and the splendour of royalty. Lewis talks about his discovery of a "cool morning innocence", and a new quality – "holiness".[11] He told his friend Arthur Greeves that holiness shines through William Morris's romanticism.[12] Lewis actually refers once to the "glories and dangers and responsibilities" attaching to monarchy in *Letters to an American Lady* (1967).[13] Although Lewis rarely uses the word 'glory' directly in this context, he implies both meanings of the ancient Hebrew words for 'glory' – the shining light and the quality that inspires awe.

Lewis asserts that Man's first duty to God and, by extension to the earthly king, is willing obedience. He looks back to the ancient Hebrews, who accepted Yahweh as King, and to His revelation to Moses. Lewis's two reasons for obedience to the divine King are because of God's declaration, 'I AM'. The first refers to His 'absolute being' and 'absolute beauty'. The second centres on God's activity and claim to sovereignty. A direct reference to Yahweh *as* King is seen in relation to "Yahweh's activity as creator" and the Israelite myth about His conquest of the primordial Dragon. Yahweh is addressed in Psalm 74: 12: "God is my King from of old, achieving victories in the midst of the earth".[14]

During a period of Atheism, Lewis found it difficult either to believe in God or to see Him as King, and thus saw no reason to obey him. After his conversion, Lewis again believed in God, initially as a Theist. Two years later, he accepted Christ as the Son of God, and believed again in the Holy Trinity. His faith restored, Lewis thought it reasonable to obey God, agreeing with Joseph Addison (1672-1719) that obedience to God makes a man happy and disobedience makes him miserable. Lewis's non-coercive idea of obedience with free will, he regards as 'loving response' to God's reciprocal love between the persons of the Trinity. Lewis's belief in obedience to the king, divine and earthly, possibly has connections with Williams's idea of co-inherence and the Pauline interchanging love of 'living-in-and-for each other'.

Williams does not, in fact, actually refer directly to obedience *per se*. Belief in obedience to God as King reflects what Lewis sees in the Psalms, especially those of enthronement, where he finds a beautiful sense of order. His notion of the obligation of obedience to the sovereign is somewhat reminiscent of the same expectation in the medieval era. For example: Richard II was jealously protective of his royal prerogative, and so governed with a strong emphasis on obedience to the monarch. Lewis, aware of the dangers of excessive use of royal power, asserted that since the Fall of Man, with Man's inherent temptation to egotism, royal power should be limited. A democracy would defend the rights of the people against evil tyranny. Like Williams (and the ancient Romans) Lewis abhorred the idea of tyranny and despotism.

Lewis had to teach some Anglo-Saxon at Oxford, notably the heroic poem *Beowulf* (c.900). In Anglo-Saxon England there was a limitation on the king's power. The "coronation ceremony . . . put limits and conditions on the king" at the same time as rallying "loyalty to his person and to the office".[15] Before the end of the seventh century, 'reciprocity' was found between the "overlord and each of his dependent kings". Even in this emergent interdependence "there existed the personal relationship of lord and man".[16] By contrast, Tolkien believed in the absolute authority of the king in Council, his 'men' being asked for advice to which he would listen.

Perhaps paradoxically, then, Lewis believed that through obedience, people find contentment. We note that Lewis, rather more than Williams, emphasised the idea that belief in God and obedience to His will are found to be reasonable. In this stress on 'reason', Lewis displayed something of the Anselmian trait of defending the faith by intellectual reasoning, rather than by debate based on the Scriptures. While still an idealist, Lewis said that he believed in 'the Absolute' (that is, God though not named as God), Berkley's God, before he saw any way of entering into a relationship with it, and that once he realised that 'the Absolute' was God, he saw Him as perfect in Himself, as did the Old Testament Hebrew people. Williams, not so ready to couch his thought in formal philosophical terms saw, like Dante and Beatrice, a theophany of the Absolute in his beloved, the Regent from God's throne.

Lewis, like Williams, believes in the idea of the 'divine order' of His very 'Being'. Lewis sees the ontological order in the sheer beauty of 'the absolute', as Williams saw in order a sense of divine perfection. There is some correlation between Williams's idea of Conformity, which may be unconsciously Pharisaic, and Lewis's concept of Order.

Lewis saw in order a sense of delight, which is a less legalistic position than Williams. To use an analogy, Lewis, for instance, saw beautiful order in getting the steps of a dance right, and in the pleasure of using disciplined skill. Lewis reminded us that John Milton (1608-1674) regarded the happy life as one of order, like enjoying a complicated dance. Both Williams and Lewis believed that in order there is constant interchange between the partners, taking turns in being reverential to each "other", even between God and Man.

Lewis discussed his concept of 'Obedience' in *A Preface to Paradise Lost* (1942), which he had dedicated to Williams. Willing obedience is due, Lewis believed, to a superior, never to an inferior. He disagreed with Milton, who asserted that only God should rule Men, and that no man is given dominion over another. Milton, therefore, denies the validity of the notion of kingship, in fact, advocating regicide in his *Eikonoklastes* (1649). Lewis believed that even order can be destroyed by obeying equals, failing to obey a natural superior or by failing to rule a natural inferior. Obedience is due, in descending steps, from God downwards. Lewis goes so far as to maintain that it is a tyrant who rules over his natural equals.

Lewis's idea of order is closely related to his notion of hierarchy. While Williams was keen to laud republican egalitarian values, Lewis was more inclined to see authority stemming from a unique being at the apex of a pyramid, the very pinnacle of Creation, to whom obedience is due. To Lewis, this Being – God, is one, transcendent and absolute, and is not 'one among others'. As a 'Supernaturalist', he believed that God is "the one original or self-existing thing . . . on a different level from, and more important than, all other things".[17]

Lewis sees a real, and historically valid, link between hierarchy and authority. For him, it was self-evident that God, who *has* no superior, wields the right to rule over all. Moreover, Lewis believed that the earthly king also has the right to rule under the authority of, and with allegiance to, the divine King, as it were to the 'High King', whose vicegerent he is in Lewis's eyes. Williams regarded the earthly king as God's Vicegerent, as did the Anglo-Saxons, who saw him as *"dei vicarius"*, Vicar of God. [18] He was, like King Arthur, anointed with oil, and set apart by God for this high office, like King David.

In *Letters to an American Lady* (1967), Lewis described Queen Elizabeth II at her coronation in 1953 as "His [God's] vice-gerent and high priest on earth".[19] This view was anticipated in *Out of the Silent Planet* (1938), where Lewis portrays the ruling angel, the *Oyarsa*, as the vicegerent of Maleldil (who represents Christ), the Sovereign with divine authority to rule and reign.

Lewis is Drawn by 'Joy' to God's Kingship

Lewis showed a predilection for monarchism in his boyhood stories of *Animal Land* written when "Jack" (as he called himself) was seven in 1905. With his brother "Warnie's" *India*, they became *Boxen*, unequivocally royal histories.[20] However, as Lewis pointed out in *Surprised by Joy* (1955), "*Animal Land* had nothing whatever in common with *Narnia* except the anthropomorphic beasts", and excluded the "least hint of wonder". Nevertheless, somewhat akin to wonder, his sense of longing – *Sehnsucht* – which he called 'Joy', with his distinctive intellectual enquiry over a period of some twenty years, led him to submit to God's kingship, the hardest part of his conversion process.[21] Lewis displayed profound belief in God's kingship, in the earthly monarch as His vicegerent and in the *democratised* kingship of the 'Everyman', that is of anyone, provided he accepts absolute responsibility for his individual role. Like Williams, Lewis believes in the self-sacrificial love of Christ, in God's immanence, sometimes emphasising His transcendence, and in the centrality of the Incarnation, Passion and Resurrection. Again like Williams, Lewis creates through his writing a greater awareness of the spiritual nature of royalty, especially that of Queen Elizabeth II, whom he saw as God's vicegerent and high priest on earth.

Lewis equates the spiritual nature of kingship in *That Hideous Strength* (1945), contrasting the spiritual and secular kingdoms of Britain, and the image of the mythical kingdom of Logres with its chief leader, the Pendragon, successor to the Christian King Arthur. The difficulty in *That Hideous Strength* is having an actual spiritual king in Ransom the Pendragon if the same spirituality underlies the monarchies of George VI and Elizabeth II. In upholding the ideal of sacral kingship, with its overall authority rooted in God, both Lewis and Williams were writing against the philosophical drift of the times. In Europe, kings and emperors were less respected in the aftermath of the Great War. Lewis's friend Owen Barfield said the prevailing atmosphere of their undergraduate days at Oxford (the early 1920s) was very much one of "secular humanism",[22] though it could be said to apply to the twentieth century as a whole. In the development of Lewis's ideas from childhood, his "stance",[23] to use Barfield's term, was not always, in spite of Lewis's upbringing, 'Christian'.

In *Surprised by Joy*, Lewis spoke of "an unsatisfied desire which is itself more desirable than any other satisfaction".[24] He had not yet become aware of the source of his "desire", his sense of longing – *Sehnsucht* – the sudden appearances of which he had referred to as 'glimpses' or 'stabs' of joy, that led him to his conversion, and to accept the kingship of God. Lewis said, "I call it Joy, which is here a technical term and must be sharply distinguished both from Happiness and from Pleasure."[25] Lewis became aware of the myth of the 'dying god', of "Pagan Christs" like Balder and Osiris. Nicolson referred, in connection with Osiris, to what he called the "legend of death and resurrection".[26] The 'dying god' myth was to become very significant with regard to Lewis's return in 1931, to a Christian "stance", through the meaning of the sacrifice of the Cross.

Lewis saw the idea of Christ as one among many 'dying gods' in Sir James George Frazer's *Golden Bough*, which was "being published when he [Lewis] was with W.T. Kirkpatrick in 1914-1917".[27] Lewis's 'stance' changed during his schooldays. Having lost his Christian faith for the time being, he did not now obey God. This was, perhaps, due to a reluctance to conform unquestioningly to a seemingly paternalistic God. This might have been because of partially repressed memories of a "mercurial"[28] father, as Lewis himself puts it, coupled with those of the tyrannical and brutal headmaster, "Oldie", of the preparatory school, Wynyard School, which was dubbed "Belsen", named after the concentration camp.[29] Lewis's army experience, which he reflected as part of Ransom's experience in the story of *Out of the Silent Planet* (1938), where "you are never alone for a moment and can never choose where you're going or even what part of the road you're walking on".[30] This demonstrates an existence without Free Will.

Before his conversion, Lewis saw the idea of having a God to obey as illusory. In a letter to Arthur Greeves of 12 October 1916, he had said, "All religions, that is, all mythologies to give them their proper name are merely man's own invention".[31] In *Surprised by Joy* he says that "all teachers and editors took it for granted . . . that . . . religious ideas were sheer illusion". He said later that when he was "demobbed" and returned to Oxford in 1919, he told himself there were to be "no romantic delusions".[32] He was still following the sceptical, if not cynical, views implanted at school, and also following the current trend.

In *The Abolition of Man* (1943), he argued that "you cannot go on 'explaining away' for ever . . . You cannot go on 'seeing through' things for ever. The whole point of seeing through something is to see something through it".[33] Lewis was still dealing with escaping from illusions when in

1922, he and Barfield had discussed in Wadham gardens "'the Christina Dream', as we called it" (after Christina Pontifex in Butler's novel",[34] *The Way of All Flesh,* 1903). The dreams that Christina "had dreamed in sleep were sober realities in comparison with those she indulged in while awake".[35] Lewis had experienced romantic longing that is the very reverse of wishful thinking. He had, around 1926, come to a state of "angry revolt" against the spell of "Christina Dreams . . . the very type of the illusions" from which he was trying to escape. His hero, Dymer, was "a man escaping from illusion". Lewis was at this time, he says, "an idealist".[36] By the time he wrote *Dymer,* he said he had rejected atheism and naturalism, in favour of idealism.[37]

Covering the whole period of his conversion process, Lewis began writing *The Allegory of Love* in 1928, to be published in 1936. In it he said that a way, other than that of allegory, of seeing the "archetype in the copy" is through "symbolism or sacramentalism". He finds "the more real"[38] experience in his symbol of joy. Lewis made a more successful attempt to explain it in *The Pilgrim's Regress* (1933), which he wrote "during his fortnight at Bernagh", on a holiday with Arthur Greeves in 1932.[39]

In the second edition of *Regress* Lewis had used the word *romanticism,* which in the third edition he calls "intense longing", thus equating it with his feeling and definition of joy. By this time he found that a "cause of obscurity was the (unintentionally) 'private' meaning [he] then gave to the word Romanticism". He describes it there as "a particular recurrent experience which dominated my childhood and adolescence and which I hastily called Romantic because inanimate nature and marvellous literature were among the things that evoked it". He added tellingly, "I still believe that the experience is common, commonly misunderstood, and of immense importance".[40] Lewis demonstrates in *Regress* both his idea of the experience of joy, and also of the idea of having to obey God, represented in *Regress* by the Landlord, who proves, in fact, to be the source of his 'Joy'.

Lewis said, "God was to be obeyed simply because He was God . . . because of what He is in Himself. If you ask why we should obey God, in the last resort the answer is, I Am. To know God is to know that our obedience is due to Him". Lewis says he had been, like Jill and Eustace in the Narnia story, *The Silver Chair,* "taken out of [him]self". One morning, two years after his conversion to theism in 1929, arriving at Whipsnade after a conversation with Dyson and Tolkien, Lewis said he believed "that Jesus Christ is the Son of God".[41]

Lewis said in the preface to the 1950 reprint of the narrative poem *Dymer* (first edn. 1926), that he had had a 'romantic longing' for the 'Hesperian or Western Garden system' of imagery, and that, by the time he wrote *Dymer,* he had come under the common obsession about 'Christina Dreams'. He says he should have repented his "idolatry". He ceased to regard the Christina Dreams as "illusions", and it seemed to him by 1929, the year of his conversion, to be reasonable and right for him willingly to obey God. It would be rash to say categorically that during this time Lewis actually became a Republican, *per se*, insofar as he seems to have equated royalism with Christianity.

Lewis told Greeves in a letter of 2 December 1918, "I have just finished a short narrative, which is a verse version of our old friend Dymer, greatly reduced and altered to my new ideas".[42] In 1927, Lewis was working on another narrative poem *The King of Drum*, hoping it would "clear things up". The re-written version, *The Queen of Drum* (published 1969), contains Christian symbolism. In 1938, Lewis asked John Masefield for his opinion.[43] Masefield said he could "feel an extraordinary beauty in the main theme – the escape of the Queen into Fairyland". *The Queen of Drum* tells us that "a King's house contains the weal of us all",[44] evincing Lewis's present enthusiasm for both Christianity and royalty.

The Queen of Drum had been written between 1918 and 1938, thus over a period elapsing Lewis's both Atheist and Christian years.[45] Lewis saw the direct connection between belief *in* God and obedience *to* Him, only *after* his conversion to theism in 1929. He said that even as "the most dejected and reluctant convert in all England", as he called himself in *Surprised by Joy*, he unreservedly acknowledged that "God was God". He was converted "only to Theism, pure and simple".[46] Lewis said that he "was permitted for several months, perhaps for a year, to know God and to attempt obedience without even raising that question", that is, the question of a future life. He "had been brought up to believe that goodness was goodness only if it were disinterested, and that any hope of reward, or fear of punishment, contaminated the will". As far as his conscious memory of it went, Lewis said, he was "least informed" over his "transition from mere Theism to Christianity".[47]

The Source of Lewis's Joy: The Divine King

Reminding us of Ransom's journey in the spaceship in *Out of the Silent Planet*, during which he had been subjected to "the tyranny of heat and light",[48] Lewis recalled in *Surprised by Joy* "certain blazing moonlit nights in that curtainless dormitory at Wynyard", always with recollections of boyhood fears. By contrast, Lewis had always thought of his early years in Ireland as a virtually idyllic "childhood", and his years of misery in public and other private schools as his "boyhood".[49]

The obstacle overcome, Lewis refers to the time that favoured *royalism*, as he discovers that the source of his 'Joy' is God. In a Bodleian manuscript he writes, "In this book I propose to describe the process by which I came back, like so many of my generation, from materialism to a belief in God". Lewis, "an empirical Theist", says that his "method" differs "from that of many contemporaries", being "out of harmony with the association lately established among us between classicism in art, royalism in politics and catholicism in religion".[50]

This remark was a paraphrase, if not virtually a quotation, from T.S. Eliot. In *For Lancelot Andrewes: Essays on Style and Order* (1928) Eliot had described himself as "classicist in literature, royalist in politics, and anglo-catholic in religion".[51] Eliot's essay describes the attitudes parodied in Lewis's 'three pale men' in *The Pilgrim's Regress*, Book Six, Chapter Two: Classicist, Neo-Angular, and Humanist (substituted for Royalist). Eliot's self-description, in turn, was a variation of a dictum of the French avant-garde journalist and critic, Charles Maurras, (1868-1952), whom Eliot likens to the Humanist Irving Babbitt.[52] For Maurras and others, monarchism was an act of political defiance in republican France. The French tradition is that of an absolute monarch, while the English ideal is normally that of constitutional monarchy, Nicolson's "parliamentary kingship".[53] However, in *early* seventeenth century England the ideal was, like the French, absolutist. Eliot asserts that although Thomas Hobbes and Bishop Bramhall (a critic of Hobbes) had "no sympathy whatever . . ." with Absolutism, "superficially their theories of kingship bear some resemblance to each other. Both men were violently hostile to democracy in any form or degree. They both believed that the monarch should have absolute power".[54] Lewis, on the other hand, said that because of the Fall of Man, "no man can be trusted with unchecked power over his fellows",[55] and for this reason he believed it necessary to have such a system of government as Constitutional Monarchy, without going as far as Milton, who for the same reason rejected hierarchical governance. Lewis's conversion to Christianity was complete by 1931, having made his "dive", an idea redolent of both self-surrender and baptism. There is, perhaps, a semi-conscious connection here with Beowulf's self-surrender in his underwater struggles with the monsters. Lewis had found Him whom he had desired. He *had* desired 'Joy', but came to realise that, as he tells us in *Surprised by Joy*, his desire was actually for "the naked Other, imageless (though our imagination salutes it with a hundred images), unknown, undefined, undesired".[56]

Lewis was led to Christianity by his love of myth and he used myth to express his own beliefs. In a letter he said, "Any amount of theology can now be smuggled into people's minds under the cover of romance without their knowing it". This 'smuggling' is what Lewis does in the space trilogy, in particular in *Out of the Silent Planet* (1938), while the theology is more directly presented in *Perelandra* (1943), which he claimed he had written for his "co-religionists", his fellow Christians. Lewis feared that Evolution theories were taking root in the popular imagination.[57] This can be seen in W. Olaf Stapledon's *Last and First Men* (1930) and J.B.S. Haldane's *Possible Worlds* (1927).There had been, indeed, projected further evolution of Man in H.G. Wells's *Time Machine* (1895). Wells, much influenced by T.H. Huxley, envisioned the degradation of Man, divided eventually into two degenerate groups, the subterranean workers, the Morlocks, and the decadent Eloi. Lewis liked the prospect of using the inter-planetary idea to counter this situation and to create a mythology based on it with which to present the Christian point of view.

The crucial word here is 'imagination', referring to the ideas taking place in the popular mind. Its interpretation means the ability to imagine or form mental images or concepts of objects not present to the senses. Owen Barfield suggested that the need had been felt for a way of distinguishing what were merely 'sweet delusions' from the "more perdurable productions" of the Romantic spirit. This Coleridge had achieved by his distinction between *fancy* and *imagination*. 'Fancy' is defined as the power of inventing "illustrative imagery" and 'imagination' as "the power of creating from within forms which themselves become a part of Nature".[58] Lewis had experienced conflict between 'intellect' and 'imagination' until the conversation with Tolkien and Dyson, leading to his conversion, when he accepted the idea that Christianity was the myth that actually happened. His imagination, "the organ of meaning" – and his intellect, "the organ of truth" were reconciled.[59]

Baptising the Imagination

Lewis hoped to "smuggle theology" into readers' minds to baptise their imaginations. He said in *Surprised by Joy* that his own imagination, though not yet his intellect and his will, had been "baptised by reading George MacDonald's *Phantastes* (1858), where he found a "cool morning innocence", and a new quality – 'holiness'.[60] Via the 'new quality' Lewis also 'smuggled' into readers' minds a rationale that supports monarchy, thus underwriting the sacred office of kingship. Lewis does *not* see God as a 'deified ruler', but rather does he see the King as His Vicegerent. Lewis also found something of this 'new quality' in William Morris. Lewis says in a letter to Arthur Greeves of 1 July 1930, that in William Morris's *Love is Enough* (1872), Morris shows that he is "aware of the real symbolical import of all the longing and even of earthly love itself . . . For the first (and last?) time the light of *holiness* shines through Morris's romanticism".[61]

In MacDonald's *The Princess and Curdie* (1883), there is an instance of the saving grace of the 'holiness' which Lewis found. Princess Irene was the daughter of "a real king – that is one who ruled for the good of his people, and not to please himself". The princess's great-great grandmother gave the gift of perception of persons to the miner's son, Curdie. He "will be able always to tell . . . when a man is growing into a beast" – in part anticipating *Perelandra*. She stresses that it is important that he does not use the gift for his own ends, or he will lose it. He wonders what will happen if he makes a mistake. She tells him that "so long as he is not after his own ends, he will never make a serious mistake".[62]

Lewis compounds his idea of the essential link between holiness and the Kingdom of God in a letter in the Bodleian Library to his friend, the American author, Sheldon Vanauken (1955) and quoted by Vanauken in *A Severe Mercy* (1977). Lewis says, initially quoting the New Testament (Matthew 6: 33):

'Seek ye first the Kingdom of God and all these things shall be added unto you'. Hopeless if it were done by your own endeavours at some particular moment. But 'God must do it'. Your part is what you are already doing: 'Take me – no conditions'. After that, through the daily duty, through the increasing effort after holiness – well, like the seed growing secretly.[63]

In his science-fiction and fantasy, Lewis aims to "create and maintain a metaphor that will serve to carry in fictional form the basic tenets of Christianity and present them from a non-Christian point of view, but without reference to normal Christian symbols".[64] In MacDonald for example, Curdie "saw high in the air, somewhere about the top of the king's house, a great globe of light, shining like the purest silver".[65] Lewis uses symbolic imagery pertaining to his ideal of sacral kingship. What is 'holy' or 'sacred' is 'set apart', consecrated or devoted to God, has His sanction and inherent mysterious power. Sacred significance comes through the enactment of a sacred ritual, such as a coronation, which action imparts spiritual grace to the participants.

Lewis said he had been greatly influenced by G.K. Chesterton's *The Everlasting Man* (1925), and "for the first time saw the whole Christian outline of history set out in a form that seemed to . . . make sense".[66] Chesterton said, "The next best thing to being really inside Christendom is to be really outside. And a particular point of it is that the popular critics of Christianity are not really outside it". Chesterton said he desires "to help the reader to see Christendom from the outside " – telling us that he proposes "to strike wherever possible this note of what is new and strange". He wants both Christendom and humanity to "stand out from their background like supernatural things".[67]

Chapter Six

Lewis and the Experience of Joy

Obedience in the Kingdom of God

There are two sides to Lewis's reasons for obedience being "in the last resort, I AM". There is firstly the Judaeo-Christian meaning in the Old Testament commentators, and secondly the Hellenistic influence, where the 'I AM' is regarded as referring to 'Absolute Being' and 'Absolute Beauty'.

Lewis's Theism and later belief that Christ is the "Son of God" demonstrate two stages in his thought, the first being belief in the God who told Moses that "I AM" had sent him; and second in God the Holy Trinity. As a Theist, Lewis said we should obey God because "I AM". Moses is told that the personal name of "the God of the fathers" is Yahweh. The more enigmatic version, "I AM", is said to emphasize God's manifest omnipresence and creative activity.

Lewis asserts in *Surprised by Joy* that "the primal and necessary Being, the Creator, has sovereignty *de facto* as well as *de jure* . . . The *de jure* sovereignty was made known to me before the power, the right before the might". In short, God has sovereignty through His creativity *and* through what He actually *is*. Lewis says that "to know God is to know that our obedience is due to Him. In His nature His sovereignty is revealed.[1]

Lewis tells us that as an idealist he believed in the 'Absolute', or "'Berkley's God'". He could not "meet" Him, adding "There was, I explained, no possibility of being in a personal relation with Him".[2] When he came to believe that the absolute is God, he was like the Old Testament Hebrews in believing in God as perfect in Himself. An important idea to Lewis, he *sometimes* sees monarchy (e.g. in the portrayal of the king as like Christ in *Perelandra* or in Jane's response to Ransom in *That Hideous Strength*) as an image of the absolute beauty and justice of God.

It is through her perfect love for God, her love for Maleldil, who in *Perelandra* is Christ the King, that the Lady, the unfallen Queen of Perelandra, freely chooses to obey Him in all things, and enjoys perfect happiness. We shall discover how her choice relates to kingship. In *The*

Pilgrim's Regress, Lewis deals with the meaning of obedience as one response, of co-inherence, rather than blindly accepting God's will. It was, indeed, Lewis's sense of joy that actually led him both to belief *in* and obedience *to* God.

The central character, John, is an allegorical type of 'Everyman', who tells the reader something of Lewis's own spiritual journey at this time. In *Regress*, the cause and object of John's intense desire, or joy, is an island. John grows up in dread of the Landlord, said to be a moral despot. During his pilgrimage, John encounters Mr Enlightenment and Nineteenth Century Rationalism (the contemporary literary movement, which still in some places belittles Lewis, as *he* had himself belittled the Modernists, and Freudianism). John meets 'cerebral' men – Mr Sensible, Mr Neo-Angular (High Church practices), and Mr Humanist. He meets Mr Broad, representing "a modernising religion which is friends with the World and goes on pilgrimage". John comes to Wisdom's house, and discovers the inadequacy of his former philosophies – Idealism, Materialism and Hegelianism. He meets the Spirit of the Age, a Giant who makes everything John looks at appear transparent, marking the ephemeral nature of prominent elements of the time. Reason comes to John's rescue. Soon he meets Mother Kirk, by which Lewis refers to Traditional Christianity, not to the Roman Catholic Church, as some have supposed. We note the Ulster-Scots use of the term Kirk, a Presbyterian expression that tacitly disguises the word Church, the word derives from the Greek Kyriakon and was borrowed by the Germanic languages. The use of which not only disguises the word 'church' itself but also emphasises Lewis's traditional notions of the Church as well as the word 'church'.

History tells him that not everyone has a picture of an Island to lead them to the Landlord, that is, to God; but they are given other pictures that will do so. History explains it is best to meet Mother Kirk at the start. When Pagans have no benefit of the Church, the Landlord "sends them pictures and stirs up sweet desire and leads them back to Mother Kirk.[3] John discovered how to reach the Island. He retraced his steps, leading away from the Island,[4] in contrast to John Bunyan's *Pilgrim's Progress* (1678, 1684).

Reason returns John to Mother Kirk, who tells him to dive down to the bottom of a pool of water and come up on the other side. He is told that all he has to do is to let himself go. Taking the risk, John let himself go and "saw the Island".[5] In an unpublished and undated manuscript in Walter Hooper's possession, a copy of which is in the Bodleian Library, Lewis wrote an account of the sense of joy he felt on becoming a Theist. In a letter to Arthur Greeves of 8 July 1930, Lewis said, "With Barfield . . . I learned to dive which is a great change in my life and has important (religious) connections".[6] In the Bodleian manuscript Lewis recalled this first dive and says, "Nothing is simpler than this art. You do not need to do anything, you need only to stop doing something – to abstain from all attempt at self-preservation – to obey the command which Saint Augustine heard in a different context, *Securus te projice*".[7]

Like John, Lewis found difficulty in the idea of obeying God, of regarding Him as King. The problem of actually submitting *his* will to God's, of making that 'dive' and abstaining from all attempts at self-preservation, he tells us in *Surprised by Joy*, with an account of his conversion, was the last great obstacle he had to overcome before his finally accepting Theism. The obstacle was that of surrendering to a God with every right to 'interfere'. Lewis had mentioned his constitutional dislike of being either imposed upon or interfered with, like Ransom in *Out of the Silent Planet*, 'Lewis' in *Perelandra* and Jane Studdock in *That Hideous Strength*.[8]

Mythology and Willing Obedience to the King

Lewis explained his intention of using fiction to express his beliefs in reality. He was "imagining out loud", and speculating "what God might have done in other worlds".[9] In *Out of the Silent Planet*, he looked at Christianity "from outside it", both outside the earth and also outside the everyday experience of the philologist hero, Dr Elwin Ransom. Lewis's ideas about kingship and willing obedience to the King are represented as he describes a contented society of three groups of non-human sentient beings, who have a belief system, to Ransom's surprise, akin to Christianity. As Ransom approached Malacandra, a fictional version of Mars, significantly he experienced a deep sense of wonder.

Ransom discovered there a theist society which believes in the Old One, in Maleldil the Young, the divine King who created the world, who lives with the Old One and in the eldils and the Oyarsas, 'tutelary spirits', one of whom they call the Bent One. Lewis explains that the Old One and Maleldil the Young represent the Father and the Son of Christianity, and that the eldila represent angels and the Bent One was Satan.[10] Ransom learns from the hrossa, one of the sentient groups, about the eldila, who convey the divine King's commands to the inhabitants, commands which should be obeyed, as though coming directly from Maleldil Himself.

Willing and immediate obedience is expected of and given by the Malacandrians, which is a happy society that does not grasp for food, which is not quarrelsome and is sufficiently continent to maintain a small enough population for the available food. Obedience is given to the divine King through obedience to the Oyarsa (the word *Oyarsa* is derived from the Greek Ousiarches, meaning 'ruling essence')[11], the planet's tutelary angel, effectively the Malacandrian vicegerent, who acts with Maleldil's authority. The Oyarsa, being an angel, and not one of the three sentient groups, is a vicegerent whose authority has a quality in it that cannot be equated with that of a human monarch. However, it is explicit in Perelandra that Lewis sees him as the right king of a planet where the Incarnation of Christ has not taken place.

Lewis regards the historic Christ, like Maleldil the Young, as the Sovereign, the King with divine authority to reign and rule. Lewis links the idea of hierarchy with appropriateness to rule. Maleldil is King and thus, to Lewis, the apex of a pyramid, the pinnacle of a hierarchy. Lewis describes a religion on Malacandra that believes in hierarchy, a belief that strongly underwrites kingship. Explaining the connection between his belief in hierarchy, kingly rule and the delegated authority of the Oyarsa, Lewis demonstrates how the persons in this hierarchy obey those above them. The hrossa tell Ransom that both Maleldil and the Oyarsa rule.

It becomes clear that the Oyarsa is acting on Maleldil the Young's authority. The sorn Augray (another sentient being) said to Ransom, "He [the Oyarsa] is the one of his kind who was put into Malacandra to rule it when Malacandra was made". The words "was put" are important because this indicates that a being more powerful than the Oyarsa had orchestrated their existence, by placing them into Malacandra, which could only have been Maleldil.. Acknowledging his vicegerency, "The voice" of the Oyarsa said, "I did not wish to stretch my authority [his angelic authority] beyond the creatures of my own world".

Further evidence for the importance that Lewis attaches to obedience to the King is seen when the *Oyarsa* told Ransom they were "both copies of Maleldil", or as we would say made in God's image. To Ransom, "it became plain that Maleldil was a spirit without body, parts or passions". Ransom had not yet realised that Maleldil is Christ, and therefore God, the one, transcendent and absolute spirit, and thus is not 'one among other' spirits. He did, however, understand that they were willingly obeying God. There is here a correspondence to the early Lewis, who was a Theist, initially unwilling to submit fully to the Christian God.

Uniquely divine authority is the underlying reason for obedience to the Oyarsa and the other eldila, whom the Oyarsa refers to as "my servants",[12] their authority stemming from Maleldil. The Oyarsa asked Ransom "what Maleldil has done in Thulcandra [earth]". He tells Ransom that soon he will end his world and give back his people to Maleldil. The Oyarsa spoke to Ransom of "Maleldil's strange wars there [earth] with the Bent One".[13] The hrossa believe that on earth – Thulcandra the 'silent planet' – their Oyarsa, the Bent One, with some eldila, rebelled against Maleldil.

Chesterton: Rebellion and the Right to Rule

Lewis believed that because of disobedience to the divine King, the Fall, God in His love took the initiative. The Malacandrians believe that though evil still persists on earth, there are rumours of Maleldil's wonderful actions to redeem His lost world. These actions refer to the Incarnation, Passion, Resurrection and Ascension of Christ. Lewis sees the Incarnation as *the* Christian miracle, and compares it with parallel pagan "invasions". In the original edition of *Miracles* (1947) Lewis said:

The fitness of the Christian miracles, and their difference from these mythological miracles, lies in the fact that they show invasion by a Power which is not alien. They are what might be expected to happen when she [earth] is invaded not simply by a god, but by the God of Nature; by a Power which is outside her jurisdiction not as a foreigner but as a sovereign. They proclaim that He who has come is not merely a king, but *the* King, her King and ours.[14]

These ideas in *Miracles* are closely derived from Chesterton's *The Everlasting Man*, where Chesterton says of such an invasion, "Royalty can only return to its own by a sort of rebellion. Indeed the Church from its beginnings . . . was not so much a principality as a revolution against the prince of the world . . . the great usurper".[15] Chesterton underlines the idea of rebellion and revolution in *Orthodoxy* when he says, "For the orthodox, there can always be a revolution; for a revolution is a restoration".[16] Lewis endorses the idea that revolution is necessary to restore a monarch in *Prince Caspian* in the *Narnia* series. The Dwarf tells the children that he is a messenger of King Caspian, who "ought to be King of Narnia" and that "we hope he will be". He says that he [the Dwarf] is one of the "*old* Narnians", and that they are "a kind of rebellion".[17]This implies that Narnia contains an undercurrent of discontent and that, perhaps, a rebellion is needed to restore the rightful King to his throne. We can infer this from the discontent of the Narnians, which indicates that whoever does rule is not doing so with consent. In *The Horse and his Boy*, the boy Shasta did not actually wish to be king, but he was told, "The King's under the law, for it's the law that makes him a king".[18] He too was restored by a rebellion, in his case the war with the Calormenes, where he succeeded his father as King of Archenland.

In *Out of the Silent Planet* Lewis displays belief in the divine revelation of wisdom to those who are already obedient to Him, to those on *His side*. The Oyarsa says to Ransom. "It is not without the wisdom of Maleldil that we have met now and I have learned so much of your world. The Oyarsa speaks of what he will do in the siege of Thulcandra "if Maleldil does not forbid [him]", again acknowledging his obedience to Maleldil.[19] The revelation of "wisdom" suggests an intervention of Providence, much like Tolkien's "chance, if chance you call it",[20] reminiscent of the statement in Perelandra, that the old philosophers had said, "There is no chance or fortune beyond the Moon".[21] Lewis, through Ransom's questions, shows that the Oyarsa of Malacandra, who is obedient to Maleldil, and has been filled with "wisdom" by Him, is effectively a Vicegerent. Through the hrossa, Lewis makes it clear that the sorns (the séroni), and the pfifltriggi are also rational beings, hnau, and speak. Ransom asked the hross Hnohra, "Which of the hnau rule"? Ransom wondered whether the *sorns* ruled, appearing the most intelligent. He was told, "Oyarsa rules",[22] suggesting a chain of command with authority from Maleldil the divine King.

The *hross* Hnohra explains that *none* of the ordinary *hnau* [the three types of sentient beings] rules, but a being who is not only of another biological species but of another kind, in fact, an angelic spirit. Here, Lewis creates a Miltonic picture of a society whose belief is wholly compatible with republicanism. He revised this picture in *Perelandra*. As was mentioned earlier, Milton had said, "Dominion absolute was given to Man in general over Beast in general, not to one man over other men",[23] if applied to Malacandra, this would mean 'not one of the *hnau* over other *hnau*'.

Choosing the King's Side

Lewis envisaged that being the "subjects of Maleldil" involves choosing to be obedient and loyal to Him which, in effect, means being on the divine King's side.[24] In *Perelandra* Lewis warns against the inherent dangers of false ideologies. Weston said, "Life is greater than any system of morality; her claims are absolute". It is vital, then, to decide whose side you are on, the divine King's, or the devil's. The physicist, Professor Weston, keen to provide a "Beyond" for Man, personifies Lewis's fear of emergent evolutionism. Weston said patronisingly to the Oyarsa, "Like Bent One better: me on his side". His accomplice, Devine is largely desirous of gold, "sun's blood", as a key to power and luxury. They intend to sacrifice Ransom, quite mistaking the inhabitants' moral and religious nature. When Augray the sorn had heard of the wars, slavery and prostitution on Thulcandra (Earth), he told Ransom it was "because every one of them wants to be a little Oyarsa himself",[25] in effect wanting to be little gods, acknowledging no superior authority.

Additionally, this is close to what will be found to be a serious breach of the right order of hierarchy, while obedience is seen to be directly related to whose side you are on. Having chosen our sides, Lewis regards it as vitally important that we obey at the moment of need, not just when we choose to. It is a matter of doing the act necessary in the present moment, which will effect its own grace like a sacrament.

Lewis exposed the dangers he saw in latent or delayed obedience. Ransom procrastinated when an eldil (an angel who brings God's commands) told Hyoi that the man, Ransom, "ought not to be there", but going to Oyarsa. Ransom chose to stay for the hunt, saying that there would be time afterwards to visit Oyarsa, and that they must kill the hnakra first. The hnakra suddenly appeared. Ransom stayed to fight the hnakra, a monstrous water-creature threatening the hrossa. Weston and Devine, probably thinking he was only an animal, shot Hyoi the hross. Ransom, when leaving, said that the hrossa would think he has run away because he is afraid to look in their faces.[26] Ransom felt guilty over the hross's death because of his procrastination. Lewis demonstrates the need to do the task which God gives us straight away, a task where we are torn, for instance, between the needs of domestic life and other possibly more inviting activities. He says that being "good" and showing "public spirit" is analogous to the examination question which, as he puts it in *Surprised by Joy*, is "to be attempted . . . by all candidates"[27] That is to say, it is a requirement. There is, of course, no analogous choice over obeying Maleldil's will in *doing* the necessary, given task immediately. In *Orthodoxy*, Chesterton speaks of the need to choose to *do* the necessary task.

> All Christianity concentrates on the man at the crossroads . . . The true philosophy is concerned with the instant. Will a man take this road or that . . . The instant is really awful: and it is because our religion has intensely felt the instant . . . it is at an immortal crisis.[28]

Lewis stresses the importance of 'being with' Christ – of being in the royal presence – as he reflects his own joy in and longing for Christ. The 'Old One' is transcendent: Maleldil was immanent as he drew near to Hyoi at the pool of Balki, who believed that his pleasure increased with time and transformed his 'Joy'.

Lewis's own longing and 'Joy' are reflected in this episode. Hyoi said "My heart has been higher, my song deeper, all my days" because of it, and this because the *hnéraki* – the death-dealing monsters – were in the pool. Hyoi said, "I drank life because death was in the pool . . . I drink it and go to Maleldil".[29] Lewis here expresses his own belief in the hope of eternal 'Joy' after death. Lewis saw the bread of the Eucharist as transformation: memory sacramentally brings the efficacy of a past action into the present – *anamnesis*. The action at the pool, somewhat akin to the Eucharist, sacramentally brought Maleldil's presence to Hyoi.

Chapter Seven
Lewis and the Hierarchy

Christ the King of Love

Lewis, like Williams, sees Christ as the King of love, of self-sacrificial love – *agape*. Maleldil, mythologically representing Christ, reigns and rules, love underlying all His commands. He engenders love for 'the Other': the Malacandrians manifest this love to each other. Hyoi said to Ransom that if another "*hnau* wanted food, why should we not give it to them? We often do", which suggests that they share willingly. Hnohra, speaking for Lewis, said that "Maleldil had made and still ruled the world . . . There are stories that he (Maleldil) has taken strange counsel and dared terrible things, wrestling with the Bent One (the devil) in Thulcandra [Earth]",[1] referring to Christ's Incarnation and loving sacrifice, it is also applicable to His temptation in the desert, and the betrayal.

Lewis sees selfless love as the way to heaven. In *The Silver Chair*, Jill and Eustace are given four sacramental signs by the King, Aslan, to guide them to go in his stead, and also to act with self-sacrificial love, bravely to attempt to rescue Prince Rilian from the evil Witch-Queen, that he may succeed his father as the 'true' King of Narnia. Lewis told his brother Warnie on 28 January 1950, "I begin to suspect that the world is divided not only into the happy and the unhappy, but also into those who *like* happiness and those who, odd as it seems, really don't".[2] Lewis speaks of the concept of heaven in *The Problem of Pain* (1940) where he says, "Love, by definition, seeks to enjoy its object: the thing you long for summons you away from the self". Becoming increasingly selfless, "Each of the redeemed shall forever know and praise some one aspect of the divine beauty better than any other creature can".[3]

Love is seen in what Maleldil intends to 'awaken' in the sentient beings and, as Lewis believed in reality, for human beings. Lewis shows the connection between God's love, and our own and the Malacandrians' need for free will. Ransom found that being sentient meant the Malacandrians have a 'soul' or 'mind' as well as a body, rather like the talking beasts in the *Narnia* stories. In *Perelandra*, the King even suggests that they "will make the nobler beasts so wise that will become *hnau* [rational beings] and

speak: their lives shall awake to a new life in us as we awake in Maleldil".[4]
Lewis said he was helped in *his* "awaking" to Christianity by Chesterton's
Everlasting Man,[5] which 'spoke' to *his* inner life, longing to be awakened to
a life of freedom in Christ, *his* King.

In *Mere Christianity* Lewis argued that, "The happiness which God
designs for his higher creatures is the happiness of being freely, voluntarily
united to Him and to each other in an ecstasy of love and delight . . . And
for that they must be free". They must have "free will . . . the only thing that
makes possible any love or joy worth having".[6] Lewis, on the importance
of Free Will, says in *Regress* that even for the Landlord, God, it is pointless
to talk of "forcing a man".[7] The grotesque idea of "forcing a man" to do
something *freely* is reminiscent of when, in *Perelandra*, Weston "hinted" that
"the King must be forced to be free".[8] This paradoxical statement reminds
us of Rousseau, who in *The Social Contract* says of the *sovereign*, in virtually
identical words, "He shall be forced to be free",[9] an apparent contradiction
in terms. If force (or fear) are enlisted to try to create freedom, the attempt
is, though of necessity, fruitless. Hnohra the hross had told Ransom that
Maleldil still ruled the world – even a child knew that.[10] Lewis remembered
being a 'child' with positive connotations. The Malacandrians with their
Free Will trusted Maleldil with 'child-like' trust.

Lewis believes that a redeemed being becomes aware of its true self, playing
its individual part in that which "floods with meaning the love of all blessed
creatures for one another, the communion of the saints".[11] The redeemed being,
he says, shall 'dance' to the 'harmony' of the "song of the Church triumphant",
and not be "like an orchestra in which all the instruments played the same
note".[12] Lewis believes harmony with the divine King is not automatic. Our
happiness, the 'harmony' to which we can 'dance', will be seriously impaired if
we ignore the needs of other people. He warns against the serious danger of
failing to have love for 'the other', and of becoming too self-absorbed.

In *The Problem of Pain*, he imagines a "jolly, ruddy-cheeked man, without
a care in the world, unshakeably confident to the very end that he alone has
found the answer to the riddle of life". The feature given to this this 'jolly
man' that makes him seem the most pathetic is that he will lose "the taste
for the *other*", and that, for him, hell will mean "to live wholly in the self and
to make the best of what he finds there". The 'jolly man' did not accept his
'absolute responsibility'. He thought and acted just for himself, and would not
wish to be 'interfered with', like Lewis himself at one time. Lewis shows how
his 'jolly man' could not possibly enjoy his potential 'democratised kingship',
nor would he accept the king as God's vicegerent. His self-obsession would
preclude acceptance even of God as King: there would be no room for Him
in his 'private life'. The 'jolly man' made his own hell. His love's object was
himself, and his love was destructive self-love. The 'jolly man' showed conceit
in supposing that he had really fathomed life's mysteries. Lewis appeared to
take the line that hell meant "the darkness outside": he had earlier explained it
as healing, since it could give a person yet another chance to repent his sin.[13]

Although a man often failed to love others, Lewis believed that God, out of love, will always attempt to rescue him from hell with forgiveness. In *The Pilgrim's Regress* (and in *The Great Divorce* 1944-45), Lewis says three things about Hell. In *Regress*, Lewis says firstly, "You must not try to fix the point after which a return is impossible, but you can see that there will be such a point somewhere". By "a return", he refers to repentance. Secondly, to reiterate, God is not able to countermand free will because "it is meaningless to talk of forcing a man to do freely what a man has made impossible for himself". Thirdly, "evil is fissiparous and could never in a thousand eternities find any way to arrest its own reproduction", emphasising that mankind is free to choose repentance, though it would be valueless to force him, rather than encourage him.

Lewis explains how hell can, he believes, perhaps deliver a person from perdition. He says, "The walls of the black hole are the tourniquet on the wound through which the lost soul else would bleed to a death she never reached".[14] Lewis speaks here of Man's propensity for having the will to do, as St. Paul admitted in his Epistle to the Romans 7: 18, what is right, but to find that instead of doing it, he does what is wrong.

Lewis believes this is an effect of the Fall, and that, because of it, no-one should have "unchecked power" over others. Nevertheless, he still unhesitatingly advocates kingship. Lewis creates, as he says, in *Out of the Silent Planet*, a picture of "what God might be supposed to have done in other worlds",[15] a reflection of earth, except that there he creates a picture of a still harmonious world, where doing Maleldil's will is regarded as entirely reasonable.

The Hierarchy of Glory

In *Out of the Silent Planet*, Lewis's very choice of metaphors highlights his predilection for a hierarchical picture of the world and of the universe itself, the divine King at the top of the pyramid and the angelic *Oyarsa* as His vicegerent.

The use of imagery can, even unconsciously, reveal a writer's thoughts and feelings. When Lewis describes the scene that Ransom saw from his spacecraft, he refers to "planets of unbelievable majesty", suggesting the glory of creation and of monarchy, divine and human. Lewis's reference to "celestial sapphires, rubies, emeralds and pin-pricks of burning gold" evokes a glorious, royal environment.[16] This reveals the authors' admiration for the aesthetic ideals associated with concepts of a heavenly firmament and 'higher power'.

Lewis's imagery here is colourfully reminiscent of Joseph Addison's poem, *The Spacious Firmament on High* (1712) and the way the "spangled heavens" proclaim "their great Original". We are reminded of the doxology at the end of the *Lord's Prayer*: "Thine is the Kingdom, the Power and the Glory". There is something of William Blake's mystical words in his *Jerusalem*, which describes his "bow of burning gold", and even to the mystical jewels of Aaron's breastplate, "a ruby, a topaz, and a beryl . . . a turquoise, a sapphire and an emerald . . . a jacinth, an agate and an amethyst . . . a chrysolite, an onyx and a jasper". The breastplate was to be made of "gold and blue, purple and scarlet yarn", on which the jewels were mounted in "gold filigree settings" (Exodus 28: 17-20, 39: 8-13). This imagery is, indeed, redolent of royal regalia.

Lewis's belief in God as King and His supremacy in the universal hierarchy are expressed in his study of Milton's *Paradise Lost*, which displays Milton's views about rulership and highlights the differences between himself and Lewis. Lewis demonstrates his own and Milton's views of the causes and effects of the Fall of Man. In *A Preface to Paradise Lost* he tells us *who* should rule, and *how* they should rule. Lewis wrote his *Preface* in 1942, the year before the publication of *Perelandra*.

Although primarily defending Milton's epic poem, he also tells us something of his own views of hierarchy. Lewis refers to "the monarchy of God", about which both Milton and Aristotle, *inter alios*, had written, of the Hierarchical conception "According to this conception", Lewis says:

> Degrees of value are objectively present in the universe. Everything except God has some superior; everything except unformed matter has some natural inferior.
>
> The goodness, happiness, and dignity of every being consists in obeying its natural superior and ruling its natural inferiors.[17]

Milton's and Lewis's idea of God was the Christian view, timeless, transcendent and, to His creatures, 'Other'.

Aristotle, however, saw God in relation to the idea of the 'Great Chain of Being'. To him, God is understood to be at the end or the beginning of a sequence of beings, and thus as 'one among others', a notion contrary to Lewis's beliefs. Aristotle's God could not, therefore, be seen as strictly transcendent, but as unique, as the first in a sequence, and arguably, the links in a chain have to obey the first link. There is, perhaps, a kind of transcendence in the 'unmoved mover' who contains all change in himself without being actually changed: he is thus 'above' the changes. The theologian Eric Mascall cites Étienne Gilson: "The first unmoved mover is very far from occupying in Aristotle's world the unique place reserved for the God in the Bible in the Judaeo-Christian world".[18]

According to Lewis, Aristotle tells us that ruling and being ruled "are things according to Nature". He cites the "soul [as] the natural ruler of the body, the male of the female", and "reason of passion". Aristotle asserts that there are "as many kinds of rule as there are kinds of superiority or inferiority. Thus a man should rule his slaves despotically, his children monarchically, and his wife politically; soul should be the despot of body, but reason the constitutional king of passion . . . A king is one who rules over his real, natural inferiors". A tyrant rules "over his naturals equals . . . even (presumably) if he rules well".

Lewis reminds us that hierarchy is a "favourite theme" with Shakespeare. "A failure to accept his notion of natural authority makes nonsense, for example, of *The Taming of the Shrew* (1590-92). With *King Lear* (1603-06), we view it in the wrong light if we do not make more than "modern concessions about parental and royal authority". With *Macbeth* (1603-07) we should "realise that the wife's domination over the king is a 'monstrous regiment'". Thus, Lewis thinks that Shakespeare agreed with Montaigne that "to obey is the proper office of a rational soul".[19] Lewis says in the *Preface* that "order can be destroyed" both by ruling or obeying natural equals, or by failing to obey a natural superior, or to rule a natural inferior. He says it would be a "confusion" to assert the monarchy of God and to reject the monarchy of Charles II, though Milton would disagree.

Referring to Milton's poem, Lewis says that Satan maintains:

that the vice-regency of the Son is a tyranny in the Aristotelian sense. It is unreasonable to suppose monarchy 'over such as live by right His equals'. Abdiel's reply is double. Firstly he denies Satan's right to criticize God's actions at all, because God is his creator.

Secondly, "as creator He has a super-parental right of doing what He will without question".

Lewis says of Milton's view of the rise of human monarchy that one of 'ambitious heart', who sins "Satan's own sin, became discontent with fraternal equality which ought to prevail among natural equals". Milton's Satan, Lewis says, transgressed 'the law of nature'. His Empire became tyrannous, his pretence to divine Right, spurious. Milton's Adam shows that in Man's 'fatherly' displeasure being declared, Man asserts the true hierarchical principle at the very moment of breaking it tyrannously. Thus, according to Milton, 'dominion absolute' was given to Man over "Beasts in general, not to one man over other men". Milton's later writings attest that he was against the Restoration monarchy of Charles II. Milton and Lewis would have disagreed on this point.

Lewis emphasised that Milton "pictures the life of beatitude as one of order, an intricate dance".[20] A central element in the image of the dance is "the reconciliation of order and freedom".[21] The emphasis is moving from moral obedience alone to include loving response, and its fruit of real joy, as we shall find in *Perelandra*, and even a softening of Lewis's ideas about hierarchy when he comes to write *A Grief Observed* (1960). The notion of "the beatitude" of order is reminiscent of the way that Charles Williams is keen to show that order is a sign of perfection, even of divine perfection. This idea is almost entirely taken from Williams, especially in his lecture on Milton's *Comus* (1634), which he gave among "the appropriate beauties of the Divinity School".[22] Williams said in his "Dialogue on Hierarchy", "In the very moment of looking down on the ranks below, the whole order is happily changed and one finds oneself looking up at the astonishing blaze of those same ranks now high and high above".[23]

Lewis shows us more of the connection he sees between hierarchy and order in his *Reflections on the Psalms* (1961). He asserts that Psalm 119, which is focused on the divine Law, conforms to a poetic pattern, with love of the poet's subject and for his delight in leisurely, disciplined craftsmanship. Lewis feels that, in itself, this lets us into the mind of the poet. It shows us what the poet felt about the Law as he felt about his poetry, and that "both involved exact and loving conformity to an intricate pattern".

Even the idea of 'conformity' reminds us of the way Williams correlated the notion of 'conformity' with the concept of 'Order'. This 'conformity' may be a latent Pharisaic conception, that is, by being self-righteous, but it may, Lewis says, "be the delight in Order, the pleasure in getting a thing 'just so' – as in dancing a minuet". The psalmist's effort to "keep thy statutes" is not born of "servile fear". Lewis unequivocally states that "the Order of the Divine Mind, embodied in the Divine Law, is beautiful".

Lewis fancies that a Chinese Christian:

whose own traditional culture had been the 'schoolmaster to bring him to Christ'" – would appreciate this psalm more than most of us; for it is an old idea in that culture that life should above all things be ordered and that its order should reproduce a Divine order.[24]

There is no suggestion of fear or coercion. In *Miracles* (1947), he says, "The partner who bows to Man in one movement of the dance receives Man's reverences in another. To be high or central means to abdicate continually: to be low means to be raised: all good masters are servants: God washes the feet of men".[25] Lewis's development of thought is seen as he includes loving response as well as moral obedience to the Head of the hierarchy according to natural ontology. Lewis took the liberal view that hierarchy is "more like a dance than a pyramid",[26] an idea very close to Charles Williams, who had said, "It is so that one hierarchy suddenly changes to another . . . With every breath the joy changes . . . If every living creature is unique, it must necessarily be so".[27] This more liberal, idealised view of hierarchy could, perhaps, succeed in unfallen worlds.

Lewis said in the preface to *Paradise Lost*, "When Donne says 'thy love shall be my love's sphere', he has for his background the cosmic hierarchy of the Platonic theologians", where every being conducts superior love or *agape* to the being below it, and inferior love or *eros* to the being above.[28] Lewis stresses the value of 'loving response', of actually *doing* the task for the present moment. In *Till We Have Faces* (1956), we see in Orual's suffering on Psyche's behalf, a vision of God's love, and His acceptance of *her* 'loving response'. In Lewis's re-telling of the Greek myth we see the Princess Orual, the heroine, act in willing exchange, as she offers to take Psyche's place as the sacrifice to the god of the Mountain. Psyche, dubbed the "Accursed", was required to make an act of Substitution for the healing of the people. She expected to die at the hands of the "Brute". Her father, a tyrannical and brutal king, feigned sadness, "hiding the greatness of his own relief" at escaping death. Orual saw herself as faceless before she was shaped by God into living stone, having previously imagined herself *as* the faceless stone goddess, Ungit: until she became her real self.

Lewis uses her story to describe a transformation, a time of spiritual growth. Orual's possessive love for Psyche gradually developed into a selfless love, through which she had let Psyche follow her love for the god, whom she "must obey".[29] Psyche agreed to *disobey* the god, and *look* at him, to 'pay' for Orual's redemption to a life of (what was in reality) Christian faith.

Orual too made an act of sacrificial Substitution, in which she becomes another sacrificial Psyche. Orual's father, the King of Glome, died and her "real reign began". She became "more and more" the Queen and less and less Orual the 'private person'. She wanted her private self to "vanish altogether into the Queen". She was growing into the person she potentially already was, chiming with St. Augustine's belief. She reigned well, if at times possessively for her country. In a dream, her father bade her to "get up" and remove her veil, a dream in which she delved down deep into the inner recesses of her mind.[30]

In a letter of 16 February 1956 to his publisher, Jocelyn Gibb, Lewis wrote, "Orual after going bareface in her youth, is made really and spiritually bareface, to herself and all the dead, at the end".[31] She would have a face and become her real self, not a mere persona, and able to 'meet' the gods face to face. Arnom the priest of Glome says of her (by then) the late queen: "Queen Orual of Glome . . . was the most wise, just, valiant, fortunate, and merciful of all the princes known in our part of the world". Her veil removed, Lewis shows the danger of her complaint that the gods take away "those we love best".[32] She had to allow her "tyrannically possessive" love to melt into selfless love.[33] She said to Psyche, "All there is of me shall be yours". Wondering how the gods can "meet us till we have faces", Orual said the priest knew that the gods "will have sacrifice; will have man".[34] In *After Ten Years* (1956), Lewis shows that when King Menelaus found Helen 'after ten years', he too had to discover for himself her real face, and see in her his true beloved, rather than "a young idealised"[35] vision of her. His right to the throne of Sparta actually depended on his marriage to the 'real' Helen, whom he loved. Lewis sees in such 'loving response' something of Christ's love, and the reciprocity involved in Lewis's idea of Hierarchy. Yet, it *does* have the notion of the Christ who washes the disciples' feet.[36] The expression 'a ransom for many' makes the name 'Ransom' highly appropriate for the hero of *Out of the Silent Planet, Perelandra* and *That Hideous Strength*.

In the mid-forties, Lewis was keen to uphold monarchism as the natural outcome of the "hierarchical principle". During the war years (1939-1945), the British royal family, with their exemplary lives, were deservedly very popular, giving the contemporary factual evidence that enabled Lewis to laud monarchy the more easily. In his essay *Myth Became Fact* (1944), Lewis quoted Jane Austen's *Pride and Prejudice* (1813), where Miss Bingley had asked, "Would not conversation be much more rational than dancing"? "Much more rational, but much less like a ball", Mr Bingley had replied. This conflates the literal dance with the dance of social manoeuvre. Lewis says, "In the same way, it would be much more rational to abolish the English monarchy. But how if, by doing so, you leave out the one element in our State which matters most"? Lewis asked the relevant question, "How if the monarchy is the channel through which all the *vital* elements of citizenship – loyalty, the consecration of secular life, the hierarchical principle, splendour, ceremony, continuity – still trickle down to irrigate the dustbowl of modern economic Statecraft"?[37] The "consecration of secular life" is the element attributed to 'holiness'. Lewis here goes further than Nicolson is able to, as he has only a secular mystique of monarchy.

A Mythical Queen's Willing Obedience

Upholding the "hierarchical principle", the ideal of sacral kingship and the "consecration" of secular life, Lewis's *Perelandra* was published in 1943. He continued "imagining", and speculating in fiction "what God might have done in other worlds". In *Perelandra*, he tackles the hypothetical event of an attack by the Devil in a hitherto unfallen world, intent on bringing its monarchy within his own tyrannical jurisdiction. Lewis makes a theological enquiry, as he said, in the mythological world, a fictional version of Venus, in the light of the Fall, and the subsequent history of redeemed Man. Lewis imagined a world populated by a king and queen, co-monarchs responsible to maintain the kingdom's loyalty to Maleldil, on which continued happiness depends. The Oyarsa of Perelandra handed over rule to them on the last day, although they were already nominally the King and Queen. A satanic attack on the "sinless waters of Perelandra",[38] already devised, was potentially capable of destroying their happiness by diverting their loyalty from Maleldil. Lewis imagined how they might be protected from such a calamity, which could subject them to temptations beyond their endurance and lead to their 'fall'.

Lewis believed that God gives individuals specific tasks, the completion of which fulfil His will. This is similar to the Platonic belief that a man has a "proper function in society".[39] To this end, Ransom was 'sent' to Perelandra to 'enact' the role of Christ, somewhat like Balder in the myth of the dying god, a myth Lewis found convincing. Ransom, symbolically Christ, is also partly parallel to Beowulf in his slaying of Grendel, as Ransom plays a part in the "cosmic war".[40] Lewis said in a letter of 29 December 1958 to 'A Lady', "Ransom (to some extent) plays the role of Christ not because he allegorically represents Him (as Cupid represents falling in love) but because in reality every Christian is really called upon in some measure to *enact* Christ's role.

Of course, Ransom does this rather more spectacularly than most. But that does not mean he does it allegorically . . . fiction chooses extreme cases".[41] In a sense he manifests democratised kingship. In the mythical world of Perelandra, Ransom ponders *his* specific task. Seeing a small dragon, he wondered, "Were the things which appeared as mythology on earth scattered through other worlds as realities", a glimpse of Lewis's belief of finding truth in myth. This is indicative to the reader that Lewis was using Ransom to vocalise his belief that truth is apparent in myth.

Lewis creates a picture of an un-fallen, or 'pre-Fall', world, making us wonder what would happen *if* an innocent Eve tasted temptation. Could she withstand it or, if she 'fell', would Perelandra be redeemed? The Queen said, "In your world, Maleldil first took Himself this form, the form of your race and mine",[42] as she and Ransom discussed the Incarnation on earth. Chesterton had said in *Orthodoxy*, "Heaven came to save mankind in the awful shape of a man".[43] The Queen asked, "Since our Beloved became a man, how should Reason in any world take on another form"? [44]

Lewis is aware that one may believe in the divine Son intellectually as Reason. The Queen, who believes He must be obeyed, more emotionally 'feels' He is also to be loved. Lewis shows that she is aware of "the reason", which she "cannot tell" Ransom, for the Incarnation on *Earth* but she does *not* seem able to appreciate any possibility of a need for Incarnation or Redemption on Perelandra.

Perhaps the Queen thought that the human form of the incarnate Christ, being like Maleldil's, underlay the King's vicegerency. When eventually Ransom saw the King, he had "a face which no man can say he does not know", which, in other words, tells us that he looked like Christ. Lewis is making here an unconscious, almost verbatim quotation from verse 22 of William Morris's *Sir Galahad: A Christmas Mystery* (1858). Morris refers to Christ as "One sitting on the altar as a throne / Whose face no man could say he did not know".[45] The Lady is seen not only as a Perelandrian Eve but also as a Perelandrian Mary. The Queen, thinking that Ransom was the Adam, the King on earth, would not command him. When she realised he was *not* a king, she then saw fit to do so. The Queen would tell Ransom of the King only that "He is himself, he is the King".[46] Lewis may have, inadvertently or otherwise, borrowed the idea inherent in the answer about Tolkien's Tom Bombadil, which Goldberry gave when Frodo asked, "Who is Tom Bombadil?" Goldberry said simply, "He is".[47]

Lewis still conjectures the plight of an un-fallen queen, as Ransom warned her of the danger of being tempted by evil. The Queen had tacitly assumed that all that was "rolling towards"[48] them was bound to be Maleldil's will, but a wrong action can be made to look innocent, a fact of which the Queen is oblivious. This idea is parallel to the Neanderthalers in William Golding's *The Inheritors* (1955) who, in primitive innocence, are similarly non-plussed by the 'new people', modern Man. The pictures in Lok's head had "showed the new people towards whom both outside – and inside – Lok yearned with a terrified love, as creatures who would kill him if they could".[49] This parallels the idea that whatever "rolled towards" the Queen was *not* necessarily God's will. She was so pure as to be somewhat naïve.

In *Approaches to 'The Inheritors'*, Kinkead-Weekes and Gregor describe Golding's Neanderthalers as "the true innocents", the harmless ones, not only "without evil themselves" but "incapable of understanding" it when it comes and destroys them. They run "to meet their killers in love", being "incapable of preserving themselves" by killing their oppressors.[50] The pure Neanderthalers were likewise unaware, in their innocence, of the possibility of evil deeds against them even being feasible.

Lewis wonders how evil could enter a perfect world: did it, perhaps, actually exist in God Himself? In *A Preface to Paradise Lost*, Lewis says the only basis for such a heretical idea is "where Adam tells Eve that evil 'into the mind of God or Man' may 'come and go' without being approved and 'leave no spot or blame'". He states that "the approval of the will alone makes a mind evil and that the presence of evil as an object of thought does not".[51]

Ransom was anxious lest the Queen should 'fall' in spite of her good intentions. This is one way in which the creator's traits are projected on to his character: Lewis's "one besetting sin is anxiety", Chad Walsh "correctly noted". This instance is not alone, many of Ransom's traits remind us of Lewis's own "convictions and consciousness".[52] Ransom illustrates Lewis's early dislike for 'interference', when Ransom said in *Out of the Silent Planet* to Weston and Devine, "As long as it [his hike] lasts you need consider no one and consult no one but yourself".[53] Lewis regarded being "interfered with"[54] by God as a thing of the past, as he said in *Surprised by Joy*. He sees obedience to God as freely choosing the "good you had got",[55] that is, given by God, and not hankering after some private desire.

In *Prayer: Letters to Malcolm* (posthumously published in 1964), Lewis regrets how "we often, almost sulkily, reject the good that God offers us because, at that moment, we expect some other good", as when the Queen 'expected' to see the King, only to find it was Ransom. Lewis clarified this "other good". He says we "are always harking back to some occasion which seemed to us to reach perfection . . . These golden moments . . . are entirely nourishing . . . if we . . . accept them for what they are, for memories".[56] Lewis surmised whether the desire to *repeat* an experience is allied to the "love of money", the "root of all evil", and therefore gives us the "security" of power.[57]

The Queen loves Maleldil and responds to His love, especially to the generosity of His gifts, by obeying Him. She thus acknowledges His kingship and His sovereignty, enjoying her life in His Presence. In *A Preface to Paradise Lost*, Lewis quoted Addison: "The great moral which reigns in Milton is the most universal and most useful that can be imagined, that

Obedience to the will of God makes men happy and that Disobedience makes them miserable".[58] The Queen realises the possibility of holding onto an 'expected good' – a 'private desire' – for too long, though *she* does not feel at all tempted to do so. Lewis wondered how long *and* how strong is our resistance. Lewis distinguished between two types of 'desire'. On the one hand, the Bent One could overwhelm the Queen with wrong 'desire', especially if he manipulated her love for the King. On the other hand, Lewis considered the joy of non-possessive 'desire'. Ransom asks the Queen whether she is "happy without the King?" Does she "want" him? She replied, "How could there be anything I did not want?" She gestured to Ransom, making "that whole world a house and her a hostess".[59] Thomas Traherne (1637-1674), the English mystic, said in *Centuries of Meditations*:

> You never enjoy the world aright, till the sea itself floweth in your veins, till you are clothed with the heavens, and crowned with the stars: and perceive yourself to be the sole heir of the whole world . . . Till you can Sing and Rejoice in God as . . . Kings in Sceptres.

Traherne signifies that everyone is a monarch of the universe. He criticises Socrates for saying in the Exchange at Athens, "Who would have thought there were so many things in the world which I do not want!"[60]

As Ransom reflected on his ancestral name, he felt that he "knew now why the old philosophers had said that there is no such thing as chance beyond the Moon . . . *ransom* had been a name for a payment that delivers". He had 'absolute responsibility' to prevent the Queen from being overwhelmed if attacked by the Devil. Ransom thought that even *should* he fail to protect her, Maleldil would redeem Perelandra by "some act of even more appalling love" than the crucifixion. Lewis tells us Maleldil was also named "Ransom", the King of self-sacrificial love. Ransom realises he was not chosen to flatter his ego, but because by having previously been taken to Mars, he had learnt "Old Solar", the language also "spoken on Venus".[61]

Before any attack took place, the Queen told Ransom about the unique command Maleldil had given them. The royal command is a mythical way (as with Adam and Eve over the apple) of symbolising the *need* for perfect and willing obedience to Maleldil, a need that requires trust, as there is no apparent reason for it. The King and Queen may walk on the Fixed Lands of Perelandra *in the daytime*, but they must *not* sleep on them at night, but remain on the floating islands.

In *Orthodoxy*, Chesterton illuminates the mythical way of explaining obedience. He says that in fairy tales happiness is contingent on the "Doctrine of Conditional Joy". "According to elfin ethics", he says, "All virtue is in an *if*". Cinderella may go to the ball in a magical coach with a magical coachman *if* she is *not* home later than midnight. Coming closer to our situation, *if* "an apple is eaten . . . the hope of God is gone". Chesterton, summing up this veto, says, "Such, it seemed, was the joy of man, either in Elfland or on Earth; the happiness depended on not doing something that you could at any moment do and which, very often, it was not obvious why you should not do"[62] it. This naturally includes obeying the Ban on the fixed Land, and its associated 'if'. Ransom and the Queen realise that because of the different geography of Earth and Venus, there *could* be no such Ban on Earth. The Lady construed that "There can, then, be different laws on different worlds".[63] Lewis says significantly in his essay, 'On Ethics', based on anthropology, "We are not really justified in speaking of different moralities as we speak of different languages or different religions . . . I deny that we have any choice to make between clearly differentiated ethical systems".[64] Lewis firmly believed that there is only one 'good', even though it may be achieved through different laws in different places.

The King Commands what is Good – Obey Him

Lewis affirmed that, "I emphatically embrace the first alternative" of the *Euthyphro* Dilemma,[65] meaning that God commands things *because* they are right, not *because* He commands them. Chesterton says in *Orthodoxy*, "The Ten Commandments . . . have been found substantially common to mankind".[66] This coincides with Lewis's beliefs about the 'one good' being brought about through different laws in different places, to conjecture what he might have thought about a surreal observation made in Tom Stoppard's play, *Jumpers* (1972).

George, a Professor of Moral Philosophy, intends to 'dispute' a paper by the recently killed Professor McFee. George points out how McFee had explained his 'relative' ideas of "the notion of filial homage" in the Atlas Mountains, a Brazilian rain forest and the Home Counties. McFee exemplified his variety of different 'goods' by saying, "Certainly a tribe which believes it confers honour on its elders by eating them is going to be viewed askance by another which prefers to buy them a little bungalow somewhere". McFee had suggested that with aesthetic judgement, so with moral judgement. "The word 'good' has also meant different things to different people at different times". In the Coda, Stoppard calls 'witnesses', one of whom, Archie, questions whether "moral values . . . are the distinguishing marks of human nature or merely the products of civilization".[67] Stoppard is neither fence-sitting nor being openly partisan. In the characters' thesis and antithesis Stoppard "satirises twentieth-century relativist thinkers – those who would claim that there are no absolute values simply "relative opinions". By holding no fixed positions, they are always "jumping". For example, the murder of McFee is covered up, "an example of how relativism extended to its extremes might extinguish all moral principle".

McFee had spoken of 'honouring elders'. George, refuting McFee's ideas, "implies that it is naïve not to *expect* such differences . . . in two widely different cultures". Stoppard does not, therefore, totally defend the idea of 'one good', though he *does* say, "The remarkable thing is the sameness of intention – the idea of honouring elders at all". In *Jumpers* we are shown a man who really "believes" in 'right' and 'wrong' – and in God.[68] This 'Sameness of intention' is gradually moving in the direction of belief in 'one good' – God's 'one good'.

In *Perelandra*, Lewis considers the laws promoting the 'one good', thereby engendering what is 'right'. The law peculiar to Perelandra is the Ban against sleeping on the Fixed Land, the law imposed by Maleldil and revealed directly by Him to her and the King. Lewis evinces his belief that it is at least possible to have direct communication of laws from God, that is to say, personal revelation of His will. This view is supported by the eighteenth-century French Jesuit priest, Père Jean-Pierre de Caussade, in his treatise *L'Abandon à la Providence Divine* (1741) – 'Self-Abandonment to Divine Providence'. De Caussade says, "God still speaks today as he spoke to our forefathers . . . a matter of immediate communication with God . . . We only truly learn when God speaks directly to us".[69] An instance of this revelation is seen when the Lady, climbing the rocks on the Fixed Land, saw Ransom shed blood when he cut his knee, and wondered if her own body would bleed if she tried cutting *her* knee. "Maleldil apparently told her not to,"[70] and she obeyed immediately.

Why, indeed, is the Ban against sleeping on the Fixed Land imposed? It is for the overarching moral reason, affecting all their subsequent choices, of having their *willing* loyalty tested. The Lady, trusting Maleldil, willingly obeys the Ban. De Caussade says of obedience, "The path of perfect faith . . . leads to the discovery of God in each moment". The answer to the question of how this is achieved is to "Obey Him in everything". The Queen feels *incapable* of being tempted to *disobey* Maleldil 'in *anything*' from within herself. To experience temptation, it must necessarily come from 'outside' herself as, indeed, Devil-promoted temptation *did*, in fact, come through the devil-inhabited Weston. The Ban *could* have been broken: the Queen could have deliberately disobeyed Maleldil and foregone the joys He intended.

In *Modern Fantasy: Five Studies*, Colin Manlove suggests the wish to break the Ban on the Fixed Land is "jumping out of flux . . . asserting one's merely personal will". He sees an attempt by Lewis to maintain a "correspondence of physical and spiritual". Even Ransom began by seeing his task as a spiritual rather than a physical struggle. Manlove says (perhaps mistakenly) that although it gives "strength to Lewis's book . . . in the end it undermines its very successes". Indeed, to break the Ban would be to assert "one's personal will"[71] against Maleldil's.[72] Manlove says Lewis lets the 'Un-man' play on the Lady's belief that "every experience offered to her must be savoured to the full" to make her at least *think* the Ban was actually *meant* to be broken, that Maleldil actually *intended* it to be, referring to the coming evil attack.

The critic somewhat perversely suggests "the Lady is only *formally* tempted", since staying on the Fixed Land "until the Un-man woke pride in her, would be out of pure love for her husband and Maleldil".[73] However, the reason for the Ban is clear. Ransom says that in obeying the other laws the Lady is doing what seems good in her eyes also, but in obeying the Ban she is doing something for which the "*only* reason" is His bidding. Living in the waves that are 'rolled towards her' symbolises the moment to moment response to God's will, as for instance, De Caussade describes it. To stay on the Fixed Land symbolises the Power to control one's life. The Queen discovers *why* she wants to obey God. She loves Maleldil, and to pull away from Him would be "cold love and feeble trust". A wish to break the Ban would be "to be able on one day to command where I should be the next and what should happen to me".[74] The 'fixed' nature of the land symbolises the rock-like security we are tempted to yearn for rather than, like Lewis at the time of his conversion, to 'let ourselves go' and trust God.

The King spoke of the "Fixed Land which once was forbidden". The Oyarsa of Perelandra said, "Maleldil puts into your hand"[75] the floating and the firm lands. It became clear the Ban is *only* a symbol, but only then. The idea that obeying or breaking the Ban would be 'out of pure love' confuses the relation between spirit and flesh over moral choice. Confusion lies in the relation of emotion that *can* actually motivate action, for instance, to actual murder. A current moral philosophical obsession with 'moral luck' suggests, for example, the 'luck' of a driver who, though very drunk, does not actually *happen* to kill anyone. This does *not* make his drunk driving moral *because* of his so-called 'luck'.

It would *neither* have been moral for the Lady to choose to stay on the Fixed Land *just because* her love for the King prompted her to do so. It would still have been disobedience, an immoral means that would certainly have determined a bad end. Manlove says the Lady has a moral dilemma. Should she, then, show her love, risking the consequences? No. She is not even tempted to do something *intrinsically* wrong, as she knows such disobedience would utterly wreck her moral standing with Maleldil.

An instance of such a dilemma is found in Charles Williams's *Shadows of Ecstasy*, where the priest Caithness shows a strong emotional hatred, if not for the man himself, of what Considine stood for – denying himself, any kind of desire, ultimately to conquer death itself. Caithness, who calls him the "Anti-Christ", said after the murder, "Out of evil, God brought forth good".[76] Although glad that Considine was murdered, he experienced a moral dilemma, having actually encouraged the killer,[77] by saying to Mottreux, and referring to the "mad ape" Considine, "If you can't cage it_____",[78] implying 'kill it'. Caithness' dilemma shows the contrast between his motive (encouraging Mottreux to *kill* Considine), and the fact that *he* refrains from *doing* so. It is evident that abstaining from murder belies what he would have *liked* to do (or persuade someone else to do), that is, kill

Considine. One's motivation may, with the courage of one's convictions, actually alter the action to which it leads, e.g. refraining from a bad action.

The Queen *could* have put love for the King before obedience to Maleldil. If she *had*, she would knowingly have used immoral means to attempt a moral purpose, and then been damned. Lewis does not minimise the responsibility of making such a wrong choice, a choice reminiscent of Thomas Middleton and William Rowley's *The Changeling* (1653), in which there is a salutary warning about the dangers, even for love, of choosing immoral means. Alsemero, whom Beatrice loves, asserts that marriage can undo the effects of the Fall. Lewis shows how the Queen, in the same way that Caithness dealt with his dilemma, abstained from a course of action (in spite of a certain appeal) *she* knew to be wrong.

This is just what does *not* happen in *The Changeling*. De Flores is called the "serpent" in Acts I and V, while Beatrice is likened to Eve – "that broken rib of mankind". Having enticed De Flores, with his own agenda – to kill her unwelcome fiancée – Alonzo (reminiscent of Lady Macbeth), says to her, "Settle you in what the act [enticement to murder] has made you . . . You're the deed's creature". She is "transformed by the deed". They both die in Act V, their souls damned.[79]

The Queen's motive to obey was simply her love for Maleldil, and as she and the King were earlier unaware of the reason for the Ban, it gave them the chance to obey solely of their love for Him. Manlove says rather cynically, "The un-man's hypothesis thus becomes no less valid for the Lady than Ransom's". The Un-man had seen no "inherent reason for the command not to stay on the Fixed Land".[80] However, the "inherent" reason was, in fact, to be able to respond to Maleldil's love with willing obedience. While the Queen was still un-fallen, Ransom realised that *he* had to obey Maleldil by doing his 'task for the present moment', that is, to kill the Un-man, *not* Weston but the Devil incarnate in Weston's body, to prevent a Fall here on Perelandra.

The Queen's Moral Peril: Tempted to Disobey

The Queen, oblivious of her imminent danger, had once said, "One can conceive a heart which did not . . . turn from the expected good to the given good",[81] although never doubting that *she* would remain loyal and lovingly obedient to Maleldil. In what De Caussade calls "obedience to the present moment", the Queen and Ransom find that the "only condition necessary for this state of self-surrender is the present moment in which the soul . . . responds to every moment of grace". The Queen's obedience to the Ban *is* her task of the 'present moment' and she is happy and at peace. What her sacramental obedience symbolises is *trust*. She does not even *need* to understand or realise that it *is* a sacrament to receive its grace.

De Caussade says about such contentment that with the virtue of the divine will every creature "is brought into the realm of his kingdom where every moment is complete contentment in God alone . . . It is the sacrament of the present moment."[82] The grace she receives is happiness and peace. By this self-surrender to God we can ourselves become kings. Lewis likewise expresses this in a letter to an American lady, where he says that we have missed the whole point of the coronation unless we feel that "we have all been crowned".[83] De Caussade says of *democratised* kingship, that people can "all surrender themselves to his action, be wedded to his purposes . . . and in the end all be participators in his majesty and privileges. It is a kingdom in which every soul can aspire to a crown".[84] All can, therefore, discover that they are, indeed, made in God's image, and enter into His joy – the same 'Joy' that drew Lewis to God.

Ransom hopes to find in the Queen, once rescued, "an obedience freer, more reasoned, more conscious than any she had known before", *if* she conquers the present temptation to disobey the divine King. Lewis shows that Ransom *must* prevent the Queen from taking the "fatal false step".[85] Suppose the Queen *were* subjected to a temptation stronger than she could withstand?

One is reminded of George Orwell's *1984* (1949) as Winston Smith became powerless to 'stand up' under the strain. One can easily argue that he needed divine redemption. The Party had reduced Smith through torture and fear to a stage where no resistance was left. The interrogator told Smith, referring to three men in "whose innocence [he] once believed", that "by the time we had finished with them they were only the shells of men". Tempted and tried beyond endurance, Smith, to whom rats were "unendurable", crumbled when he was faced with a cage of "enormous rats".[86] He heard the door click against the rats, preventing them from biting him. Unable to stand up under the treatment, and beyond human help, Smith's only rescue would have been through grace, which the secular Orwell cannot invoke.

However, Lewis, as a Christian can and, indeed, *does* look for the Queen's deliverance from overwhelming temptation. Ransom realised that it was *his* 'absolute responsibility' to prevent the Queen of Perelandra from experiencing excessive temptation and 'falling from grace' – part of his democratised kingship. Lewis believed that loyalty to Christ the King of love involved taking sacrificial risks. In Ransom's case, this meant being ready to deal physically with Weston, as the 'Un-man' (the devil in Weston's body). Ransom had free will to choose to do – or not to do – this. He was not forced, as this would have nullified any virtue in his making the 'right' choice, that is, choosing the King's side. Lewis showed how the Queen was, in fact, vulnerable to Weston's devilish temptations, even though she profoundly loved, and was determined to obey Maleldil. Her very innocence made it difficult for her to be aware of the dangers. The risk lay in the possibility of choosing a private desire, however laudable in itself, in preference to obeying God.

Chapter Eight
Lewis and the Ideal of Kingship

The King's 'Miracle' and the 'Unman'

Weston, the Devil's physical representative is present as a manifest reality. Where, Ransom wonders, is Maleldil – or at least, *His* representative? A miracle is needed to rescue the Queen. Ransom came to realise that "He himself was the miracle". One of Maleldil's purposes was to "save Perelandra not through Himself but through Himself in Ransom".[1] Ransom sees that he would need to fight Weston not 'spiritually', as he had thought, but physically, if he is to attempt to kill him. Would *he* be able to stand up physically against Weston, who taunted him with the idea that many who fought him thought that God would help them? Weston jeeringly asked a question that referred mockingly to the crucifixion, "Could He help Himself?"[2] Christ *did* patiently stand up under His suffering where, Lewis believed, perfect love paid the terrible price of absolute Evil. However, there is another side to the coin. In his *Preface*, Lewis refers to *Paradise Regained* (1671): "The perfect manhood which Adam lost is there matured in conflict with Satan, in that sense Eden, or Paradise, the state of perfection, is 'regained'".[3] The devil-inhabited Weston had said with dreadful effect, "I *am* the Universe. I, Weston, am your God and your Devil. I call the Force into me completely". Weston's face was "twisted out of all recognition".[4] Observing this grotesque transformation, Ransom was here like Syme in Chesterton's *The Man Who Was Thursday: A Nightmare* (1908) who, we are told in Stephen Medcalf's 'Introduction', when going to meet his six colleagues was "terrified by their appearance of having, each in his own way, passed outside humanity".[5]

The now devil-possessed Weston subjected the Queen to a subtler and mentally crueller temptation than Eve herself had undergone in the Garden of Eden, and systematically worked to destroy her innocent obedience to Maleldil. Weston deviously suggested to the Queen that "the wrong kind of obeying itself can be a disobeying". The Queen replied, "How can we not obey what we love?" Maleldil might not *always* actually *want* to be obeyed, he suggested. It was this "idea" that admitted "the whole flood of suggestion" to her mind.[6]

Weston invited, like Faust, the 'Force' into himself. The Faust myth itself is a warning against pride. The Faustian character type is only concerned to achieve his purpose by whatever means, and leads to a loss of humanity as it involves a compact with the devil. The earliest known Faust-figure is the magician Simon Magus, who tried to buy with money the power to confer the gift of the Holy Spirit. (Acts 8: 18-19).[7] The fanatically held ideology to which Weston clings is the 'Life-Force' of emergent Evolutionism. The French philosopher, Henri Bergson (1859-1941), in his *L'Évolution Créatice* (1907) said that he was well aware of "the conflict between evolution and religion". He held that the "*élan vital*", a 'Life-Force' was popular probably because he had tried "to develop a non-Darwinian evolutionism that made room for religion, albeit not for orthodox Christianity," backed by both scientific and philosophical arguments.[8] Lewis said in *The Discarded Image* (1964), "Quasi-religious responses to the hypostasised abstraction *Life* are to be sought in Shaw or Wells or in a highly poetical philosopher such as Bergson, not in the papers and lectures of biologists". [9] Lewis's designation of Weston as the 'Un-man', literally a person below the status of a man, reflects the use of similar expressions in German, e.g. *Unmensch*, *Übermensch* and *Untermensch*. Weston was wedded to what he saw as the *spirituality* of the life-force. When he eventually called "that Force" into himself he was, in effect, calling on the Devil for his aid, as he said that Ransom's God and his Devil were "both pictures of the same Force".[10]

Weston became less than a man, an *Unmensch*, as he relinquished his very humanity in his vain attempt to be spiritual; this is a classic instance of the Faustian contract. In *Orthodoxy*, Chesterton said,

> The greatest disaster of the 19th century was this: that men began to use the word 'spiritual' in the same way as the word 'good' . . . It encouraged mere spirituality. It taught men to think that, so long as they were passing from the ape, they were going to the angel. But you can pass from the ape and go to the devil[11]

and this is precisely what Weston did.

According to the Faust myth, he who calls on the Devil for his aid relinquishes his soul. Such a fate is found in the writings of Goethe, Christopher Marlowe and to some extent in Thomas Mann's *Doktor Faustus* (1947). Here, the composer, Adrian Leverkühn, made a pact with the devil. He said, "Since my twenty-first year I am wedded to Satan . . . because I would win glory in this world".[12]

The expression *Untermensch* was coined in Nazi Germany to denote a person regarded as racially inferior, e.g. a Jewish or black person. At the other extreme, we meet the grotesque concept of the *Übermensch*, the Superman with the Will to Power (*der Wille der Macht*), the concept coined by the Nihilist philosopher Friedrich Nietzsche in *Also Sprach Zarathustra* (1883-05), far from popular with the British Allies in wartime. The notion of a 'Superman' was adapted in England by George Bernard Shaw for his play *Man and Superman* (1905), where he refers to the idea of Evolution and the life force. The echo of Nietzsche's *Übermensch* is deliberate. The very idea that human beings might one day evolve into *Übermenschen*, Supermen, was for Lewis the most recent variation of the serpent's temptation to Eve: 'Ye shall be as gods'.

Being involved in aiding such an evolution to do its work could also be used to justify many horrific atrocities against other species, on earth or even on another planet, or against so-called inferior races. The whole scheme sails close to Hitler's dream of a master race, the idea Lewis vehemently attacks in *That Hideous Strength*,[13] with the concept of being ruled by an autocrat.

A stark contrast exists between Ransom's Christian idea of the spiritual and Weston's distorted picture, where he would give the life-force free reign, inevitably leading to a totalitarian state, ruled by a tyrant. The difference is vividly illuminated in the 'Talks and Essays' of the German writer, Thomas Mann, who frequently adversely criticised the German dictator, Hitler. Mann said, "Let's get rid of this big-mouthed propaganda Boss from Hell called Goebbels who, a cripple in body and soul, gives credence to his lies before God with inhuman (*unmenschlicher*) disdain and seeks to elevate (somebody) to World Ruler." After he had written about Goebbels, saying that "Politics is Inhuman", Mann relates an ironic, Weston-like description of Hitler's would-be killer as told by the Nazis. In view of the date of Mann's 'Essays', it is even possible that Lewis may actually have read them before he wrote about his own 'Unman'. Mann wrote that one Uhl, intent on killing the Führer, "was a sub-human . . . with a gun and a diabolical smile".[14] Mann's reportage sounds just like Weston, with his inhuman appearance, his callous attitude, the parallel name, Un-man, and is especially evocative of Weston's "devilish smile".[15]

Un-mensch is, in fact, an ordinary German word meaning 'inhuman creature'. Mann, actually saw Hitler himself, like the *unmenschlich Goebbels*, as an *Unmensch*. In *That Hideous Strength*, Lewis satirises just such an 'inhuman' state, and an attempt to set up a race of Supermen, as a timely warning.[16] The idea of losing one's rational soul is in line with George MacDonald in *The Princess and Curdie* (1883), where some people, over a long time, "if they do not take care, go down the hill to the animal's country". The grandmother explains to Curdie: "Many men are actually, all their lives, going to the beasts".[17] Here we see a Victorian, moralised version of quasi-Darwinian reverse evolution, such as is found in Charles Kingsley's *The Water Babies* (1862-63).

Lewis tells us that Weston had not become an Unman overnight, but had been losing his humanity over many years. In *Perelandra*, he says, "Weston was not now a man at all. The forces which had begun, perhaps years ago, to eat away his humanity had now completed their work. The intoxicated will which had been slowly poisoning the intelligence and the affections had now at last poisoned itself".[18]

Ransom felt alone as he strove to play his part – to 'enact' the role of Christ and to kill the Unman. The Bible says that God is faithful, and never fails us, even when we feel alone but, as Chesterton asks, 'Does He ever fail Himself?' He tells of how, in the Passion, the cry from the Cross "confessed that God was forsaken of God".[19] In *A Grief Observed*, Lewis says, "C . . . reminded me that the same thing happened to Christ: 'Why hast thou forsaken me?'" Here Lewis described *his* sense of being forsaken when he needed help in his grief over his wife, Joy's death. Lewis had said that he turned to God only to find "a door slammed in my face", and "after that, silence". He asked himself, "Where is God?" Lewis said he had felt God's presence in the happy times, but asked where He is when He is needed. Lewis made it clear that his marriage to Joy was the completion of him as a man, and that he yearned to know that she still existed somewhere. Lewis answered his own question. He said, "I have gradually been coming to feel that the door is no longer shut and bolted. Was it my own frantic need that slammed it in my face?"[20]

However, neither Ransom nor Christ had made God seem absent by anything like Lewis's "frantic need". In *A Grief Observed* Lewis did not imagine himself to be God's presence, as Ransom was called to be on Perelandra. It is through Christ Himself, then, *in* Ransom that Perelandra would be rescued. Lewis explains why Christ's risen life affects Perelandra as well as on earth.

In *Mere Christianity*, Lewis imagines a toy soldier who obstinately objects to being "brought" to life. "He will not be made into a man if he can help it". The human in Christ "came to life again. The man in Christ rose again: not only the God . . . We saw a real man. One tin soldier – real tin, just like the rest – had come fully and splendidly alive". The difference here, Lewis says, is that "When Christ becomes a man it is not really as if you could become one particular tin soldier. It is as if something which is always affecting the whole human mass begins, at one point, to affect the whole human mass in a new way".

Lewis says that this '*something*' is "that the business of becoming a son of God, of being turned from a created thing into a begotten thing, of passing over from the temporal biological life into timeless spiritual life, has been done for us".[21] Further personal revelation from Maleldil occurs when Ransom had heard a "Voice", the voice who told him His name was Ransom, the voice telling him he must kill the Unman. It was not a *physical* voice in the ordinary sense of the word: Ransom was convinced it was Maleldil's Voice. Lewis believed in personal revelation. For example, the Queen several times tells Ransom that Maleldil is 'telling her' something. For instance, when Ransom asked her, *apropos* of the age of another world, Malacandra, "How do you know that?" she replied, "Maleldil is telling me".[22] The voice that Ransom heard was not a kind of hallucination or even imagination. The Old Testament maintains that it was not Elijah's imagination when God's voice spoke to *him* when, fleeing from King Ahab and Queen Jezebel, a voice asked him what he was doing there.

Ransom's experience of revelation through the voice is paralleled in *one* of the two voices that Christopher Martin 'heard' in William Golding's *Pincher Martin: The Two Deaths of Christopher Martin* (1956). He *imagined* he heard the voice say, "And last of all, hallucination, vision, dream, delusion will haunt you. What else can a madman expect?" Then God's Voice, and no hallucination, asked him, "Have you had enough, Christopher?", i.e., enough "surviving". Martin's first reaction was to say, "You are a projection of my mind". Realising it *was* no illusion, he said, "I could never have invented that".[23] Martin said to God, "You gave me the power to choose and all my life you led me carefully to this suffering because my choice was my own".[24]

Unlike Ransom, Martin did *not* choose 'the gift that was given'. Golding said that Christopher, the Christ-bearer, has become Pincher Martin, who is little but greed. Just to be Pincher is purgatory; to be Pincher for eternity is hell".[25] Ransom and Martin experienced revelations, differently received. According to Chesterton, those who denounce revelations denounce dogmas. In *The Everlasting Man*, he says, "What a denouncer of dogma really means is not that dogma is bad: but rather that it is too good to be true. He refers to the liberal nature of dogma, and how the "truth has made us free". He concludes his discussion by saying that "the moral of all this is an old one, that religion is revelation".[26]

The voice had revealed to Ransom that he must actually *kill* Weston: "This you must do". Ransom felt a sense of "lawful hatred" for what was corruption itself. He fought with Weston and "heard its jaw-bone crack". We note that the possessive adjective that is used here is '*its*', not 'his'.

Lewis attacks the destructive claims of Nihilism, as the Un-man tries to convince Ransom of the truth of Materialism: "The only point in anything is that there isn't any point". In the dark, the Un-man seized Ransom and dragged him under the water to where it was "no longer warm". Eventually, Ransom hurled a large stone at Weston's face, killed him, and pushed his body over a cliff into a "sea of fire".[27]

In Lewis's Paradise world of *Perelandra*, Ransom obediently fulfilled his task of rescuing the Queen from the wiles of the devil. The Oyarsa of Perelandra then handed over the rule of the planet to King Tor and Queen Tinidril. The naming of the beasts by King Tor in *Perelandra* is, to an extent, reminiscent of Williams's *The Place of the Lion* (1931), the book that prompted the start of the friendship between Williams and Lewis. In the chapter "The Naming of the Beasts", Anthony appears to his beloved Damaris to be like the Adam in an old picture. "Anthony – Adam . . . called and he commanded . . . Living creatures showed themselves . . . By the names that were the Ideas he called them . . . duly obedient to the single animal who was lord of the animals, they came".[28] There is a long tradition of Christian Platonism in Charles Williams.[29] The naming in Williams is symbolic of God's order in creation and reminiscent of the "cosmic significance" in Yahweh's Victory over the "Chaos Powers".[30]

However, in *Perelandra* the beasts are not 'Chaos' but are simply beasts, like the named beasts in Genesis. Lewis refers to Adam as King when in his *Preface* he says Adam's kingly manner is the "outward expression of his supernatural kingship of earth and his wisdom . . . Eve . . . is made so awful that with honour he may love [her]".[31]

The King and Queen are now established and Ransom has accomplished his 'function', his 'task for the present moment', on Perelandra. With Ransom, "the submission of the individual to the function is already beginning to bring true personality to birth".[32] However, Lewis shows that it is not primarily a matter of a man or woman's 'value' *per se* that underlies the choosing of a vicegerent, that is to say, a monarch.

In *That Hideous Strength* (1945), Jane Studdock, the wife of Mark, a research sociologist, meets a man whom she instinctively regards as her superior, recognising his position in the hierarchy. The man is Ransom, who is paradoxically both a king and *not* a king. In a conversation with Merlin, Ransom explains that in the order of Logres he "may be Pendragon", (Chief or King). In the order of Britain he is "the King's man", a subject of King George VI, crowned and anointed by the Archbishop. In spite of the paradox, Jane, for the first time in years, "tasted the word *King* itself with all linked associations of battle, marriage, priesthood, mercy and power".[33]

Lewis again portrays Ransom with his wounded heel as Mr Fisher-King, the wounded King, and the Head of a Christian community in a reference to the 'dying god' myth. Lewis explores further how individuals must make conscious choices over right and wrong, between Christ and the Tyrant. Here, Lewis presents the tyrant as the Head of the National Institute of Co-ordinated Experiments, whose aims ostensibly show that "Man has got to take charge of Man. That means, remember, that some men have got to take charge of the rest".[34] This is a notion that goes utterly against Lewis's beliefs about the hierarchy and the correct criteria for some ruling over others.

Lewis believed that eventually it would not be '*some* men' ruling over others but, as the Italian physiologist Filostrato says, it will be *one* man. This is always the case in totalitarian states, as with Stalin, Mao and Hitler. The head of the French scientist, Alcasan, guillotined for murdering his wife, is the official Head of the N.I.C.E. the National Institute. He (or 'it') parallels the dehumanisation of Weston the Un-man in *Perelandra*, underlining Lewis's belief in the gradual abolition of humanity discussed in *The Abolition of Man* (1943).[35] Ransom's community opposed the evil machinations of the N.I.C.E. Lewis describes how the National Institute strove to do on an even bigger scale what Weston had essayed earlier, that is, virtually to create a world of Un-men.[36] Of the technological control of the populace, and the dangerous misuse of scientific knowledge, Lewis said in *The Abolition of Man*:

> No doubt those who really founded modern science were usually those whose love of truth exceeded their love of power . . . The regenerate science which I have in mind would not do even to minerals and vegetables what modern science threatens to do to man himself.[37]

A Spiritual Kingdom

Lewis endeavoured to merge the mythical Logres with contemporary Britain. Ransom was not only the Head of the Company, but also the Pendragon, the Chief, from the Brythonic *pen*, a head, and *dragwn*, a dragon, a guardian of treasure. Calling Ransom 'Pendragon' corroborates the idea of the Company as a living remnant of Logres. Jane Studdock has "Vision", which is the power to dream realities.[38] Lewis's Jane calls to mind an idea in *The Romance of the Rose*. The author of the earlier part of *The Romance of the Rose*, c.1225, Guillaume de Lorris, said, "For my part I am confident that a dream may signify the good and ill that may befall people, for many people dream many things secretly, at night, which are later seen openly".[39] Jane had a "gift", that of seeing "real people" in her dreams, dreams that led her to meet Ransom, and eventually to joining the "King's side", and to becoming a Christian. Jane had learned from Miss Ironwood, a "doctor", that she (Jane) had a "gift" of dreaming about "real people". In fact, she dreamed about a man "all golden and strong",[40] with a beard. Meeting him in the waking world, she recognised Mr Fisher-King.

Lewis's vision of the Fisher-King is enhanced as Ransom invited Jane to stay while he had lunch. A tray was brought in "bearing a glass, a small flacon of red wine, and a roll of bread". Ransom "broke the bread and poured himself out a glass of wine".[41] This priest-kingly activity has strong Eucharistic overtones. It was, in fact, *Melchisedec* who, as the Priest-King of Salem, in biblical tradition made the first offering of bread and wine long before the Eucharist was first celebrated.[42] In *The Figure of Arthur* in *Arthurian Torso* (1948), Charles Williams quotes Robert Paululus (c.1178), with perhaps, the Fisher-King in mind, "No longer the old Melchizedeck, flesh born of flesh, but the new man, spirit born of spirit, offers the invisible offering of flesh and blood through the oblation of earthly food".[43]

Lewis emphasises the connection he sees between the allegiance to royalty and the need for obeying a call to duty immediately. Ransom said he lives "like the King in *Curdie*",[44] in which the miner's son Curdie braves dangers from goblins to save the princess to whom he owes allegiance. In MacDonald's *The Princess and the Goblin* (1872), "The king, who was the wisest man in the kingdom, knew well there was a time when things must be done and questions left till afterwards".[45] This echoes De Caussade's idea of "obedience to the present moment".[46]

Ransom owes allegiance to Maledil, Christ the divine King, and therefore endeavours to save the Company and Britain-Logres from the N.I.C.E. Ransom's Company is reminiscent not only of Williams's idea of a 'company' but also of the Pauline ideas expressed in Lewis's essay *Membership* (1945). Lewis advocates neither an excess of "solitude" nor of "our modern collectivism", but rather the idea of being "members" of a "Body", Christ's "mystical body".

St. Paul, Lewis says, meant by "*members* . . . what we should call *organs*, things essentially different from, and complementary to, one another". Lewis asserts that "the society into which the Christian is called at baptism is not a collective but a Body . . . that Body of which the family is an image on the natural level". Lewis says he believes that God did *not* create "an egalitarian world", and that "if we had not fallen . . . patriarchal monarchy would be the sole lawful government".[47] It is a big "if": we *are* a fallen race, not to mention Lewis's surprisingly unargued position.

Lewis says, "As organs in the body of Christ . . . we are assured of our eternal self-identity".[48] In *Mere Christianity* (1952), he speaks of Christ as "*the* new man".[49] In *That Hideous Strength*, the N.I.C.E. parodies the idea of the 'New Men'. Filostrato says, "Our Head [Alcasan], is the first of the New Men . . . It is not Man who will be omnipotent, it is some one man . . . it may be you. It may be me".[50] In tyrannical regimes, ostensibly oligarchies, in practice only *one* man rules (whether that is Hitler, Stalin or Orwell's 'Big Brother'). The true New Man has 'put on Christ' by obedience and submission to the 'function'. In *That Hideous Strength*, the struggle between king and tyrant unfolds as the efforts to get Jane to the N.I.C.E., and Mark to Ransom's company, become stronger. They are brought together *through* the Company after a strained relationship.

On Earth, Lewis sees hope for Logres (the Pendragon's land) in the restored trust and loving obedience of Jane and Mark, hope in a democratic Christian monarchy, symbolised by the Pendragon. Lewis sees this monarchy in the war-dominated reign of King George VI. In *That Hideous Strength*, Mark had seen "the picture of the King [George VI] which hung above the fireplace", a deceptive symbol of royalty, used by the evil Director of the N.I.C.E., one Wither, to give an impression of credibility to his wicked practices. Merlin had asked whether there was any help in "this Saxon king of yours who sits at Windsor", referring to King George VI. Lewis, seeking to make the realm of the Pendragon and the modern United Kingdom coalesce, explained through Ransom that "he [the King] has no power in this matter", but that he did not, in fact, wish to overthrow him.

Ransom said that "the Faith itself [was] torn in pieces since [his] day . . . The Christians are but a tenth of the people. There [was] no help there".[51] It is clear that King George is *not* the spiritual healer who can challenge the N.I.C.E., as Ransom had told Merlin. This function is reserved for the Pendragon, and is not here fulfilled by the King. The Pendragon is involved in the function of the vicegerent, endeavouring to show the mythological idea of restoring England's healthy state through his symbolic function.

Lewis indicated that England needed to be 're-Christianised' by the Pendragon, so that it could become 'Logres Regained'. The presentation of the symbolism of the healing powers of the mythological Pendragon is a little strained, as Ransom is now, in fact, actually back on earth, and *not* on the mythical world of Perelandra, but also because Ransom has spiritual powers, which are implicitly denied to King George VI. The relation between symbol and reality is severed. The difficulty of reconciling this situation perhaps presented a problem to Lewis, who actually brought the Pendragon into the 'un-mythic' land of England of c.1945, in *That Hideous Strength*, where the Pendragon is *not*, in fact, King George VI.

This whole problem was not present to Williams in his *Arthuriad*. Lewis does, however, produce an anomalous situation regarding monarchy by creating an alternative royalty in the person of the Pendragon, without any line of royal descent. There is a difficulty in the curious kind of 'ordination' in the Pendragon, whom Lewis sees, like the constitutional monarch of the House of Windsor, as a 'spiritual' king.

Another difficulty is seen in the contrast between the symbolism of the physical fight with Weston, the "bridge by which something else had invaded Perelandra", the Devil incarnate in Weston's body, and the horrifying scene at Belbury. The symbolic struggle with evil, the "lawful hatred"[52] on Perelandra, is, indeed, convincing. Ransom's function is altered when he returns to earth, the 'Silent Planet'. Here he is not on a mythological world, but literally 'down to earth', where killing Weston is not seen as killing a Devil-embodied person but, by some, as murder. We remember that Perelandra is 'mythical' and symbolic, but that earth is not and this provides a stark contrast between the fantastic and the realistic. It is one thing to have killed the Un-man, but quite another matter when back on earth to kill people at Belbury.

Nevertheless, it is of contemporary Britain –'Logres Regained' – and its royalty of which Lewis writes. Still upholding the ideal of the Christian constitutional monarchy, Lewis said in a letter of 10 March 1959 to Patricia Hillis, "The world of fairy-tale, as the world of Christianity, makes the heart and imagination royalist in a sense which mere politics hardly [touches].[53] What my stories do is to liberate – to free from inhibitions – a spontaneous impulse to serve and adore, to have a 'dearest dread'".[54] Perhaps the most telling evidence for the correlation of kingship and responsive love is found in Lewis's *Letters to an American Lady*.

In the letter of 10 July 1953 to Mary Willis Shelburne, in reply to her asking him about the coronation of Queen Elizabeth II, Lewis said:

People did *not* get that fairy-tale feeling about the coronation. What impressed most who saw it was the fact that the Queen herself appeared to be quite overwhelmed by the sacramental side of it. Hence, in the spectators, a feeling of (one hardly knows how to describe it) – awe – pity – pathos – mystery. The pressing of that huge, heavy crown on that small, young head becomes a sort of symbol of the situation of *humanity* itself; humanity called by God to be His vice-gerent and high priest on earth, yet feeling so inadequate. As if He had said, 'In my inexorable love I shall lay upon the dust that you are glories and dangers and responsibilities beyond your understanding'. Do you see what I mean? One has missed the whole point unless one feels that we have all been crowned and that coronation is somehow, if splendid, a tragic splendour.

Lewis advocates a democratic *and* a democratised kingship (or queenship), *not* based on 'equality', but on individual acceptance of absolute responsibility. Lewis calls the crown a symbol of "the situation of *humanity*", a symbol embodied in the Queen's function as Vicegerent.[55] Lewis tells how Ransom, who willingly accepted *his* individual responsibility, as De Caussade put it, "can aspire to a crown",[56] and was instrumental in preserving Logres within England, a Christian kingdom with the spiritual monarch Lewis saw in Queen Elizabeth II at her coronation.

Although Lewis had created a most curious situation, with the co-existence of both King George VI *and* the Pendragon, in his letter of 1953, he vigorously asserts the *spirituality* of the British monarchy, and sees in it the Mystery to which Nicolson had referred, and that King James I assumed, as Williams said in his biography.

The Development of Lewis's Ideal of Kingship

In his youth in Ulster, Lewis, a nominal Christian, accepted the Kingdom of God and of Christ. A loss of faith in his schooldays occasioned a serious change in Lewis's ideas, preventing belief in either the divine King or *Christus Rex*. His friend Owen Barfield had said that Lewis's "stance", as he put it, in the development of his ideas, in spite of his upbringing, was not always Christian.[57] When Lewis was demobbed in 1919, he thought, "You cannot go on 'explaining away' for ever . . . You cannot go on 'seeing through' things for ever. The whole point about seeing through something is to see something through it".[58]

In 1922, he discussed with Barfield the 'Christina Dream', as they called the sense of illusion in Samuel Barber's novel, *The Way of All Flesh* (1903).[59] In 1926, he came to a state of "angry revolt" against the dreams. His eponymous hero, Dymer, in his poem *Dymer*, was "a man escaping from illusion".[60] By the time he wrote *Dymer*, Lewis, showing further development, said he had rejected atheism and naturalism, in favour of idealism.[61] He was working on another poem, *The King of Drum*, in 1927. Re-written as *The Queen of Drum*, it contains Christian symbolism, and tells us that "a King's house contains the weal of all",[62] indicating emergent growth towards Christian kingship. Until 1929, the year of his conversion, Lewis *may* have equated royalism with Christianity, with the fractured societies of Ireland that attends this assumption.

It is, in fact, highly unlikely that a man brought up in a Protestant-Unionist Ulster middle-class background, with its political conservatism and monarchic sympathies, would even consider such a transfer of loyalties. However, when he *was* converted, a major development in Lewis's thought, it was "only to Theism, pure and simple", when once more acknowledging that "God was God", he thought it reasonable and right to obey Him. Lewis explained that "God was to be obeyed simply because He was God . . . because of what He is in Himself". The reason for obeying Him, in the last resort, Lewis said, is because "'I am'". Two years after his conversion to theism in 1929, after a conversation with Dyson and Tolkien, Lewis made in 1931 the most significant advance in his developing ideas yet. He said he believed "that Jesus Christ is the Son of God",[63] a belief in *Christus Rex* from which he never looked back.

Lewis's beliefs in God and the idea of God as King clearly converge. He said the matter was "complicated . . . The primal and necessary Being, the Creator, has sovereignty *de facto* as well as *de jure* . . . The *de jure* sovereignty was made known to me before the power, the right before the might", that is to say, God has sovereignty through His creativity *and* through what He actually is. In *Surprised by Joy* (1955), Lewis said that "To know God is to know that our obedience is due to Him. In His nature His sovereignty *de jure* is revealed".[64] Lewis retrospectively reviewed the development of his religious thought; he said that while an idealist he believed in the Absolute, or "'Berkley's God'". He could not "meet" Him. Lewis said, "There was, I explained, no possibility of being in a personal relation with Him".[65] When he came to believe that the Absolute really *was* God, Lewis, like the ancient Hebrews, believed in God as perfect in Himself, and as the heavenly King.

In *The Allegory of Love*, begun in 1928 and published in 1936, having had eight years in which his ideas could mature further, Lewis said there is another way than allegory of seeing that the "archetype in the copy" is through "symbolism or sacramentalism". He found "the more real"[66] experience in his symbol of Joy, and explained this better in *The Pilgrim's Regress* (1932). In the second edition of *Regress* Lewis used the word *romanticism*, which in the posthumous third edition he calls "intense longing", equating it with his definition of Joy. He said of his 'stabs' of Joy, "I still believe that the expression is common, commonly misunderstood, and of immense importance".[67] He said in a Bodleian manuscript that he recalled learning to dive with Barfield, and that "Nothing is simpler than this art . . . you need . . . to abstain from all attempt at self-preservation".[68]

Lewis wrote an account of the Joy he felt when he became a theist and accepted the kingship of God. He tells of the discovery that the source of the Joy he wrote about in the Bodleian manuscript is, in fact, God. He refers to the time that favours *royalism*, as he describes his return to faith. He speaks of the "association lately established . . . between classism in art, royalism in politics, and catholicism in religion",[69] echoing Eliot. Lewis parodies Eliot's essay in his 'three pale men' in *Regress*, substituting Humanist for Royalist: Eliot's essay is itself a variation of Charles Maurras. This is important since being a monarchist in France and England have been very different, the French tradition being that of an absolute

monarch, while the English ideal after 1649 has been, and still is, one of
constitutional monarchy. Lewis, unwilling to endorse tyranny, takes the
ideal of monarchy further. He says because of the Fall "No man can be
trusted with unchecked power over his fellows",[70] stating the need for a
type of government such as democracy.

Having himself been led to Christianity by his love of myth, Lewis's
ideas of kingship continued to develop when he decided to use myth to
express his beliefs. He began to write *Out of the Silent Planet* in 1937,
the first of a trilogy of science fiction. He did what he called 'smuggling'
theology into peoples' minds. *His* mind had been "baptised" by reading
George MacDonald's *Phantastes* (1858), where he found a new quality –
'holiness'.[71] Lewis's evolving ideas about kingship and willing obedience to
the King are represented in *Out of the Silent Planet* (1938) as he portrays a
contented society that has a belief system akin to Christianity – with a divine
King, Maleldil, who created the world, who lives with the Old One (the
Father), and in eldils (representing angels) and the *Oyarsas*, tutelary spirits,
one of whom, the Bent One, represents Satan. The inhabitants willingly
obey Maleldil, who represents Christ. Lewis appears to have moved in a
surprising direction. He creates a Miltonic picture of a society whose belief
is wholly compatible with republicanism, though he reverts in the second
book of the trilogy, *Perelandra*.

In *Out of the Silent Planet*, Lewis heightens the paradigm in which his idea
of kingship operates. He presents the king's antithesis; the contrast of the
juxtaposition inevitably sharpens the image of the ideal. Weston personifies
Lewis's objection to 'emergent evolutionism'. He announced "Me no care
Maleldil. Like Bent One better: me on his side",[72] deliberately aligning
himself with the Devil, a Faustian action. Maleldil, however, epitomises
a more positive development in Lewis's idea of kingship, as He actively
engenders love for others, for instance, the self-sacrificial love shown by
Queen Orual in *Till We Have Faces* (1956), when she offered to take Psyche's
place as the sacrifice demanded by the god of the mountain.

Lewis continued to develop his ideal of kingship in *A Preface to Paradise
Lost*, ostensibly about Milton's God but really about Lewis's. Written in
1942, the year before the publication of *Perelandra*, he expounds his ideas
about Hierarchy, telling us *who* should rule, and *how* they should rule. He
refers to "the Hierarchical conception", and the "monarchy of God", who
Lewis says has no "natural superior".[73] Developing the ideal further, Lewis
tackled the hypothetical situation of what might happen to an un-fallen
world and its monarchy *if* Satan attacked its innocence. He explored this in
Perelandra, where the Queen believed she would remain loyal to Maleldil,
though her failure, Lewis suggests, would have caused "some act of even
more appalling love" than the Crucifixion.[74]

Lewis portrayed his concept of democratised kingship. This is a kingship
offered to those who accept their individual responsibilities, as Ransom
did in *Perelandra*. Ransom, with his significant name, realised that he had

absolute responsibility to prevent the Queen from being overwhelmed in the event of an attack by the Devil, incarnate in Weston. Maleldil did not intend to save Perelandra "through Himself but through Himself in Ransom".[75] Weston cruelly tempted the Queen to disobey Maleldil. Ransom, realising that he must fight Weston *physically*, ultimately killed him, removing the threat to her innocence.

It is not until the third book in Lewis's trilogy, *That Hideous Strength* (1945), that we discover Ransom's enthronement to his democratised kingship. He returns to earth from the mythological planet Perelandra, to become Mr Fisher-King, a remnant of Logres and the Pendragon. There he takes a meal of red wine and a roll of bread, a priest-kingly activity with strong Eucharistic overtones. Lewis returned us to the 'real', un-mythic England in spite of a certain difficulty in reconciling the presence of both the Pendragon and the constitutional monarch of the House of Windsor, King George VI. Lewis said in Perelandra, "The triple distinction of truth from myth and of both from fact was purely terrestrial".[76] The crisis of monarchy, brought about by the Abdication of King Edward VIII in 1936, helped to confirm the 'Mystique' of the kingly office, the Mystique to which Nicolson referred, and the attendant responsibilities to be borne by the king. Williams said in an unpublished letter to Anne Ridler, *apropos* of the Abdication, that King George VI was "anointed and crowned", much as I could wish otherwise".[77]

Lewis's ideal of kingship is most clearly displayed in his *Chronicles of Narnia*, written in the 1950s. The stories allegorically reflect Christian ideas. In *The Lion, the Witch and the Wardrobe* (1950), Lewis portrays an Anselmian view of salvation through Substitution and, as in his space trilogy, 'smuggles' ideas into people's minds. In *The Last Battle* (1956), Lewis makes a daring apocalyptic development when the High King of Narnia, King Peter, is asked by Aslan, who allegorically represents Christ, to "Shut the Door" – the door that had *appeared* to lead nowhere. King Peter took this brave step, and the land of Narnia came to "an end". Narnia had apparently been, according to Lewis, a "Shadowland". Lewis portrays the "Great Story", as he calls it, the story that "goes on for ever", envisioning Paradise, which he described as "England within England".[78]

Monarchy and Middle-Earth

Chapter Nine

Tolkien and the Historical Notion of Kingship

> In Middle-earth dwelt also
> Gil-galad the High King.
> J.R.R. Tolkien, *The Silmarillion* (1977), p. 254.

An Inkling

J.R.R. Tolkien (1892-1973), a gentleman and a scholar, looked to the monarchy of England, and specifically to Victoria, Queen and Empress, to strengthen his British colonial identity, a monarchy whose family name, like his own, was of German origin. Unlike Williams and Lewis, Tolkien was a Roman Catholic, though like them a royalist. Tolkien's ideas about kingship stemmed partly, he says, from his beliefs. They also came from his deep interest in the history of the Anglo-Saxons, their kings, and the wealth of Early English literature, especially that encapsulating the concept of kingship, for example the heroic tale of *Beowulf*.

J.R.R. Tolkien's circumstances and home background were different again from those of both Williams and Lewis. Tolkien was born of English parents in Bloemfontein in South Africa in 1892. His great-great grandfather, in fact, came to England from Saxony in the eighteenth century. Tolkien regarded his "German name with pride", though the main part of his descent, he insisted, was "purely English". He had "a taste" for 'Germanic languages', and respect for "the Germanic ideal".[1] Tolkien's father, Arthur, emigrated from Birmingham to South Africa to take up a post with the Bank of Africa. He acquitted himself well, and in 1890 became manager of an important branch of the bank, where a house was provided and the income was adequate. He married Mabel Suffield, in 1891. They led there a life that "was by no means uncomfortable". The house was "solidly built", and had a very large garden. There were "servants in the house". When John Ronald was born he had a "nurse who had been engaged to look after him".[2] Tolkien's early life, in a professional home, where he enjoyed the comforts of a prosperous family and a loving atmosphere that was both devout and loyal to the British

Crown, led directly to his own fidelity to the king. In a letter of 7 June 1955 to W.H. Auden, Tolkien says he is not "a 'democrat' in any of its current uses: except that I suppose, to speak in literary terms, we are all equal before the Great Author".[3]

Tolkien and the Historical Notion of Kingship

Tolkien ordered Middle-earth: he saw divine kingship 'reflected' in the rulers of Middle-earth. His ideal of kingship, inherent in his fiction rather than stated in discourse, is discernible in what he calls "Story", set in a "Secondary World".[4] As a devout Christian he believed, like Williams and Lewis, in God and in the Kingship of Christ, the divine King who "reigned from the tree".[5] However, in his 'Story', he tries not to parody Christianity because it would create allegory, of which he says, "I dislike allegory in all its manifestations".[6]

Williams had not spoken directly about 'obedience' to God or the King, but had encouraged co-inherence, the Pauline reciprocal living in-and-for each other. Lewis, on the other hand, had quite unequivocally looked for obedience both to the heavenly and the earthly kings although, like St. Augustine, and thereafter Lewis, he was looking for a willing compact rather than an enforced compliance. Tolkien, however, shows that his mythological god, Ilúvatar, *is* obeyed by His angels, the Ainur, but in a way that is (with the exception of Melkor) what might be called 'Collegiate', that is to say, willing response to His generosity-led commands. His very act of Creation is the result of the divine utterance, "Eä! Let these things be!"[7]

The idea of an 'absolute' monarch was central to Tolkien's philosophy. Acting as God's vicegerent, he exacts obedience after taking heed to the thoughts of His councillors. In the draft of a letter of 1963, he describes his ideal king as "monarch with the power of unquestioned decision in debate";[8] he is referring to his fictional King Aragorn II's Great Council. Here, we are reminded of the Great Councils of King Richard II, a monarch particularly pertinent to Tolkien because of his interest in Shakespeare's play and the literary culture of that epoch. Richard II, very conscious of the obligation of obedience to the monarch, emphasised his royal Prerogative, although he *did*, in fact, listen to advice proffered by the magnates, the nobility. They had "no power to make a statute", and even their unanimous advice the king should "reject" if he thought it "*inutile*". Unlike Aragorn's councillors, Richard's magnates were latterly "so sharply rebuked and reproved by the king that they dared not speak the truth concerning his welfare and that of the kingdom". It was, indeed, Richard's over-emphasis on the Prerogative, the duty of obedience to the king and the magnates' "rebellion" that led to his deposition.[9]

On the one hand Williams and Lewis are both constitutional monarchists, Williams believing that a monarchy should benefit from the inherent egalitarian qualities of a just republic, whereas Lewis looks for a democratic realm in which the king, God's vicegerent, is willingly obeyed. Tolkien, on the other hand, has a more Absolutist approach to monarchic government and, according to his biographer Humphrey Carpenter, is "'right-wing' in that he honoured his monarch and his country and did not believe in the rule of the people".[10] Tolkien reflects the attitude of the Stuart king, James I, and his belief in the 'Divine Right' of kings, with the 'passive obedience' of the people. This doctrine of monarchy was successful under James but disastrous under Charles I, who took the 'right' to impossible extremes and acted tyrannically. The tragic ends of King Charles I and his ancestor, Richard II were, in the last resort, due to their political over-reaching. Tolkien, aware of this, decreed that his Kings of Númenor, appointed by the Valar (angels) so that their kingship was ratified by Ilúvatar, eventually suffered a similar fate. The last king, Ar-Pharazôn, became a tyrant. His growing obsession with self-aggrandisement led him to attempt to wrest immortality from the Valar (those of the Ainur who entered Arda, the Earth, as demiurges to help to complete it), whom he defied by sailing against the Ban to the Undying Lands.

Ilúvatar, to prevent the thwarting of His commands, caused Númenor to sink under the sea, divine retribution reminiscent of that brought down in ancient Israel by Manasseh's 'lawless reign'. Tolkien uses the word *King* in his mythology for the tyrant Morgoth the Vala, the notable exception to those who willingly obeyed Ilúvatar. With Morgoth's rebellion began many thousands of years of bitter struggle between good and evil. Tolkien's word *Vala* calls to mind the symbolic poem by William Blake, originally called *Vala*, written and revised 1795-1804, and renamed *The Four Zoas*. Blake elaborated his own cosmic mythology, presenting characters from his earlier symbolic works, including one named Orc, another word used by Tolkien, signifying a degraded Elf, tyrannically enslaved by Sauron, Morgoth's lieutenant.

Morgoth, a type of devil, who malevolently desired to be King of the Earth, attempted to wreck all that Ilúvatar had created, and to subdue Elves and Men to his own egocentric will. Here we see not so much a Fall of Men as of angels. Tolkien portrayed his idea of active evil (that is, conscious immorality, as against the mere absence of good) as the Shadow – the absence of light, especially in the person of Morgoth's lieutenant. Sauron was originally a Maia (a lesser angel) whose iniquitous lust for power spread insidiously into the whole earth. An instance of this expansion is when Sauron lured nine leaders of Men (some of whom were Kings) into his service with the deceitful promise of a Ring of Power. Their King, the Witch-King of Angmar, epitomised evil in action in his long and bitter enmity with the true King of Gondor, King Aragorn II, Tolkien's ideal king. In a seemingly endless struggle, culminating in the War of the Ring, Sauron had desired to dominate the whole world, though in the end unsuccessfully.

There is some comparison between the tyrannical and evil Witch-King and Lewis's anti-Christ figure, the Unman, in *Perelandra* and, to a much lesser degree, Williams's King Cradlemas in the *Arthuriad*. Lewis's Unman was, indeed, a man who, devil-inhabited, epitomised reverse evolution. Weston, the Un-Man, unsuccessfully tempted the Queen of Perelandra, to disobey Maleldil. Williams's Cradlemas was regarded as a tyrant, though *not* a barbarian, but only the last "sinister representation of the Roman civilisation".[11] However, Tolkien's Witch-King is an utterly evil figure whose downfall was precipitated by succumbing to the offer of enormous power. He continually strove to destroy the true King, Aragorn, of elven and angelic descent, who had fought long and hard against Sauron, and whose Northern Kingdom, Arnor, he had already ruined.

Tolkien shows no ambivalence over the need to fight to free the people of Middle-earth from the tyrants, Morgoth and Sauron, whereas Williams was ambivalent about the use of force. Lewis was quite willing to see an armed struggle, for instance to restore the true King of Archenland in *The Horse and his Boy* (1954). It is significant that Tolkien and Lewis both served as soldiers in the First World War, whereas, for reasons of health, Williams did not. The importance of this biographical fact is stated as Tolkien and Lewis both demonstrate the necessity of removing unlawful rulers. Focusing on the removal of tyrants, reminds us of Aristotle's notion that "Tyrants were men who seized kingship, and perverted it for their own benefit".[12]

The very antithesis of the persistent devilry of the rebellious Vala, Morgoth, (also known as Melkor) is the gracious royalty of the King of the Valar, Morgoth's brother, Manwë. He is referred to in *The Silmarillion* (edn. 1977) as "the first of all Kings", and moreover, as having been "appointed to be the vicegerent of Ilúvatar, King of the world of Valar and Elves and Men, and the chief defence against the evil of Melkor". Tolkien tells us that Manwë, "has no thought for his own honour, and is not jealous of his power, but rules all to peace", this subtly understates the depth of his benignity.[13]

In a letter of 25 April 1954 to Naomi Mitchison, Tolkien said that his story is "cast in terms of a good side, and a bad side . . . tyranny against kingship".[14] This struggle unfolds first between the two archangels, Manwë and Morgoth, and much later between King Aragorn and the Witch-King, Aragorn's "hereditary foe" in the War of the Ring. In Ar-Pharazôn, the Witch-King, Morgoth and the other would-be King of the Earth, Sauron, Tolkien epitomised his revulsion for tyrants in Sauron.

This is reminiscent of the "morbid horror" the Romans felt about tyranny. They felt that tyranny was an abomination; this is implied by the view of monarchy, which had been jaded by the misuse of power in prior regimes, described retrospectively by the republican establishment, in view of the tyrannous "legendary Tarquins of the sixth century" (BC).[15] Tolkien insisted that the battles between the forces of good (the Elves and Men) against those of evil (manifested as tyrannies and perversions of power) were not intended to be an allegory of World War I, of Nazism, nor yet of tyrants like Hitler, Stalin and Mao, in spite of the *applicability* (a term he used for apparent alignments) to modern history. A reader may be tempted to align

Tolkien's 'Story' with modern History, rather than a reflection of universal truths. One may argue that some of his writing was inspired by his time fighting in the First World War, though an unconscious impression of an experience is not to be confused with *allegorical applicability*.

Williams had spoken of the glory attaching to kings, heavenly and earthly. Lewis, not overtly referring to royal Glory, nevertheless speaks of the glory of light and that which evokes awe. Tolkien tells of glory and splendour in *The Book of Lost Tales* (edn. 1983), when the Ainur "bowed" – an action that itself suggests majesty – to Ilúvatar, as He "unfolded a history" unequalled in its "glory" and "splendour",[16] reminiscent of when "the Glory of Yahweh was entering the sanctuary".[17] A more direct reference to the glory of the King is seen after the eventual fall of Sauron. In the rejoicing at what Tolkien calls the Eucatastrophe, the sudden joyous turn, the messenger sings, "Sing and be glad, all ye children of the West, for your King shall come again", a song that echoes Psalm 24 to the King of Glory", interpreted traditionally as Christ, to come in.[18]

Yahweh is surrounded in His Glory by "His divine court", a mythical idea borrowed by the Hebrews from the Canaanites.[19] Tolkien's mythological god, Ilúvatar, is likewise surrounded by *His* Court – the Ainur – one of several parallels to be discovered between Yahweh and Ilúvatar, who dwells beyond the world and is transcendent, leaving it to the Valar to govern the affairs of Arda, the World of Elves and Men. Ilúvatar willed (even before the beginning of Time) Joy for Man and the Elves. Christopher Tolkien, J.R.R. Tolkien's third son, calls this "Finrod's exalted vision of the original design of Eru [another name for Ilúvatar, meaning the One] for Mankind".[20] Finrod was, in fact, the Elven King of Nargothrond, and the first Elf to have dealings with the Three Houses of Men, the Edain (the Elf-friends).

Williams and Lewis had both referred to atonement through Substitution, whereas Tolkien suggests that, to prevent the wiles of Morgoth from permanently undermining His 'Purpose' of joy, Ilúvatar would ultimately need to intervene (as indeed the ancient Hebrews believed that Yahweh would intervene on Israel's behalf) and the One "himself enter into Arda, and heal Men and all the marring" caused by Morgoth. Finrod actually guessed that "Eru would come *incarnated in human form*" which, Tolkien says, would "surely not be parody, but the "extension . . . of the theology of Arda into specifically, and of course centrally, Christian belief".[21] Tolkien presents us overtly with the counterparts of *two* Persons of the Holy Trinity, Ilúvatar the All-Father and the Secret Fire – a Pentecostal image – which he said in a letter to Clyde Kilby, "was the Holy Spirit".[22] Tolkien rather narrowly avoids what he called 'parody' by leaving the Incarnation of the Son as a future projection. By naming this 'parody' for the imitation of Christianity, Tolkien is indicating that the danger is that the thing imitated will then be spoiled.

The King of the Valar, Manwë, is named as Ilúvatar's vicegerent. In *Morgoth's Ring*, Tolkien describes the Valar as "certain angelic Beings" who were "agents and vicegerents of Eru (God)". There is a reference to the "Majesty of the Ainur", with its resonances of royalty.[23] The Ancient Hebrews had, indeed, regarded their king, the Davidic king, as vicegerent, as the "Messiah of Yahweh . . . specially commissioned by Yahweh for this high office". As God's vicegerent, the Hebrew king was responsible for the "administration of justice within his realm".[24] The Anglo-Saxon king was also, as "king by the grace of God, *dei vicarius*",[25] vicar of God, thus His vicegerent. He was regarded, like the Israelite king, as the judge who brings justice to his realm.

The historian of Anglo-Saxon England, Chaney, cites one of the major sources on the structure of Anglo-Saxon society, the so-called *Institutes of Christian Polity*, which, he says, is "generally attributed to the authorship of Archbishop Wulfstan (d. A.D. 1023)", a "royal counsellor" and the author of homilies in the vernacular. The *Institutes* is "almost the only work in Old English and one of the earliest anywhere to define the duties of the various classes of society". The *Institutes* assert that "a Christian king is Christ's deputy", His vicegerent. It also discusses the "kingship of God" and speaks of the "Glory of kings". Of the earthly king, it says it is "befitting a righteous king" to be guided to "just judgement".[26] *The Cambridge Guide to Literature in English* says that Wulfstan had written 'The Cannons of Edgar' and the 'Institutes of Polity' as well as "many lesser-known pieces", implying a certain importance to the 'Institutes'. The Bishop also "contributed to the vernacular version of the Benedictine office" – again an unusual practice at the time.[27]

There are further parallels between the kings of ancient Israel and Tolkien's divinely-appointed Kings of Númenor. In their 'cult' (as John Eaton and others refer to these groups), the Israelite kings literally led the people to the high places. The theologian, John Eaton, says, "The chief officiant in principle was the king". It is "especially the king's high priesthood which was renewed in this festival". Eaton refers to the New Year festival, when the king prayed for the kingship and the people's welfare in the coming year. In the three Númenórian festivals the kings led their people to the Hallow, a high place for the worship of Eru Ilúvatar for a similar purpose, reflecting the time when the Kings of Israel had played a corresponding role. Both the Hebrew and Númenórian festivals took place in open-air Shrines. The parallel functions of priest-king in these pilgrimages suggest, perhaps, Tolkien's belief, not only in kingship *per se*, but also in its sacramental quality. Eaton sees the loyalties of Yahweh and King Solomon "almost merging"[28] in Psalm 2, while in Psalm 72 we find the 'peace and prosperity' that is attached to Solomon.

Solomon's vicegerency here parallels that of an Anglo-Saxon king who, like Solomon, engenders 'Peace and Plenty', reminiscent of Alexander Pope in *Windsor Forest* (1713, line 42). Tolkien had, as Tom Shippey said, "done his best to root his *Silmarillion* in what little genuine Anglo-Saxon tradition he could find".[29] His intention was, in fact, to write a mythology for England, and he gave much thought to the matter. Lewis points out in *The Discarded Image* that in medieval times the "very words 'story' and 'history' had not yet been desynonymised".[30] Tolkien clearly wrote his 'Story' as *though* it was 'history', we know it as fiction, but we, nevertheless, tend to give it credence. Christopher Tolkien said that his father "developed certain original theories, especially in connection with the appearance of Hengest in the Old English poem, *Beowulf*.[31] In 'Beowulf: The Monsters and the Critics' (1936), a lecture Tolkien gave to the British Academy, he called the days of the heroic events in the poem "heathen, noble, and hopeless". He referred to the "central position the creed of unyielding wills holds in the North".

In the "history of kings and warriors" the poet sees that "all glory . . . ends in night", and perceives the "common tragedy of inevitable ruin". Tolkien sees in Beowulf a hero (later in the poem a king) who, a pagan, (though the author of the poem is, like Tolkien himself, a Christian), has the "noble pagan's desire for the *merited praise* of the noble – the idea expressed in the Anglo-Saxon term *lof*. He expects the pagan's 'just esteem' embodied in the word *dom*. To achieve *lof* and *dom* meant the hero had to offer "absolute resistance, perfect because without hope".[32] Tolkien exemplifies this northern "theory of courage" in King Aragorn, his ideal king, when he exhorts the 'three hunters', Gimli, prince of the Dwarves, Legolas, prince of the Elves and himself the Ranger of the North (not yet King) to follow their friends, now in enemy hands, to act with courage , even if without 'Hope'. In *The Lord of the Rings: The Two Towers*, Aragorn says to them that "with hope or without hope we will follow the trail of our enemies".[33] Like Aragorn's faithfulness to the hobbits, Beowulf has the 'highest loyalty' a man can have. Man is "engaged in a battle he cannot win".[34]

Beowulf's heroism is of the very highest. Aragorn, likewise, is engaged in a battle he does not *know* that he can win in the War of the Ring. There is, perhaps, a certain parallel in the long struggle between the heroic King Aragorn and the tyrannical Witch-King of Angmar and the prolonged encounters between the hero Beowulf and the inhuman 'Monsters'. Tolkien's heroic kings have their roots in the distant past and were, Shippey thought, 'calqued' on the Anglo-Saxons, though *not* to be equated with them. There is something of the reciprocity found between the "overlord and each of his dependent kings" in Anglo-Saxon England, and the just King Aragorn who, like the Anglo-Saxons, would not use his soldiers' loyalty to enhance his own personal glory. In seventh-century England, "there existed the personal relationship of lord and man",[35] a relationship that existed between Aragorn and his friends the Hobbits, friends who were also soldiers. Tolkien had been a military officer, and had based the character Sam on his batman. Frodo and Sam reflect the relationship of an officer and an ordinary soldier, Tolkien saw Sam, nevertheless, as the hero of his 'Story'. As a sacral monarch, he was like the Anglo-Saxon Saint-Kings, Oswald and Edmund. Aragorn did not, of course, follow a Cross when he went into battle, but he *did* wear his Elfstone, the mythological equivelant. Tolkien's Ideal King, Aragorn, like the *Rex Pacificus* of the Anglo-Saxons, and the king of the ancient Hebrews, brought peace, prosperity and justice to the lands. Like King Edward the Confessor, King Aragorn has "the hands of a healer", which is how he the "rightful king could ever be known".[36]

Tolkien's Ideas Discovered in 'Story'

Tolkien began to demonstrate his beliefs that come together in his ideal of kingship when, in 1917, he wrote 'The Fall of Gondolin', which became 'Of Tuor and the Fall of Gondolin' in *The Silmarillion*. Tolkien had, then, already started to write his 'Story', set in Middle-earth, the body of legend he "could dedicate simply to England", as he told Milton Waldman in a letter of 1951.[37] Tolkien reveals through 'Story', that is, the fictional narrative form, an underlying belief in God the Creator, in the devil and in the divine vicegerent, the 'arch-angelic' and the earthly kings. The Creator's "original design . . . for Mankind" is that an eternally joyous state, which I have called 'Collegiate Joy', would be brought about through the intervention of "Eru [the One] . . . incarnated in human form,[38] an idea that tends to echo the Christian Gospel.

Tolkien's ideas of 'good' and 'evil' are mythologically presented as Ilúvatar, Morgoth (the dark enemy) the "prime power of evil"[39] who had assaulted the last elvish stronghold of King Turgon in "The Fall of Gondolin", Manwë the King of the Valar, the Elven Kings, the Dwarf Kings and the Kings of Men. Tolkien, as a mainstream Christian, believed profoundly in God and, though he strives to avoid writing what he called "a parody of Christianity",[40] he comes close to it in *Morgoth's Ring* (Volume 10 in the *History*, which he had not actually published). The *History* consists of twelve volumes of Tolkien's writings, edited and published by Christopher Tolkien, the first part appearing ten years after his father's death. The *History* is edited versions of J.R.R. Tolkien's texts, where the author gradually develops the 'history' of the Elder Days, while the published *Silmarillion* is intended by its editor to be "a completed and cohesive entity", and is, as Shippey saw it, "the latest work of its author", in spite of Christopher Tolkien's "assurance that a very high proportion of the 1937 'Silmarillion' text remained into the published version".[41]

By 'Collegiate Joy' I mean the cohesive, joyous society of the Valar, later Elves and Men, engendered by Ilúvatar, the Creator, who is *not* Himself *part* of the 'college' – not one of the Ainur – the panoply of angels. To obviate error, Tolkien may have refrained for this reason, and also, perhaps, to avoid allegory, from using the word *king* for Him. Indeed, he may also have wished to avoid the earthly stricture of naming Him as 'king'.

Tolkien's ideas and beliefs are largely to be deduced from those apparent in his stories. He is quite clear about his intention: his remarks in a letter of 10 April 1958 to C. Ouboter are pertinent regarding any deliberate meaning or "message" through his mythology. He said:

> As for 'message'; I have none really, if by that you mean the conscious purpose in writing 'The Lord of the Rings', of preaching, or of delivering myself of a vision of truth especially revealed to me! I was primarily writing an exciting story . . . such as I find personally attractive."

He added significantly, "But in such a process inevitably one's own taste, ideas and beliefs get taken up.[42] Tolkien held that through 'Story', especially mythological story, truth *could* perhaps, be expressed in a way that no other medium can achieve. For example, Tolkien wrote *Mythopoeia* (1931) after the significant conversation in Magdalen College with Hugo Dyson and C.S. Lewis, as Christopher Tolkien has told us in the Preface to *Tree and Leaf*.[43] Tolkien and Dyson had convinced Lewis, contrary to his assertion that myths are lies "breathed through silver", both that "myths could convey important truths" and that the incarnation, crucifixion and resurrection of Christ could be perceived as God's own myth , "conveying a meaning" beyond our reasoning.[44]

Shippey reminds us that the word "*spell*" embodies what Tolkien meant by "fantasy" – something unnaturally powerful (magic spell), something literary (a story), something in essence true (Gospel) – the "gód spel", the "good story". Tolkien asserts that the Gospels have the "supremely convincing tone "of Primary Art, of Truth".[45] In *On Fairy-Stories*, he says that the peculiar quality of the "joy" in Fantasy can be experienced as a sudden "glimpse" of the underlying reality or truth. Fairy-story depends on the nature of Faërie – the Perilous Realm. Fantasy has the power of giving to "ideal creations" the inner consistency of reality in a secondary world. Inside it, what the author says is "true", and accords with the laws of that world. Tolkien sees a parallel between the underlying reality or truth discoverable in *his* 'Story', with the "supremely convincing tone" of the Gospels and its relation to the Old Testament. Tolkien says, "This story has entered History and the primary world",[46] a story that begins and ends in joy, a story that shows the "inner consistency of reality". The relation of the Gospels in 'looking back' to the Old Testament is parallel to the necessity of 'looking back' at the long history of the Númenórian Kings in Tolkien's Story, which has its own ending "in joy" in *The Return of the King*. The Gondorians (and the reader) become more aware of the significance of King Aragorn as they 'look back', an action parallel to a Christian 'looking back' at the Old Testament, to understand better the full meaning of the accounts of Christ's life in the Gospels . In *The Birth of the Messiah*, Professor R.E. Brown says that "one may speak of the Gospels developing backwards". He suggests that by 'looking back' from the Resurrection, "the disciples came to a more adequate understanding of who Jesus really was".[47]

The Devices of 'Looking back' and 'Mediation'

Of the benefits of 'looking back', Lewis said in *Miracles*, "Only Supernaturalists really see Nature. You must go a little way from her, and then turn round, and look back. Then at last the true landscape will become visible".[48] Tolkien wrote of the 'history', to which Aragorn's kingship 'looked back', in a letter of 20 September 1963 to Colonel Worksett:

I am doubtful myself about the undertaking [to make the *Silmarillion* consistent with *The Lord of the Rings*].[49] Part of the attraction of The L.R. [*The Lord of the Rings*] is, I think, due to the glimpses of a large history in the background: an attraction like that of viewing far off an unvisited island, or seeing the towers of a distant city gleaming in a sunlit mist. To go there is to destroy the magic, unless new unattainable vistas are again revealed.[50]

Christopher Tolkien said of the 'new unattainable vistas', "*The Silmarillion* . . . in its longer form, was bound to begin at the beginning. How could 'depth' be created when you had nothing else to reach further back to"? He says that in *The Silmarillion* "there are explorations to be conducted in this world with perfect right . . . and it is proper to attempt to comprehend its structure in its largest extent, from the myth of its Creation".[51] However, Genesis chapter I implies just such an illimitable vista by a "rigorous obliqueness"[52] by not saying *who* God actually *is*. At the beginning of *The Silmarillion* we are told, before Creation takes place, of the existence of Eru, the One. To read *The Silmarillion*, Christopher Tolkien advocates placing oneself "imaginatively" at the end of the Third Age – within Middle-earth – "looking back" at the point of Sam Gamgee's "I like that!" – "adding, 'I should like to know more about it'". Sam's delight was for the poem that Gimli recited in Moria, which itself 'looks back' to the "mighty kings in Nargothrond and Gondolin".

Christopher Tolkien suggests that "the literary 'impression of depth'", regarding *The Lord of the Rings*, "cannot be made a criterion by which a work in a wholly different mode is measured". To do that would imply the history of the Elder Days is of no more significance than as an "artistic" background for the later book. Somewhat ambiguously, he adds such a "looking back" if "understood mechanically", simply *as* a backcloth to *The Lord of the Rings*,

> as if a fuller account of the mighty kings of Nargothrond and Gondolin would imply a dangerously near approach to the bottom of the well, while an account of Creation would signify the striking of the bottom and a definitive running out of 'depth' – nothing to reach further back to . . . The very fact that '*The Lord of the Rings* . . . establishes such a powerful sense of a real time-structure . . . provides this necessary vantage point.[53]

Christopher Tolkien appears to have held two different positions. First, that it is feasible to "look back" at the Elder Days *only* from a historical perspective – that is, from a great distance in time – as though the dimly apprehended events' "attraction lies in their very dimness". At the same time, he was saying, "This is not how things work, or at least not how they need work".[54] In other words, one may enjoy purposely 'going back' to experience the events as and when they took place. This can either be interpreted as an incongruity on behalf of Christopher Tolkien, or as the truly polysemous nature of the vision of Middle-earth, which may be taken as both literal and figurative – both real and imagined. This feature of Tolkien's mythological 'history' reminds us of the way in which we can interpret medieval 'history', according to Lewis's assertion.[55]

When Christopher Tolkien came to publish *The Silmarillion* and *Unfinished Tales* (1980) he changed his theory to the latter view, that everything can, in fact, be seen close up. At least in *The Hobbit* we look through Bilbo's eyes as 'mediator'. "There is in *The Silmarillion* "no 'mediation' of the kind provided by the hobbits".[56] In the volumes of *The History of Middle-Earth*, Christopher Tolkien uses his father in the place of Bilbo: at least some of "The Silmarillion" was actually heard orally by Christopher Tolkien from his father. This will surely prove a feast for 'reader response' theory, which will be saved for another study. Listening to the developing 'Story' apparently changed Christopher Tolkien's 'reception' of it. He found it natural to see his father as the mediator.[57]

This deliberate 'looking back' is a structural device that creates verisimilitude: the reader more readily 'receives' the story as though it were about actual historic people, whose way of life had been philologically deduced. Tolkien thus populates an entirely imaginary world through a philologist's view of *invented* languages. Of these languages and those who ostensibly spoke them, and the world in which they lived, it is difficult to realise, as Christopher Tolkien said, that the whole thing "exists only in the mind".[58] He told me he may have said this "in opposition to those who claim to find its origin in some known part of the physical world".[59]

J.R.R. Tolkien intensifies the illusion at the beginning of his writing in *The Book of Lost Tales: Part I*, Book One of *The History of Middle-Earth*, by appearing to have 'discovered' the story via the mediation of one Eriol, who in turn had heard it from the Elves on Tol Eressëa, the Lonely Isle. The Elves, looking even further back, had actually *known* the Valar, the angelic 'Powers', who had been allowed to enter the World by the Creator Himself, so providing evidence for truth.

The reception of *The Silmarillion* is more convincing, then, to the reader who 'looks back' with Sam and experiences the 'return of the true king', though it should be remembered that this is, in fact, not actually a myth of *The Silmarillion* but is peculiar to the different creative effort of *The Lord of the Rings*, in which Tolkien was influenced by "things Celtic".[60] Such a joyous outcome Tolkien refers to as a "Eucatastrophe", the word he had coined for a "sudden joyous turn" in *On Fairy-Stories*.[61] The King's 'return' followed the (at least temporary) victory over evil, symbolised as the shadow in the person of Sauron, Morgoth's erstwhile lieutenant. The 'joyous turn' is completed by the restoration and coronation of Aragorn, Tolkien's true and ideal king. The 'looking back' is not entirely conscious to the reader, and is better regarded as the moment of realisation that the sudden joy stems from an event that fits the "inner consistency of reality" in his 'secondary world' where, as Tolkien said, what the author relates is "true", and which echoes that in the primary world. The reader ponders the source of the "joy" and the nature of the 'glimpses' seen in the "story" that took place in "*Faërie*: the Perilous Realm".[62]

Tolkien's extraordinarily consistent secondary world is found to be complete with its own myths, history, languages, palaeography, flora, fauna, geography, geology and theology, orders of being, and is "a world full of creatures beyond count", as C.S. Lewis reminded us.[63] Tolkien has created an unusually (perhaps uniquely) highly developed and comprehensive secondary world. He may have been influenced to an extent by William Morris's *The Well at the World's End* (1896), and probably by his other romances, as a stage for the enactment of Tolkien's own myth. Tolkien's 'stage' for his 'myth' actually *feels* like this world, although he had altered some of the geography. His 'Shire', for example, through rich and vivid description, is reminiscent of the English midlands, especially of Worcestershire and Warwickshire. The reader *feels* at home there, as many have asserted, making the mythical world evocative and convincing. The Elvish and dwarvish languages, and those of men, develop with philologically realistic changes as the peoples move, both in time and place. The reader gradually becomes aware of the extent of any changes and development in Tolkien's own "ideas and views". Not actually *caused* by the passage of time, any development in his concepts is manifested in his writing, which itself took place over many years."

The reader discovers and understands the underlying theology both by process of mediation, as, for example, by Eriol, or later the imaginary Anglo-Saxon, Ælfwine, through gradual revelation, and by an increasing awareness of the actual beliefs of the characters as the Story unfolds. The central myth spans some thirty-seven thousand years, presented as though actual history, itself ostensibly 'discovered' by the author.

An exploration of the history of the Elder Days, the history and Tolkien's creation myth will facilitate the discovery of the extent to which Tolkien's view of kingship changed over the years. As a scholar, Tolkien had moved "freely in the early Middle Ages". His main tendency was politically "monarchic". However, the one exception is his "Shire", where for a thousand years the Hobbits "got on very well" without a king, with merely "titular Thains" and a Mayor.[64] However, the Thain *represented* the King, whose territory included the Shire, though for many years his 'return' was awaited with little expectation. This is also a reflection of Tolkien's scholarship, as early peoples native to Britain also lived in small societies with, what we call now, civic leaders.

Tolkien's ideas underwent a sea-change in 1937 when he began work on *The Lord of the Rings*, specifically working on the Shire and its Thain. He said in a letter of 21 February 1958 to his son Christopher that "an enquirer had asked him what *The Lord of the Rings* was "all about". He had said that "It was an effort to create a situation in which a common greeting would be *"elen síla lúmenn' omentielmo"* – A star shines on the hour of our greeting.[65] This can be seen as a greeting that implies a sense of wonder at the world given to us by God. Chesterton, like Tolkien's Elf, felt that we need to view the world so as to combine the ideas "of wonder" and "welcome". Tolkien, himself much influenced by Chesterton, manifested both wonder and welcome in his Shire, seen *inter alia*, in Frodo's delight in "woods and fields and little rivers".[66]

Chesterton believed in the "ordinary man". Tolkien, more of a royalist, made it clear that *his* 'ordinary man', Sam, neither *could* nor could *want* to be a king. Tolkien's shining example of *his* "sane" and "ordinary" man Sam, whom Tolkien himself had called the "chief" hero of *The Lord of the Rings* in the 1951 letter to Milton Waldman.[67] Chesterton's ordinary man "had one foot in Earth and the other in fairyland".[68] This duality reminds us of Smith, in Tolkien's *Smith of Wooton Major* (1967). In fairyland, on a walk "without a guide", Smith hoped to discover the "further bounds" of the land. He saw, "far off" one of Tolkien's 'unattainable vistas' – a "great hill of shadow", and "the King's Tree springing up",[69] an event redolent of when, in *The Return of the King*, Aragorn saw "there sprang a sapling tree no more than three foot high",[70] a sign of hope for the future of the royal house. Tolkien, like the Anglo-Saxons, presents his just kings as in direct descent in the royal line, *and* receiving the approbation of the people. This is precisely the situation in *The Lord of the Rings*, when Aragorn is brought before the people, the direct heir of King Isildur, Elendil's son. The Lord Steward, Faramir, asks the people, "Shall he be king and enter the City and dwell there? And all the host and all the people cried *yea* with one voice".[71]

It is germane to our consideration of Tolkien's presentation of his mythological god, Ilúvatar the divine King, to remember that he believes that a writer, especially when he is 'creating' – or sub-creating – a secondary world, is acting in his most god-like manner. For many years, Tolkien "held to his theory of 'sub-creation', which declared that since the human imagination came from God, then its products must come from God too". With the "Elvish craft" of Fantasy in mind, we remember that in *On Fairy-Stories*, Tolkien said that "God is the Lord" – and thus the creator – "of angels, and of men", adding significantly, "and of elves".[72]

The creative co-operation of the Valar is exemplified in *Lost Tales*, where water was mostly "the dream and invention of Ulmo",[73] though in *The Silmarillion*, Ulmo simply "turned his thought " to water, and the Valar began their "great labours",[74] their 'demiurgic' activities, developing what was already created. We see that, in *The Silmarillion*, Tolkien has moved away from the idea of the 'demiurge' to that of God having created everything *ex nihilo*, in tune with orthodox Christian belief. In making a reflection or echo of Anglo-Saxon *praxis* in validating a king, Tolkien employed the device of 'looking back', thus creating a sense of believable history in the reader's mind. In 'mediating' his own myth *through* English history, which is (at least partly) recognisable to the reader, Tolkien continued to speak in a way that a reader 'receives' the 'Story' as being something 'true'.

Chapter Ten

Tolkien and the Divine Court

Ilúvatar the Creator and His Court

By 'looking back', we can trace Tolkien's ideas of his creation myth from
the first appearance of Ilúvatar and the Ainur in *The Book of Lost Tales: Part
I*, Book One in *The History of Middle-Earth*, which J.R.R. Tolkien began
writing in 1916-17, when he was twenty-five years old. Here, we find
that depth was *not* an illusion. It becomes apparent that the "history of the
history" of Middle-earth developed seldom, as Christopher Tolkien says, "by
outright rejection – far more often it was by subtle transformation in stages",
and that the legends "can seem like the growth of legends among peoples".
There is much in the old manuscripts that Tolkien "never (so far as one can
tell) expressly rejected".[1]

Did Ilúvatar create the world by royal command, or did He ask for the
help of assistants, that is, did demiurgic assistants take part in the creation,
or only in the further development of the world? When, then, *did* Ilúvatar
and the Ainur, one of whom, Manwë, was called "the first of all Kings"
in *The Silmarillion*, first appear in Tolkien's legendarium, that is to say, his
mythology as a whole?[2] Tolkien wrote "The Music of the Ainur" in *Lost
Tales* while working on the Oxford English Dictionary, between 1918 and
1920. Eriol asked his host, Lindo, about the Valar (those of the Ainur who
entered Eä, the created order). "Are they the Gods"? He was simply told, "So
they be". The Elf Rúmil told him, "Ilúvatar was the first beginning . . . the
Lord for always who dwells beyond the world; who made it and is not of
it, but loves it", which states that Ilúvatar was definitely outside the creation
as the 'first beginning' and Creator, and as such has parental love for the
world. As Christopher Tolkien said, the account of the "Music" continued
"to be ascribed" to Rúmil, a "philologist" on Tol Eressëa. Eriol asked, "What
was the Music of the Ainur"? Rúmil said, "Behold, Ilúvatar dwelt alone.
Before all things he sang into being the Ainur first". He revealed to them
through "themes of song . . . many of the great and wonderful things that he
devised . . . and now they would make music unto him . . . about his throne".
Ilúvatar "propounded" a mighty design, "unfolding a history", showing the
"glory of its beginning and the splendour of its end".[3]

In his Creation myth in "The Silmarillion", Tolkien uses imagery of themes of music, given to the Ainur (the angelic Powers), by the Creator, Ilúvatar, reflecting the medieval depiction of the angels singing "continuously around the throne of God". Bradford Lee Eden says that, as a medievalist, Tolkien knew the medieval concept of the "music of the spheres", itself grounded in ancient and classical philosophy, and "discussed and theorized by Plato and Aristotle". The concept would have been "deeply ingrained" in his education and in his Roman Catholic upbringing. The "most commonly quoted source" of material connected with the medieval concept of "the music of the spheres" is Boethius (c.480-524) and his model of "cosmological theory" which tells of the harmonizing by "a chain of beings" that help to "produce the plenitude of creation". Tolkien did not, Eden says, refer to his use of the medieval concept in his own mythology.[4] Nevertheless, Ilúvatar's angels *did* sing round His throne, reflecting the medieval notion of the 'Music of the Spheres'. Tolkien set his 'Story' in the dim and distant past, long before the Middle Ages. His use of 'melody' by Ilúvatar in creating His world is reminiscent of Boethius; but it was meant to subtly suggest to the reader a much earlier time. However, by *maintaining* the medieval image, Tolkien enhanced the acceptance of his 'history' as truly ancient, because, as a 'modern', the reader would *feel* that he has 'looked back'. Tolkien had deliberately *not* 'discarded the image'. Lewis referred in *The Discarded Image* to "attempts to get in all the phenomena known at a given period" as a "Model", one that will be "ruthlessly smashed", that is then 'discarded'. "In every age the human mind is deeply influenced by the accepted 'Model' of the universe."[5] The reader, therefore, *feels* that the 'history' of Ilúvatar's 'creation' is 'true'. Tolkien said in *On Fairy Stories* (1964), "The story-maker proves a successful 'sub-creator'. He makes a Secondary World which your mind can enter. Inside it what he relates is 'true': it accords with the laws of the world".[6]

In part like Yahweh, Tolkien's mythological god, Ilúvatar, had engendered a joyous society for Elves and men. The Collegiate Joy, as I call it, is manifested when, in *The Silmarillion*, Ilúvatar said to the Ainur, "I will now that ye make in harmony together a Great Music",[7] an activity that requires a fine sense of order and, indeed, of willing co-operation. In "The Music of the Ainur" in *Lost Tales*, the Ainur "bowed" and were "speechless", both images suggesting royal presence, the words "glory" and "splendour", which is significant as it reinforces the symbolism. Ilúvatar asked them to "exercise [their] minds in adorning the theme", His design, which the Ainur "began to fashion . . . into great music".

Ilúvatar referred to a theme for the Ainur to adorn, through which He revealed the forthcoming 'history'. He told them "a mightier far [Music] shall be woven before the seat of Ilúvatar by the choirs of both Ainur and Men after the Great End". This is an anthropomorphic image that reflects Ilúvatar's omniscience. In *The Book of Lost Tales*, Melko thought to "interweave matters of his own vain imagining". He looked for the Secret Fire that "giveth Life and Reality", and did not find it, for it "dwelleth with

Ilúvatar".[8] As I said, Tolkien told Clyde Kilby "very specifically . . . that the Secret Fire sent to burn at the heart of the World in the beginning was the Holy Spirit".[9] We see, implicitly at least, two persons of the Holy Trinity mirrored in Ilúvatar (the Allfather) and in the 'Secret Fire'.

Christopher Tolkien said that "the great theme that Ilúvatar propounded to the Ainur was originally made somewhat more explicit", referring to his father's text – "The story that I have laid before you", then, he says, "in the last version of the *Ainulindalë*, written more than thirty years later". He points out that in "The Music of the Ainur", in *Lost Tales*, Ilúvatar said, "Even now the world unfolds and its history begins".[10] As Christopher Tolkien also said, the most significant difference in this early form of the history, which began with the beginning of time, is that "the Ainur's first sight of the World was in its actuality, not as a vision that was taken away from them and only given existence in the words of Ilúvatar: *Eä!* Let these things Be! (*The Silmarillion*, p.20)". The myth of creation emerges from the 'first beginning' and with "solidity and completeness".[11] Regarding his creation myth, J.R.R. Tolkien tells us himself in "Athrabeth Finrod Ah Andreth – "The Debate of Finrod and Andreth" in *Morgoth's Ring*, that the Valar, "certain angelic Beings (created, but at least as powerful as the gods of human mythologies)", were the "agents and vicegerents of Eru (God)". The 'debate' was written, Christopher Tolkien tells us, "at a later time" than the rest of the writing in *Morgoth's Ring*, and he says he would "place the work in 1959".

J.R.R. Tolkien elaborates the work of the Ainur as agents and vicegerents when he says, "They had been for nameless ages engaged in a demiurgic labour completing to the design of Eru the structure of the Universe (Eä)". In "Myths Transformed" in *Morgoth's Ring*, we are told that "in the demiurgic period, before the establishment of Arda 'the Realm' . . . the Valar in general . . . were labouring in the general construction of Eä (the World or Universe)".[12] In *Lost Tales*, Ilúvatar devised that Men should "design their life beyond even the original Music of the Ainur".[13]

The idea of designing, shaping or fashioning Man's lives occurs also in *The Silmarillion* and in "Morgoth's Ring" in the 'C' manuscript (so called in Christopher Tolkien's *History*) of the "Ainulindalë". This is J.R.R. Tolkien's last but one version of 'The Music', written *after* the completion of *The Lord of the Rings*. There is mention already in *Lost Tales* of Man's 'new' gift – the "free virtue" to order their lives. With regard to Ilúvatar's purposes, we see in this gift what Christopher Tolkien calls the "different fates of Elves and Men". In *Lost Tales*, we are told that it is "one with this gift of power" ('one with' referring to the gift of freedom) that men "dwell only a short while in the world alive". Men *are* assured of joining "in the Second Music of the Ainur", whereas the fate of Elves is, by contrast, that they shall dwell "till the Great End", even for thousands of years; but that "what Ilúvatar has devised for Eldar beyond the world's end he has not revealed even to the Valar".[14] In *The Silmarillion*, Tolkien includes explicitly the "gift of freedom", and the gift to "seek beyond the world"; and he now calls "Death" the "gift of Ilúvatar", an altogether later development. Tolkien explains that "Ilúvatar knew that Men, being set amid the turmoil of the Powers of the world, would stray often, and would not use their gifts in harmony."[15] In short, they die comparatively young to obviate the charge of corruption with the loss of their intended joy.

Kingship and the Ainur: God's Vicegerent

In *The Shaping of Middle-Earth*, in 'The Quenta', "the greater part" of which was written, Christopher Tolkien says, in 1930, we are told that "after the making of the World by the Allfather, who in Elvish tongue is named Ilúvatar, many of the mightiest spirits that dwelt with him came into the world to govern it". Christopher Tolkien says this opening section "is the origin and precursor of the *Valaquenta*", as can be seen in such wording as "who in Elvish tongue is named Ilúvatar", here and in *The Silmarillion* (p.25). It seems "likely enough" that it was "a condensed synopsis".[16]

Indeed, it says nothing about whether the world was brought into being by a royal command, like Eä, or whether the Ainur played what Tolkien called a 'demiurgic labour', that is to say, whether they played a subordinate but constructive role in its unfolding, its creation. Even its unfolding could be seen *either* as its creation *ex nihilo*, that is, given being, *or* as co-operation in developing the already created world. In *The Shaping of Middle-Earth*, are 'The Earliest Annals of Valinor', earliest as they were followed in the 1930s by a second version, and even more significantly, *after* the completion of *The Lord of the Rings* and "very probably in 1951-2", by another version – 'The Annals of Aman'. They certainly "belong", Christopher Tolkien says, "to the same period as the Quenta, but also . . . they are later then the Quenta".

We are simply told of Creation that "At the beginning Ilúvatar, that is, Allfather, made all things, and the Valar, that is the Powers, came into the World",[17] which annalistic style gives us only a very "condensed" version of the narrative. The story of 'The Lost Road', in *The Lost Road and Other Writings*, was presented to a publishing company in 1937, the year that saw the beginning of the writing of *The Lord of the Rings*. With a brief reference to Creation, Elendil relates the story to his son, Herendil, who thus mediates it to the reader. He said, "The Father made the World for elves and mortals, and he gave it into the hands of the Lords, who are in the West . . . There is Ilúvatar, the One; and there are the Powers . . . Ilúvatar designed the World, and revealed his design to the Powers".[18] Once again, there is no sign of demiurgic activity: Ilúvatar had both made the design *and* given it 'Being'. Christopher Tolkien tells us that up till now, in the history of the history, there had been "only one account of the Creation of the World", written in Oxford in 1918-20. The manuscript of this version of the "Ainulindalë" was used for "massive rewriting many years later, when great changes in the cosmological conception had entered". There were two texts, in the *History* referred to as 'A' and 'B'. Christopher Tolkien says, "In many details of expression A was closer to the old *Tale*".[19]

In the text of the 'Ainulindalë' in the *Lost Road* (1987, edn. 1991), Rúmil told Ælfwine,

> There was Ilúvatar, the All-father and he made first the Ainur, the holy ones, that were the offspring of his thought . . . Ilúvatar called together all the Ainur . . . the glory . . . and the splendour . . . amazed the Ainur, so that they bowed before Ilúvatar and were silent . . . Of the theme that I have declared to you . . . I desire now that ye make in harmony together a great music.

As in *Lost Tales*, we see royal deference within the imagery in the bowing, the silence and the words "glory" and "splendour". Ilúvatar clearly engenders a joyous society. Tolkien's ideas develop in the *Lost Tales* as He told the Ainur that the 'greater music' will be made "by the choirs of both Ainur and the sons of men after the Great End". Christopher Tolkien points out that in the first revision (in the thirties), the sentence was changed to "by the choirs of the Ainur *and the Children of Ilúvatar* after the *end of days*".[20] The published *Silmarillion* also has the more comprehensive promise. Referring to creation, effectively as in *Lost Tales* so in the version of the 'Ainulindalë' ("already in existence"[21] in the thirties), in *The Lost Road*, Ilúvatar said, "I have given being unto all": Creation had been entirely His. The Ainur adorned Ilúvatar's theme. Apart from decorating the melody, there is no suggestion of any 'demiurgic' (that is, 'co-creators' or helper's) activity. We hear of Manwë that "he is not fain of his own honour, nor jealous of his own power". In *The Lost Road* Tolkien adds "but ruleth all to peace", and is "king in this world of Gods and Elves and Men".[22] This anticipates the idea in the "Words of Pengolod" that follow the actual 'Ainulindalë' in the 'C' text, Tolkien's last but one version of 1948 in *Morgoth's Ring*, written *after* the completion of *The Lord of the Rings*, where Manwë "ruleth all to peace",[23] almost identical to the *Silmarillion*.

However, Tolkien's use of the word *king* in the "Quenta Silmarillion" in *The Lost Road* was in a bad sense, when "Morgoth forged for himself a great crown of iron, and he called himself the King of the World", an action reminiscent of Aristotle's idea that tyranny is a perversion of kingship for one's own purposes. Between December 1937 and January 1938, Tolkien was revising the "opening chapters" of the "Quenta Silmarillion".[24] Tolkien's attitude to the word *king* was markedly warm as he came to work on *The Lord of the Rings*, towards the end of 1937, especially noticeable with regard to Aragorn. He had already used the term *king* for Manwë in "The Silmarillion", largely completed towards the end of the same year.[25] As Tolkien says in a letter to Milton Waldman (of a London publisher), "probably written late in 1951", "We are to see the overthrow of the last incarnation of Evil . . . and the return in majesty of the true King",[26] Aragorn. In a letter of 2 December 1953 to Robert Murray, Tolkien says, "The religious element is absorbed into the story and the symbolism".[27]

In *Morgoth's Ring* is the third version of 'The Annals of Valinor', now 'The Annals of Aman', a work, which, as Christopher Tolkien has said, "undoubtedly belongs with the large development and recasting of the Matter of the Elder Days that . . . [Tolkien] . . . undertook when *The Lord of the Rings* was finished". It "stands in close relationship to the revision at that time of the corresponding parts of the 'Quenta Silmarillion' . . . the text that had been abandoned at the end of 1937". Telling us nothing further of the creation myth, the *Annals* begin, "At the beginning Eru (the One) Ilúvatar made Eä, the World that is, and the Valar entered into it", and again we hear that Melkor "claimed the kingship".[28]

In the 'Ainulindalë' in *Morgoth's Ring*, Ilúvatar commanded them to make "a Great Music" and, symbolising His ultimate purposes, said, "A greater still" will be made by "choirs of the Ainur and the Children of Ilúvatar after the end of days", and then, "take Being". These statements accord with the published *Silmarillion*, where the Ainur saw not only the "vision" of the world, but also "the coming of the Children of Ilúvatar": "they were conceived by him alone", as in the published *Silmarillion*. Tolkien refers to the "Majesty of the Ainur",[29] with resonances of royalty, also as in the *Silmarillion*. However, Melkor wanted "subjects and servants", like Satan in *Paradise Lost*, based on St. Augustine's *De Civitate Dei* (XIV, II), to be "called Lord, and to be a master over other wills". He claimed the earth as his "own kingdom!"[30] Manwë reproved him. Melkor displayed the image of a tyrant, in line with the *Silmarillion*, where Melkor "desired rather to subdue to his will both Elves and Men".[31]

Christopher Tolkien opines, the "central shift" in the Creation myth lies "in the fact that in the old form" when the Ainur "contemplate" the world, find joy in it and desire it, it had already "been given Being by Iluvatar", "though in C it is a Vision that has not been given Being".[32] In the post-*Lord of the Rings* version of the "Ainulindalë in *Morgoth's Ring*, there is an important development. The "Vision" *was* "taken away and hidden", and the Ainur perceived "a new thing, Darkness",[33] as in *The Silmarillion*. The really significant development in *Morgoth's Ring* is when Ilúvatar, knowing the "desire" of their minds, gave the royal command, "Let these things Be!" Curiously, he did *not* say even now, "Eä!" He promises to send "the flame imperishable", the Holy Spirit, "into the Void . . . and the World shall Be", as in *The Silmarillion*. The other new thing and "no vision" that Ilúvatar made was "light, as it were a cloud with a living heart of flame",[34] whereas in the *Silmarillion*, although they *did* see "a light", the new thing that Ilúvatar had made was "Eä, the World that is".[35] The Valar, entering the World, found the "Great Music had been but the growth and flowering of thought . . . and the Vision only a foreshowing . . . [of] the World . . . and they must achieve it". They laboured "in wastes unmeasured and unexplored",[36] entering on definite demiurgic activity, a distinct development from the pre-*Lord of the Rings* B manuscript of the 1930s, as in the new version the Valar worked long in shaping the world, though not in giving it 'Being'. This demiurgic activity persists in *The Silmarillion*, where "began their labours . . . in ages unaccounted and forgotten".[37]

In *Lost Tales*, Melko (as he was then still called) as one of the Valar, had also worked on the World, but not co-operatively, and had even devised things "out of harmony" with Ilúvatar's mind. But he would *never*, he said, "seek to do aught against the lordship of Manwë".[38] Although Melkor had not, in fact, in that *first* version of "The Music", claimed the Earth as his "own kingdom", he does so *now* in the post-*Lord of the Rings* version in *Morgoth's Ring*, as in *The Silmarillion*. Manwë sternly reproves him, "This kingdom thou shalt not take for thine own, wrongfully, for many others have laboured here no less than thou".[39] However, in the story of "The Lost Road" in the book of that name, Melkor (there called Akar), said that he "desired the World to be a kingdom unto himself". In spite of Manwë's reproof, in 'The Lost Road' in the book of that name, Akar, another name for Morgoth, also claimed the kingship of earth. He said that he "desired the world to be a kingdom unto himself." The matter of wrongful kingship had not been included in the 'Ainulindalë' of the thirties. There, in *The Lost Road* Manwë, Morgoth's brother, had been called "king in this world of Gods and Elves and Men."[40]

Melkor's intended usurpation is the first instance in the 'Ainulindalë' of the form of *king*, coupled with his self-styled royal title in *The Lost Road*, when Manwë, using his authority as Ilúvatar's vicegerent, reproved him, a response that survives in *The Silmarillion*. This implies concepts of kingship on both their parts, if not directly related to Ilúvatar, except in so far as Manwë is His vicegerent, and acts as king, with His delegated authority. In the 'Valaquenta' in *The Silmarillion*, those of the "Ainur who desired it" entered the world, and, as "it was their task to achieve it", had long "laboured in the regions of Eä", until "the Kingdom of Earth" was made.[41]

After the publication of *The Lord of the Rings*, in 'The Later Silmarillion' in *Morgoth's Ring*, Manwë is referred to as "the first of all kings, lord of the realm of Arda". The manuscript dates, as Christopher Tolkien says, from as early as "December 1937 – January 1938", and "used for the '1951 revision'".[42] The word 'realm' suggests a crowned King: in *The Silmarillion*, he is given the title "King of the World of Valar and Elves and Men". In the 'Valaquenta' in *The Silmarillion*, we read only of the "Lords of the Valar", and the Valier (their 'wives'), "The Queens of the Valar". In the 'Ainulindalë' in *The Silmarillion*, the "Great Ones", the Valar, sometimes array themselves "like to the shapes of the kings and queens of the Children of Ilúvatar".[43]

Tolkien made his final position clear about the function of the Ainur in the 1951 letter to Waldman. He says the Ainur "are as we should say angelic powers, whose function is to exercise delegated authority in their spheres (of rule and government, *not* creation, making or remaking) . . . Their power and wisdom is derived from their knowledge of the cosmogonical drama, which they perceived as a drama (that is as in a fashion we perceive a story composed by someone else), and later as a 'reality'"[44] In the letter to Waldman, Tolkien said, referring to the Ainur, that he "meant to provide beings of the same order of beauty, power, and majesty as the gods of higher mythology, which can be accepted – well, shall we say baldly, by a mind that believes in the Blessed Trinity",[45] perhaps an unconscious acceptance of a link between God and Ilúvatar. Tolkien meant that his angels can be accepted by an orthodox Christian, who believes in the doctrine of the Holy Trinity.

Ilúvatar, God's Kingship and the Old Testament

Ilúvatar the Creator of Eä 'reflects' the Judaeo-Christian God, whether called Yahweh or God the Father, who is held to be Creator of Heaven and Earth. Tolkien avoids parodying Christianity by *not* including the doctrine of Creation through the Word. We would, of course, expect to find, in view of Tolkien's beliefs, in Ilúvatar an image of the divine King found in the scriptures, of Yahweh in the Old Testament, and in the Father in the New Testament. Ilúvatar's image is perceived through an 'Elven screen', woven in *Faërie*, imagined, or better, *discovered*, in mythological story. However, Yahweh, sometimes called by the same name as the Jebusite god El Elyon (in the so-called Elohistic document, or strand of tradition) is in fact, in Genesis 14:19 and 22, "described as 'creator of heaven and earth'",[46] a definition equally applicable to Ilúvatar, who alone gave Being to Tolkien's World. God is seen in Genesis 1 as the Creator who gave royal, authoritative commands. Having created the heavens and the earth, He created light, after which the angels were created. The Ainur, however, already existed when Ilúvatar gave *His* command.

Since Tolkien said that "inevitably" in Story, one's own "ideas and beliefs get taken up", it is noteworthy that in the dénouement of his Story, the date of the fall of the tyrant Sauron's tower is significant, with specifically Christian association, 25 March, the Feast of the Annunciation of the Blessed Virgin Mary. Tolkien knew the traditional Roman Catholic interpretation of the Bible generally, especially of the Book of Psalms. The Jesuit, Richard Clifford says:

> When the kings ceased in Israel after the sixth century BC, people prayed the Psalms for a new Davidic king . . . The process illustrates liturgical poetry becoming text, i.e. lifted up from its immediate liturgical context to a new use. Since God is the author of the Psalms, they are valid for new situations.

The Church wanted authoritative, sacred words that teach unerringly about Christ as King; there is little wonder that they turned to the Psalms. Clifford sums up the authority of Scripture, and the 'new' meaning attributed to the psalmic texts by way of Christologisation by saying that:

> The authority of the Psalms comes from their being the word of God, scripture. Thus they transcend their original situation and become texts for new environments. The New Testament depicts Christ doing what Yahweh did in the Old Testament. Psalms praising Yahweh therefore praise Christ . . . The Psalter, part of the scriptures, was especially authoritative for the new Church.[47]

The image Tolkien would have found in Psalm 23, for example, would have been an image of God who is "prominent as King". The psalm is "appropriate for David the shepherd-king", who is "personally" conducted by Yahweh the Shepherd-King.[48]

Tolkien was familiar with the account of the Fall, its repercussions and divine intervention in the light of it, culminating in the Incarnation, the Resurrection and the Ascension. He may have known at least some of the scholarly exegeses of biblical texts, that is, those written during his lifetime. Whether or not Tolkien actually knew the scholars' writings, they nevertheless serve to clarify the picture *we* see of God in the Scriptures, and find 'reflected' in Tolkien's Story. In his Creation Myth, Tolkien's model for kingship is God as the Creator, presenting us with a perfect paradigm of God's Kingship compatible with Judaeo-Christian belief. We cannot, of course, actually *know* to what extent, if any, Tolkien deliberately aligned his mythological Creator, in his imaginary history, with Yahweh the God of the ancient Hebrews, as portrayed by the Old Testament. Christopher Tolkien had asserted that he knows "of no evidence deriving from [his] father specifically supporting the idea that he to any extent 'modelled' Ilúvatar on Yahweh".[49] Nevertheless, in spite of Christopher Tolkien's statement, I would suggest that J.R.R. Tolkien, as an informed Christian, *unconsciously* modelled his mythological god on the Judaeo-Christian God as a by-product of the socio-cultural background of the author's life.

We can, indeed, be aware of certain parallels that can be found implicitly in Tolkien's imaginary story. I said that he expressed his ideas primarily through story rather than in discourse. Yahweh is presented 'in Story' in the Old Testament, where the Hebrews focussed on what God had *done* for them, such as bringing them out of bondage in Egypt. However, scholars have made a composite 'theory' of God's Kingship, culled *from* that story. There is, indeed, a striking resemblance between the scholars' 'theory' of the divine king in the Old Testament and Tolkien's 'theory' of his mythological divine King, Ilúvatar.

In order to assess the parallels it is important to consider both the Isrealite Kings with the Númenórian kings, with positions as possible vicegerents. The Old Testament scholar, John Bright, in *A History of Israel* (1960), says the "covenant was Israel's acceptance of the overlordship of Yahweh", and that here the notion of God's "rule" over His people, "the Kingdom of God", had its start. Israel's tribal organisation was itself "a theocracy under the Kingship of Yahweh". His symbols of kingship were "the Ark", which was His "throne, the rod of Moses was His sceptre, the sacred lots his tablets of destiny". Some of the "earliest poems" hail him as *King*, examples of which include Exodus 15:18; Numbers 23:21; Deuteronomy 33:5; Psalm 29:10ff, and Psalm 68:24.[50]

The Israelites were "forbidden to have dealings with any divine suzerain but Yahweh", thus regarding God as the King to whom the Israelites owed allegiance. The vassals of the King of the Hittites were similarly constrained by alliances within the empire. Any disloyal action would "destroy the peace of the community". The fact that the covenant between God and the Israelites follows the "pattern of a suzerainty treaty" is of "profound theological significance". The relationship is one of mutual trust between a King and his people. Israel's "God-King was . . . a cosmic God who had chosen her in her dire need", and Israel had "primarily to accept the rule of her God-King". In spite of borrowing of "language and form", Israel's Old Testament eschatology was not seen "as a borrowing from Israel's pagan neighbour", nor from "the later royal cult".[51] In the pre-exilic days of the local shrines in Northern Israel, according to several scholars, the Psalms had a *cultic* function. Yahweh's "gracious acts" towards Israel were "recited in the cult". The use of the term 'cult' here does not refer to an esoteric, unorthodox section of society often involving peculiar practices, but it is meant in the sense of ancient Israel. The 'cult' involves the expression of the worship of Yahweh, according to the accepted, normative faith of the people, it is found in religious *praxis* which employs ceremonial, ritual and (early on) animal sacrifice.

Israel trusted in the "coming days when Yahweh would intervene decisively in Israel's behalf". The idea of a future hope, Israel's Old Testament eschatology, was there as part of Israel's normative faith. The pagan religions developed nothing remotely "resembling an eschatology". Yahweh came to Israel in Egypt "as a God who called his people from nothingness into a new future and into hope". In early Israel, the God-King's direct leadership of His people was "through his spirit-designated representative", a judge whose "authority was not absolute, nor permanent, nor in any case hereditary", and he (or she) was "in no sense a king". Some scholars have argued that in adopting kingship, Israel also adopted "a pagan theory of kingship" and a "ritual pattern" for expressing it. This theory asserted that the king was regarded as a divine or semi-divine being, who on the occasion of the New Year festival, "in the role of the dying and rising god of fertility, ritually re-enacted the struggle of creation and the victory over the powers of chaos, the sacred marriage and the god's resumption of his throne", reminiscent of Nicolson's "vigorous incarnation of fertility", from which, he believes, arose the "legend of death and resurrection".[52]

The Old Testament scholar, John Bright suggests, perhaps rather categorically, that "there is no real evidence for the existence of any such single ritual pattern and theory of kingship throughout the ancient world, and much to the contrary." There is no evidence for any such *pagan* "theory of kingship" as *this* throughout the ancient world except, perhaps, in Egypt. Such an essentially pagan pattern would have been "incompatible with normative Yahwism". The early "cult, however, did not centre in a sacrificial system, but in certain great annual feasts". The Book of the Covenant lists three (Exodus 23:14-17; 34:18-24) "at which the worshipper was expected to present himself before Yahweh: Unleavened Bread (and Passover), Weeks, and Ingathering". The feasts were all older than Israel, and were (except Passover) agricultural, and "borrowed . . . from outside", that is, originally from paganism. Psalms of Canaanite origin were "adapted for Israelite use" (e.g. Psalms. 29, 45, 18 etc.), and new ones composed.[53]

It is likely that *some* features of Israel's royal ideology *would* have been
"borrowed" from the Canaanites, as Israelite monarchy was itself an
"innovation". Features *becoming* acceptable to Yahwism were features
concerning royal cultic shrines. The Israelite national shrine was "constructed
on a Canaanite pattern", with "doubtless borrowed features of its cult – and
of its ideal of kingship". "Covenant obligation" was conceived as a "purely
cultic matter": the demands were met at the national shrines. For the future,
"Israel trusted in the coming of the Day of Yahweh". Israel had hoped, then,
for the 'coming of God', even before the days of the monarchy, with the
attendant notion of His 'rule', which very rule had its beginning in "the
ancient Mosaic covenant".[54] The monarchy in Judah, on the other hand,
"was given legitimacy . . . by Yahweh's eternal covenant with David". Each
king, as "Yahweh's anointed 'son' (Psalm 2:7 etc.) would be protected from
his foes". Eventually, the dynasty would "gain a domain greater than David's,
with the kings of the earth fawning at its feet (Psalm 2:7-11; 72: 8-11, etc.).
Theologically, the moral obligations "proper to Yahwism were imposed on
the king (e.g. Psalm 72"), who was to "maintain justice". The promises were
"sure and unconditional (Psalm 89: 1-4, 19-37; Samuel 7: 14-16)". The
official cult was, by "sacrifice and offering and by ritual reaffirmation of the
promises, to assure the well-being of the nation". Of sacrifice in the cult in
early Israel, we are not "well-informed". The Temple was the "successor of
the shrine of the tribal league", such as those at Shechem, Bethel and Dan.[55]

The institution of kingship, then, "originally foreign to Israel", had found
a place in Yahwistic theology. Israelite kingship was, as elsewhere, a sacral
institution. An "official notion of kingship" was annually affirmed in the
cult. The king played a "leading role", especially in the "autumnal feast of
the new year". The nature of the royal cult and the ideology of kingship have
both "provoked endless debate . . . leaving us to infer what we can from
isolated passages, particularly from The Psalms, regarding the interpretation
of which there is no unanimity". Bright says, for example, that "Israel's king
was called Yahweh's 'son', but in an adoptive sense only (cf. Psalm 2:7); he
was Yahweh's vicegerent". The "theology of Davidic kingship is best seen in
the royal psalms, which . . . are all pre-exilic".[56]

In *The Psalms in Israel's Worship* (1962), Mowinckel maintains that the
Psalms are best understood when seen "in the right cultic connection",[57]
since they originated in the cult. The 'right cultic connection' was generally
of psalms "adapted" for use in the three "great annual feasts", as Bright said.
The Old Testament scholar John Eaton, in *Kingship and the Psalms* (1986),
supports Bright's view of the king's "leading role" in the autumn (that is the
New Year) festival. He says that, in the rites, the "chief officiant was the king;
the unity of kingship in the divine and human spheres also entailed that such
ceremonies of the gods had direct bearing on the king's life and welfare". It
is "especially the king's high-priesthood which was renewed in this festival".
Eaton explains that the Israelite king "had a pre-eminence as one brought near
to God" and imbued with "his 'holiness', which afforded communion". His

ordination involved his sanctification, as God poured "over him the 'oil of his holiness'". In Psalm 110:4, from such ceremonies, God names the king "priest for ever". The king's office is in "the succession of the ancient Melchizedek's, he is priest-king of the supreme God, the Creator".[58] Concerning the king's role as Yahweh's vicegerent, in Psalm 4, "the speaker is . . . demanding respect both for himself and for Yahweh, the two loyalties almost merging". In Psalm 72, both God *and* the King of Israel are besought to bring justice and peace simultaneously, the King acting as God's vicegerent. "The king, enabled by God, is to rule with compassion, bringing prosperity to society and nature and enjoying lasting, world-wide dominion".[59]

In 1982, Goulder wrote *The Psalms of the Sons of Korach*, where, in his own reconstructions of the Psalter, based on evidence which purports to come from the sons of Korah, he sees two sequences of Tabernacles Psalms. Each begins with a song of the pilgrims on arrival at an ancient shrine. Goulder maintains that Psalm 45 was used at the wedding, or rather the annual ritualistic 're-marriage' of King Ahab and Queen Jezebel, which took place at the Autumn Festival. The King himself led the annual pilgrimage, a journey of many miles from Samaria to Dan in the far north. As God's 'representative' of the Ancient Hebrews, the King was regarded as having a special relationship with God, in the Psalter the word 'I' usually referring to him. The King also led the rites when the Israelites arrived at the shrine. Of the psalmody allegedly used at the Festival, Goulder suggests that Psalm 45 was sung, not at the 'bamah', the High Place, where the sacrifices were offered, but in "conjunction with rites of enthronement: the king is pictured seated on his throne, with the new queen standing on his right". The throne is in "an open space", not in "a hall".[60] Whatever credence we give to Goulder's colourful conjectures regarding the autumn festival, it is, nevertheless, generally agreed that the King of Israel played a central part.

Examining the picture provided by members of the Oxford Old Testament Seminar enhances the validity of the contention that Tolkien created in his mythological god, Ilúvatar, as a 'paradigm' of the Judaeo-Christian God. The members explored for three years (October 1994 – June 1997) the theme of "King and Messiah". The findings of the Seminar are published as a collective volume, and underline the Hebrew belief in Yahweh as *King*, indeed for a time the *only* legitimate monarch over Israel. The Seminar considered the place of the Israelite King in relation to God and the people when once the monarchy *was* established, including the King's role and Jewish 'hope' in a 'future ideal king'. They reflected on God's ultimate purpose for Man, the messianic hopes of Jewish eschatology. Of the image of *King* for God, Alison Salvesen, in the Seminar's "Proceedings" said, "Though God in Ancient Hebrew does not have a crown, he does have a throne, symbolizing his kingship". This creates for us a modern picture of the place of the king and God as King in ancient Israel.

The clearest description of God as King is in I Kings 22:19, where Micaiah describes his "vision of the Lord seated on his throne, with the whole host of heaven standing around him". Isaiah also had a vision of "the Lord sitting upon a throne" (Isaiah 6:1), and says, "The Lord says; 'Heaven is my throne'" (Isaiah 66:1). The throne, much "more central" than royal regalia to the concept of kingship, is "the key symbol of monarchy in Ancient Hebrew, not just of God's rule and Israelite kingship, but of Pharaoh in Egypt (in the Pentateuch) and Ahasuerus in Persia (Book of Esther), spanning the biblical world and its literature".[61]

Of God's *kingship*, Coverdale's translation of Psalm 45, a wedding psalm, verse 7 has: "Thy seat O God endureth for ever: the sceptre of thy kingdom is a right sceptre", where the word "seat" is equated with God's "throne". John Day says, "The more natural way of taking *'elohîm* in Psalm 45:7 is as a vocative, hence 'Your throne, O God, is for ever and ever', as it was in all the ancient Versions",[62] thereby stressing that it is God's *own* kingship that is meant. Elohîm is "God in the plural".[63] Tolkien would probably have taken the idea of God's "throne" lasting "for ever" as referring to the Son. The words of the psalmist are christologised as addressing Christ the King, redolent of Fr. Clifford's idea that "psalms praising Yahweh therefore praise Christ".[64]

S.E. Gillingham argued that Psalm 72 is an accession or coronation psalm, in which the people and a cultic leader pray for the king to uphold "justice" so that "peace and prosperity" may persist in his reign. Of all "so-called Messianic psalms", we see here something of Jewish Hope in the "merging of a present political reality with an idealized future hope", making it "more open than others to an eschatological interpretation".[65] The link between God and the "political reality" to which Gillingham referred, is considered by the Oriel Professor, John Day, in the "Proceedings", where he says there is an "intimate connection" between God and "political reality". The "connection" is one that "bears witness to strongly opposed beliefs about the monarchy", for instance, whether it was "divinely ordained, or evidence of rebellion against God". Be that as it may, the idea of a Messiah is one, he says, that "presupposes that a day will come" when God will "find means of intervening to establish his own rule". Judaism was "most inclined to believe in intervention through God in person". Isaiah reads, "Behold, a king will reign in righteousness". *Every* king should reign in righteousness. Any differences between the royal psalms and the messianic hopes of "late Jewish apocalyptic" should not obscure the belief that "God is interested in the world order and has specific and detailed plans for it". Barton asserted that in earlier texts the "king who will exercise rightful dominion over all nations will be the king who attends to the needs of the poor and needy", as, perhaps, "exemplified" in Psalm 72. This hope in the coming of God to reign in righteousness "is part of the ideology of kingship outside, and indeed long before, Israel's monarchy". The Jewish belief that God would "in the last days" include the Gentiles, and the Christian belief that "these last days had begun", have roots that go back well before the exilic period, and "are bound up with kingship from early times". The important "underlying" belief here is that God "must have benign purposes for the whole world he has made".[66]

The Old Testament sees it as the King's duty to "ensure that justice and righteousness prevail in the land". Another aspect of Psalm 45:7 is seen as the psalmist says to the Israelite King, and to God, thereby linking them both, "Your divine throne endures for ever and ever", perhaps suggesting, John Day says, that his throne is *like* God's. King Solomon, he adds, "is said 'to sit upon the throne of the kingdom of the Lord'" in I Chronicles 29:23, but is not therefore addressed as God. In Isaiah 9:7, the "ideal future king" is also referred to as 'mighty god'".[67] Like David the "shepherd-king", in Psalm 23, he is interpreted as a prophecy of Christ. Christopher Rowland says in the "Proceedings", "The kingship of God plays an important part in the Gospels as the key component of Jesus' message".[68] As a Christian, the Kingship of God would have been a central belief to Tolkien, as would the Kingship of Christ who, as Clifford said, is seen in the New Testament as "doing what Yahweh did in the Old Testament".[69]

A sign of Ilúvatar's *kingship* is Tolkien's use of the word *seat*, in *The Book of Lost Tales*, Ilúvatar told the Ainur they would sing the mightier music before "the seat of Ilúvatar . . . after the Great End",[70] betokening eternity in Paradise. This anthropomorphic image of the word "seat" is symbolic, like that of Yahweh's "throne" with "all the host of heaven standing beside him" in 1 Kings 22:19. Ilúvatar ruled the Valar, *his* heavenly host, as a "theocracy" under his "kingship", as Bright said of the "Kingdom of God".

In parallel to Yahweh, Ilúvatar is the sole Creator of Tolkien's World and, indeed, of the whole Universe. Neither Yahweh nor Ilúvatar required demiurges to create it. Ilúvatar, like Yahweh, gave the royal word of command. He simply said, "*Eä*! Let these things Be!" to give His world being. There are further parallels in these creative acts. Tolkien's Ilúvatar created "of his thought",[71] while Yahweh created through His Wisdom, the personification of a characteristic of God. We are told that "The Lord created me [Wisdom] at the beginning of his work" (Proverbs 9:22). Wisdom "is an attribute or activity of God himself, by which he created all things . . . This conception is an important element in the Old Testament doctrine of Creation and a pointer to the New Testament doctrine of the Logos [Word]".[72]

The Ancient Hebrews regarded Yahweh as 'Other', as majestically tran-scendent. According to Bright, God was "elevated above personal contact with human affairs", and there was "even a growing reluctance to utter the divine name. When the name Yahweh ceased to be pronounced is uncertain, but by the third century there seems to have been a general prejudice against it".[73] Yahweh's "rule" as Israel's *King*, to which Bright referred, is put into effect through His Immanence. As Stalker says, "God does not 'dwell' in the tabernacle – he dwells in heaven – but he 'settles impermanently' upon it". He is "present with his people" at the Tent of Meeting. Thus solving the problem of immanence and transcendence, "the bridge is effected by the idea of his 'tabernacling'".[74]

By contrast, Ilúvatar is, as Verlyn Flieger says, "a strikingly remote and disengaged figure", with "little or no interaction in his world". He leaves it to the Valar "to concern themselves" with the affairs of the world. He rules, then, through them. Ilúvatar indeed gives the world 'Being', but the Valar *do* act as sub-creators in a way that "takes them a good way beyond the conventional view of angels". They are, Flieger suggests, to an extent "more comparable" to *Elohím*, God "as multiplicity", not suggesting several Gods, but rather "God in all his aspects". The comparison is between *Elohím* and the "multiplicity of Eru's [Ilúvatar's] thought who are the Valar". However, Tolkien makes it "clear that Manwë is not God but a secondary figure",[75] as seen in the 1951 letter. In the draft of a letter, after one in 1958 to Rhona Beare, Tolkien said the Valar "take the imaginative but not the theological place of 'gods'".[76] Hebrew angelology involves angels "who were elemental spirits connected sometimes with natural phenomena like the wind, clouds, fire, etc. ",[77] who have something in common with the Valar as 'spirits' of Water (Ulmo); of the Winds (Manwë); and of Fire (Melkor). The care the Rabbis took "to insist on the distinction between God and the angels" is paralleled by that between Ilúvatar and the Valar, though, as Flieger implies, the Valar receive greater power than God gave the angels.

There is a clear parallel between Barton's "benign purposes" of God for Man, and those of Ilúvatar. The hope in God's "reign", he said, was "bound up with kingship from early times" and, as Bright said, was there "as part of Israel's normative faith". The idea of a divine 'purpose', with a coming Day of God, is also there in Tolkien. Rúmil had told Eriol in *The Book of Lost Tales* that Ilúvatar "dwells beyond the world", thus manifesting His transcendence, and that He not only "made" the world but "loves it".[78] Ilúvatar, like God, as Barton puts it, has "benign" purposes for the Ainur and the Children after the end of days. His purpose is symbolised by the Greater Music that shall be made before Ilúvatar, which Christopher Tolkien in *Morgoth's Ring* called "Finrod's exalted vision of the original design of Eru for Mankind", that is to say, Man would live in hope of eternal joy. As King Finrod surmised, "This is the last foundation of *Estel* [hope], which we keep even when we contemplate the End: of all His designs the issue must be for His Children's Joy".[79]

This essentially 'Collegiate Joy', shared in community – of God's coming Kingdom – is not a possessive, private pleasure, but essentially joy symbolised by the Ainur singing their themes of music *together* in heavenly harmony, as Ilúvatar had indeed bidden them to do. At 'the heart of the matter' of the parallels between Yahweh and Ilúvatar *is* 'Collegiate Joy'. The whole question of the relation of Biblical and Tolkienian concepts is complex, as, indeed, is that of Hebrew eschatology itself.

There was, of course, no *immediate* equivalent to collegiate joy in Genesis, there having been no primordial college of angels disclosed as the first-created beings. However, in Job 38:4-7, we have what Irwin calls an "impressive sketch of creation", though it is not, he says, "at all in accord with prevalent ancient theories, such as we find in Genesis 1. It is rather an imaginative sublimation of building done by man".[80] It has been suggested that the passage in Job, beginning, "While the morning stars sang together and all the angels shouted for joy" is:

the nearest parallel [to angels having been there from the beginning] . . . The implication is that this happened at Creation which Job did not share in. But in revealing it to Job, God may be said to admit him to a knowledge of it, and by a Christian to anticipate the knowledge we have through the Incarnation.[81]

In his essay, "Introduction to the Book of Job", Chesterton says that even upon the "meagre information" we have in Job 38: 4-7, he cannot help feeling that the sons of God "must have had something to shout about". He speaks of the snow and hail as "treasury that He has laid up against the day of battle – a hint of some huge Armageddon in which evil shall be at last overthrown"[82] – and that therefore universally collegiate joy shall become a reality.

In *Temple Theology: An Introduction* (2004), Margaret Barker says of "Day One" of Creation that the "second temple priests wrote Genesis I and were silent about the angels of Day One". She adds, "The angels were the Fullness of God, because they were aspects of God", an idea reminiscent of Flieger. We see something here of the 'multiplicity of God' of *Elohim* – a plural word, as Bright said. Day one, Barker maintains, "in the Genesis account corresponded to the holy of holies", and as Philo was "emphatic" to stress, was "not to be understood in the chronological sense for there was no time before the visible world was created".[83] In Barker's *The Great High Priest: Temple: The Temple Roots of Christian Liturgy* (2003), she says, "The Book of Jubilees describes how the ministering spirits were created on Day One", where we find: "The angels of the presence, the angels of sanctification, the angels of the spirit of fire, the angels of the spirit of the winds, the angels of the spirit of the clouds and darkness and snow and hail and frost (Jubilees, 2:2)".

Ilúvatar Himself engenders a spirit of cohesive community in the Ainur, and later, in Middle-earth, though Wood *does* come rather close to implying that Ilúvatar might be regarded as one of the Ainur, and not only 'aspects of God', which clearly He is *not*. Regarding the Valar as 'aspects of God' does leave open the possibility of mistaking Tolkien's intention. Ilúvatar is depicted as being *with* the Valar, *his* 'choir of angels', like Yahweh with "the whole host of heaven standing around him". In Tolkien's Story in Middle-earth, God is seen as 'the One', monotheistically as in the Old Testament. In Genesis 1:26, God says, "Let us make man in our own image". In *The Gospel According to Tolkien: Visions of the Kingdom in Middle-earth* (2003), Wood suggests that if not simply the royal plural, "the pronoun [us] may point to the heavenly court, as if God employed intermediate beings to assist him in his action". Here we see again the possibility of demiurges who do more than merely 'adorn' what was already created.

Later scholars taught that the angels were created on days two or five, but *not* on the first day. This was, Barker explains, to "emphasize that no angel had been the co-creator".[84] It is notable that Tolkien's mythological God, Ilúvatar, had *no* 'co-creator', but that, nevertheless, "He made first the Ainur, the Holy Ones",[85] and that they are, indeed, reminiscent of the spirits of fire, winds and frost in Jubilees. However, we see in the symbolic myth of the Yahwist's account of the Garden of Eden, or in its Persian form of Paradise, "a symbolic pattern of the underlying causes of all God's activity in Creation and Redemption". The ideas which could "only be said in myth and symbol . . . run on through the whole of Scripture, and in the Apocalypse of St. John". There "we hear of the One who is 'the beginning of God's creation' (Revelation 3:14), who had prevailed where the first man had failed, saying, "To him who conquers I will grant to eat of the tree of Life, which is in the Paradise of God" (Revelation 2:7).[86]

Something of the Christian interpretation of that eschatology is found in Tolkien's picture of the Valar around Ilúvatar, an instance of his "absorbing" into his story something of his Roman Catholicism. He is 'reflecting' his Christian belief into his creation myth, and revealing God's purposes with the benefit of theological hindsight. The Old Testament concept of the 'purpose' of God is 'reflected' onto the Valar, the angels. In a sense, it is God's own joy within Himself, in His "multiplicity" as *Elohím*, which we see *mythologically* portrayed in Ilúvatar, though without *theologically* erroneously supposing Him to *be* an Ainu.

In the 'Ainulindalë', in the collegiate joy occasioned by Ilúvatar, Tolkien has 'taken up', and incorporated in his 'Story' the Christian view of Joy, that it was, in fact, from the first *meant* to be experienced *corporately*. Tolkien, by 'looking back', imputes to the joyous society of the Valar (apart from Melkor) the Christian ideal of joy, also exhorted by St. Paul. Tolkien shows how peace and joy (reminiscent of the peace and *plenty* of the Anglo-Saxons) is to be experienced in the Kingdom in a cohesive society, and not merely separately by individuals. The "peace of the community" is what Bright said would have been destroyed if the Israelites had broken their "allegiance" and been disloyal to Yahweh, their "divine suzerain", their King.

Tolkien 'looked back' to the messianic hope of the Israelites, eventually realised in Christ. The 'future Hope' had been "recited", as Bright said, "in the cult". The people trusted that there would be a "coming day" when Yahweh would "intervene" on their behalf. They believed, as Barton said, "in intervention through God in person". In parallel with the Israelites' Hope, there was in *Morgoth's Ring*, an expectation that one day Ilúvatar would need to 'intervene in person' because of what was, in Christian terms, the Fall, here the fall of the angels through Melkor. Such an intervention would bring about Ilúvatar's purposes in spite of Melkor's attempts to foil them. "They say", Andreth said, "that the One will himself enter into Arda, and heal Men and all the Marring from the beginning to the end". As I said, King Finrod had guessed that redemption would come through Men, and that "Eru would come incarnated in human form".[87]

Tolkien felt this "surely" was not parody, but merely the "extension" of the theology of Middle-earth into "Christian belief".[88] Without falling into *imitatio*, Tolkien created a parallel between the Old Testament and his mythology in his King of the Valar, Manwë, Ilúvatar's vicegerent, and Melkor, who parallels the Devil. As *King* of the angels, Manwë is the royal counterpart of Michael who, Turner says, is perhaps "the greatest of the seven archangels of Judaism". Revelation 12 is "more Jewish than Christian". Here, "Michael, not Jesus, is the conqueror". The time has come "when the struggle with Antichrist must begin". Figuring in apocalyptic literature from Daniel onwards, the story of Michael has been "somewhat Christianised" by its author, John. The "contest" is between good and evil, "represented" by Michael and Satan respectively. The question was asked, "Who is like the beast?" The answer is the devil (Revelation 13:4)? This "is reminiscent", says Turner, "of the probable meaning of Michael's name: 'who is like God?'" [89]

Part of this "struggle" between good and evil is seen in a likeness between Yahweh and Ilúvatar. The royal function as Yahweh's "priest-king" resembles the thrice yearly pilgrimages to the Hallow on the mountain called Meneltarma in Tolkien's *Unfinished Tales*. The Númenórian festivals, when the Kings led *their* people to the Hallow to worship Eru Ilúvatar, reflect the three festivals when the King of Israel was the "chief officiant", as Bright said, when his "high-priesthood" was "renewed". However, Tolkien looks to a later time when Númenórian pilgrimages no longer took place. He says in a letter of 4 November 1954 to Robert Murray, "The 'hallow' of God and the Meneltarma had perished, and there was no real substitute. Also, late in Númenórian history, when the 'Kings' came to an end there was no equivalent to a 'priesthood': the two being identical in Númenórian eyes". [90] In *Unfinished Tales*, King Tar-Palantir "went at due times" to the Hallow. The original practice of the Númenórian Kings was to go "thrice" every year, when "none might speak any word, save the King only". He offered prayer for the coming year at the *Erukyermë* in spring, in praise of Eru at the *Erulaitalë* in midsummer, and thanksgiving to him at the *Eruhantalë* in the autumn. [91] In the ancient Hebrews' autumn festival, Bright tells us, "The covenant with David inevitably tended to crowd the Sinai covenant and its stipulations into the background". [92] "The three annual festivals" of the Hebrews were "related to agriculture". The three "annual pilgrimages were Canaanite festivals taken over by Israel", the "erection of Solomon's Temple . . . led to the introduction at the autumn equinox of a New Year festival on the Babylonian model". [93] During the "early period of the Hebrew monarchy a great New Year festival was celebrated with appropriate ritual in which the kingship of Yahweh and his triumph over the forces of evil opposing his purposes of blessing for Israel and the world were depicted in the form of a dramatic myth". [94]

It is significant that as well as the Hebrew's autumn (New Year) festivals, there were also those of the ancient Celts. The archaeologist Simon James cites a quotation from Tolkien: "Anything is possible in the fabulous Celtic twilight, which is not so much a twilight of the gods as of the reason". [95] Humphrey Carpenter, Tolkien's biographer, tells us that in a lecture in 1955, Tolkien said "much of value in the way of autobiographical comment". Referring to his recently published *The Return of the King*, Tolkien said that the large "work" he had just presented "contains . . . much of what I personally have received from the study of things Celtic". [96]

The archaeologist, Barry Cunliffe says, "The Insular literature and the remarkable calendar found at Coligny near Bourg, dating from the late first century BC, enable an approach to be made to Celtic concepts of the time". There is a fragmentary bronze calendar, divided into columns indicating "propitious or unpropitious times", and recording "two festivals". In the Celtic "agrarian and pastoral" society, the New Year was marked by a festival, *Samain*, each 1 November for the "well-being of the tribe".[97]

In *their* festivals, Tolkien's Númenórian Kings "ascended the mountain on foot followed by a great concourse of the people"[98] to a "high place . . . open and unroofed",[99] akin to the pattern of the Israelite kings, except that the Israelite shrines, though on 'high places', were not precisely on 'mountain tops'.

The striking connection between Israelite and Númenórian pilgrimages, though not exactly parallel, is that both festivals focus on kingship, and on God's blessing on the people through prayer, praise and thanksgiving, offered by the king. The parallel priest-king functions indicate Tolkien's belief not only in the sacral nature of kingship, but also, perhaps, that he saw the two functions , like the Númenórians, as being 'identical', virtually a sacramental kingship.

King Aragorn II, a 'type' of Christ – the Priest-King *par excellence* of the order of Melchizedek – is discovered in the rejoicing at the end of *The Lord of the Rings*. As Tom Shippey says, the messenger sings a song as Sauron's Tower of Barad-dûr falls, the "stylistic model" of which is undoubtedly the Psalms. We see as I said, in the words "Sing and be glad, all ye children of the West, for your King shall come again", "echoes" of Psalm 33, and of the words "Lift up your heads, O ye gates, and be ye lift up ye everlasting doors, for the King of Glory shall come in" of Psalm 24. The way that we, in modern times, have Christologised the psalms is evident in "the traditional answer" to the question, "Who is the King of glory?" – Christ.[100]

Tolkien's ideal king, Aragorn II, is descended from King Isildur, brother of King Anárion, son of King Elendil. Members of the Faithful, the Elf-friends, those Númenórians who remained faithful to Eru Ilúvatar, escaped to Middle-earth, and founded new kingdoms in Gondor and Arnor. Arnor later fell to the King of Angmar, to be restored by Aragorn when he 'returned' as King of both kingdoms. They were the epitome of a 'faithful remnant', the few who stayed loyal to God. The 'remnant' faithful to Ilúvatar, Aragorn's ancestors, parallels the 'faithful remnant' of Israel, who remained 'loyal' to Yahweh and who, as Bright says, "perpetuated" Isaiah's teachings with "the notion of the coming King of the line of David, the Messiah". Israel looked for a "prince of David's line", who would set up his "beneficent and righteous rule", and who would govern as no other "Davidide" had ever done, that is, as "Yahweh's charismatic vicegerent".[101] In a parallel way, when the 'true king' had returned, the Gondorians (and the reader) came to see, by 'looking back' at *their* history, who Aragorn really was. We see in Aragorn a 'type' of Christ and, as Tolkien said in the 1951 letter to Milton Waldman, "the return in majesty of the true King".[102]

Chapter Eleven
Tolkien and the Ideal of Kingship

Tolkien and Heroic Kingship in Anglo-Saxon Literature

King Aragorn II, the 'true' King of Gondor, like the Anglo-Saxon *Rex Pacificus*, is a hero who will bring peace and plenty, and Justice to his realm. Tolkien wanted to ground his mythology in English tradition. In *The Book of Lost Tales* (edn. 1983), Christopher Tolkien says his father had early intentions of involving Eriol with Hengest and Horsa, thus "showing the direction of [his] . . . thought at that time", but "abandoned the writing of the *Lost Tales* before he reached their end".[1] In *A History of the English Church and People*, Bede tells us that "the Angles or Saxons came to Britain at the invitation of King Vortigern in three longships . . . Their first chieftains are said to have been Hengest and Horsa.[2] As Shippey says:

> . . . Eriol [was] as it were a dual ancestral figure . . . In Tolkien's thinking, Ottor / Eriol was by his first wife the father of Hengest and Horsa, in early but authentic legend the invaders of Britain and the founders of England. By his second wife he was to be the father of Heorrenda, a harper of English (and Norse) legend, about whom nothing else is known – an image, therefore, of the fantastic 'lost' tradition which Tolkien was about to invent.[3]

The apparent historicity of Tolkien's Story is enhanced as we link his own Eriol / Ælfwine stories to the semi-legendary account of the Jutish kings, Hengest and Horsa. "Among the very earliest outlines [of the stories] . . . and headed 'Story of Eriol's Life', the mariner who came to Tol Eressëa is brought into relation with the tradition of the invasion of Britain by Hengest and Horsa in the fifth century.[4]

Christopher Tolkien had said that his father gave much time and thought to this matter, and "developed certain original theories, especially in connection with the appearance of Hengest in *Beowulf*".[5] He translated and gave lectures at Oxford on the Finn and Hengest "Fragment" and "Episode", a published version of which has been edited by his ex-pupil, Alan Bliss, who says there is a close link between the *Finnesburg* Fragment and the story "very allusively related in *Beowulf*". Tolkien calls the associated passage in *Beowulf* the 'Frisian disaster *or* massacre'. That the references in *Widsith*, the Episode in *Beowulf*, and the fragment of a poem – *The Fight at Finnsburg* – "all refer to the same persons Finn (King of the Frisians) and Hengest is almost the only certain thing about them".[6]

Tolkien says that the fragment's accidental ending does not prove that the "preoccupation of the episode with the situation after the fight is peculiar, or that the position of Hengest after the fight was not also to the author of the fragment the chief part of the tale (quite different as his style, treatment and objects were to those of the author of *Beowulf*)", who was more concerned with King Beowulf, son of Scyld, and Hrothgar, King of the Danes. Tolkien tells us that we see from the episode that eventually, Hnæf, for the time being assumed to be the 'young king' of the Fragment, "was slain in the defence and . . . one of the cruces of interpretation – the son also of Finn and his wife Hildeburgh".

The "chief crux" of interpretation, Tolkien says, is that:

we find Hengest surviving and a mysterious peace patched up, neither the terms nor the reason of which can be understood at a glance . . . the references to the *wealaf* (1084, 1098) ['the survivors of the disaster' as Alexander translates it in *Beowulf*, 1995, p.73] are clearly both difficult and both of first importance. There is a funeral by burning, marking a pre-Christian heathen tale.

It is "evident" that the first need is to clarify, where possible, the identity of the named figures in the tale. The expression '*Hengest sylf*' does not necessarily imply that Hengest was a king or prince, but it does show that he was of "special importance" in the tale.[7] Hengest appears to be the leader of the 'defenders', and the "chief party" to the treaty with Finn, and "it is *his* feelings after its conclusion that are dealt with". Hengest's position was possibly like that of Sigeferth, who is *Secgena leod*, not a 'king of the Secgan' but a prince whose sword is now at the service of Hnæf, though he may have been more famous.

Hengest's relations with Finn, not with Hnæf, are "primarily defined by *wrecca*, an exile or *gist*, a guest. But Hengest was *not* precisely a *wrecca*, 'in exile', but had come on a visit "which had ended disastrously ", as the name *Freswæl*, what Tolkien named 'Frisian Disaster', implies. Significantly, Tolkien writes that "outside the Finn-story the name *Hengest* is unknown in literary or historical documents or traditions, except as the name of a Jutish adventurer who with his brother Horsa came to England".[8] Finn and Hengest's story in *Beowulf* (lines 1066-1159) relates events that took place in days that, in 'Beowulf: The Monsters and the Critics' (1936), Tolkien calls "heathen, noble, and hopeless". Tolkien sees no "discrepancy between theme and style", and says that in *Beowulf*, we have an "historical poem about the pagan past", by a poet who, 'looking back', found "something permanent and symbolical". The poet 'found' a "fusion . . . of thought and deep emotion". Tolkien refers to the "central position the creed of unyielding wills holds in the North". In the "history of kings and warriors" the poet sees that "all glory" ends in "night", and perceives the "common tragedy of inevitable ruin". He feels this 'ruin' the more *"poetically"* being removed from the despair, and yet views (from outside) the "despair of the event" while having "faith in the value of doomed resistance".[9]

The minstrel in *Beowulf* sings "in Heorot [meaning 'hart', a royal animal, Hrothgar's hall] of the Creation and the lights of Heaven". Tolkien says the poet reveals "a direct contrast of youth and age in the persons of Hrothgar and Beowulf". To depict Hrothgar's "nobility" and the "desire of good for truth", Tolkien says that the poet, when "delineating the great King of Heorot", turned to the Old Testament. Tolkien's reference to Hrothgar as the "great King" expresses the high esteem in which he holds the splendour of royalty. Compared with Hrothgar, the poet depicts Beowulf as "a young knight, who used his gift of *mægen* to earn *dom* and *lof* among men and posterity".[10]

By *mægen*, Tolkien refers to the possession of "a favour of God", to 'might, a comment by the Christian poet himself telling a story of "heathen heroes". By *dom* and *lof*, the poet refers to two similar, though *not* synonymous, meanings, of which the basic sense is "the noble pagan's desire for the *merited praise* of the noble". The more precise meaning of *lof* is "ultimately and etymologically *value, valuation,* and so *praise*", whereas *dom* means rather *"judgement, assessment,* and in one branch *just esteem, merited renown"*. To the Christian *lof* tended towards ideas of 'heaven', and *dom* ideas of the judgement of God. The word *lof* continues to have for Tolkien a rich, ancient and "pagan" meaning, "the praise of one's peers". There is in *dom* a unity with *lof*. "Hrothgar expands", Tolkien says, "on lines found elsewhere, either in great elaboration as in the *Fates of Men*, or in brief allusion to this well-known theme [about heaven] as in *The Wanderer* 80ff."The *Seafarer*, "proclaiming" that 'all men must die', continues by saying that "Therefore it is for all noble men . . . that ere he must go hence, he should merit and achieve on earth" the praise (*lof*) of the living who commemorate him after heroic deeds against the devil, that "his *lof* may live with the angels for ever".

To achieve the desired *lof*, in those quite literally *hopeless* days, meant being heroic and offering "'absolute resistance, perfect because without hope'". This notion is an intrinsic part of the "theory of courage, which is the great contribution of early Northern literature". The "heroic figures, the men of old . . . remained and still fought on until defeat". Thus, the "temporal defeat . . . is no defeat, for the end of the world is part of the design of the Metod, the Arbiter who is above the mortal world". There is, Tolkien says, "in *Beowulf's* language little differentiation of God and Fate . . . he definitely equates *wyrd* [meaning fate] and *metod* [meaning God or Lord] ". The worth, the *lof*, of "defeated valour in this world is deeply felt".[11]

In *The Two Towers* Aragorn says that "with hope or without hope we will follow the trail of our enemies",[12] exhorting the 'three hunters' to act with courage if without 'hope'. For Tolkien, the author of *Beowulf* shows the lasting value of "man's struggles in the dark". The poet describes man, "fallen and not yet saved", as "disgraced but not dethroned",[13] a description very reminiscent of Tolkien's own line in *Mythopoeia* in virtually identical words. Aragorn is 'not yet saved', having lived in pre-Christian times. Aragorn is, indeed, seen as a type of Christ but, as Shippey said, "Too conscious an approach to 'mythopoeia' would have ended only in allegory",[14] presenting Aragorn allegorically as a Christian 'figure' like a saviour. Tolkien says, "The poet of *Beowulf* saw clearly: the wages of heroism is death". Man shows his "highest loyalty" in being "engaged in a struggle which he cannot win". This 'highest loyalty' is found in Beowulf as one who is regarded as "The prince of the heroes of the North", an image suggesting genuine approbation of royalty. The pinnacle of heroism is seen in both the Norse and English form of the story alluded to in *Beowulf*. This heroic height has two "features: the dragon, and the slaying of him as the chief deed of the greatest of heroes". There being a dragon, followed by the killing of the dragon is "No idle fancy", but has origins in fact and invention, "the dragon in legend is a potent creation of men's imagination". Tolkien says that the "large symbolism" of the 'monsters' as foes, not only as personifications of evil, comes near the surface, but does *not* "break through" and become allegory. In *Beowulf*, the symbolism refers to a man facing an enemy, the dragon – a *feond* – a word applicable to the enemies of Beowulf and Wiglaf. Such an enemy is more evil than any human enemy, "treading the named lands of the North".[15]

We find in the heroic stories the esteem in which the old heroes were held. In 'heroic situations', "we could see the exaltation of undefeated will, which receives doctrinal expression in the words of Byrthwold at the battle of Maldon . . . [and the] paradox of defeat inevitable yet unacknowledged", even the defeat of "kings and champions". Tolkien regards the preservation of *Beowulf* as having been "by chance (if such it be) from the dragon of destruction".[16] The attribution of its 'preservation' to "chance" is reminiscent of when in *The Fellowship of the Ring*, Tom Bombadil at least *suggests* it was by divine intervention that *he* was brought to the Hobbits' rescue "by chance", adding "if chance you call it".[17]

In Tolkien's account of it, *Beowulf* is "a contrasted description of two moments in a great life", moments that move between Beowulf's youth and his age, his "first achievement and his final death". The "tragedy of Beowulf" is contained between lines 1888 and the end, though without the first half of the poem, there would be no "direct contrast of youth and age in the persons of Beowulf and Hrothgar". The basic division of the poem, Tolkien suggests, is between lines 1 and 2199, and 2200 to 3182, with a subdivision between 1888 and the end. In the second half, the reader cannot be sure of the "literary experience" that the hero will not perish. Disaster is at hand: triumph is over, and there is the "inevitable victory of death". Beowulf is "an heroic figure of enlarged proportions". He faces his "final foe", not a Swedish prince, nor even a treacherous friend, but a dragon. It was, indeed, "treason that destroyed the Scylding dynasty". If the hero falls, Tolkien says, "before a dragon, then certainly he should achieve his early glory by vanquishing a foe of similar order".[18] The "conquest of the ogres" comes at the right moment.

In his youth, Beowulf destroyed the 'monster' Grendel and also his mother, achieving a second major victory. It was not until his old age that he finally overcame the dragon, the placing of which momentous event "is inevitable: a man can but die upon his death-day". Beowulf's foes were inhuman, making the story "more significant" than this imaginary poem of a great king's fall. It "glimpses the cosmic" and ponders the "fate" of "human life and efforts". It reflects on the life of an 'Everyman' "until the dragon comes",[19] and refers to death and maybe to the approach of war with Hitler.

Beowulf's trust had been in his "own power and will". He had lived "according to his own philosophy", and was rewarded by "the praise of his peers during his life and after his death". Any Christian notion of 'heaven' had to be "rigidly excluded". The 'great King of Heorot' does *not* refer to "heavenly bliss", even in his sermon. Beowulf's spirit "departed to whatever judgement awaits such men". As a young man, Beowulf had affirmed that *dom* – merited renown – was the "prime motive of noble conduct".[20]

Beowulf and Hrothgar are "quite distinct", Tolkien says, and Hrothgar is always seen as a "wise and noble monotheist", and was modelled, "it has been suggested in the text [of *Beowulf*] on the Old Testament patriarchs and kings". But Beowulf rarely refers to God and largely regards him as "the arbiter of critical events", and makes little differentiation between fate and God, the Anglo-Saxon *Wyrd* or *Metod*. Beowulf ascribes his victories to 'luck'. In the poem, he says of his conquest of Grendel's mother in the water-den, "I survived that fight / not without difficulty; but my doom was not yet" (lines 2140-1).[21]

Beowulf was not guilty of the crimes of "perjurers and murderers". It was said, "He was a king / blameless in all things . . . Half a century / he ruled it [his land] well" (lines 1885-86 and 2207-08). In the last four lines of the poem, it says Beowulf "was of all the world's kings / the gentlest of men, and the most gracious, / the kindest to his people, the keenest for fame".[22] Does this refer to 'Fame' in the perspective of God, or his peers? As a 'good pagan', Beowulf would have hoped for *dom*. The poem ends with the word *lofgeornost* – the most desirous of glory – the "summit of the praise" of the dead hero. As a Christian, the *author* would have seen it as being in God's eyes, and with His approval. Beowulf's reward would be "that his *dom* shall live". The idea of "lasting *dom*" is, as Tolkien says, "capable of being Christianised; but in *Beowulf* it is not Christianised". There is "evidence" in the poem "of the author's own view of the destiny of the just pagan". Beowulf becomes "much more like Hrothgar".[23]

However, Beowulf's funeral is not Christian. The poet reveals Beowulf's own thoughts. Expressing his opinion, he expects the "recognized virtue of his kingship". He had really trusted in "his own might". The poet saw the possession of this 'might' as *mægen* – a "favour of God". The "supreme quality of the old heroes, their valour", was given by God, and as such, could be "admired and praised".

The poet says that when "the dragon's ruinous assault" on Beowulf was reported, Beowulf "was filled with doubt and dismay". Tolkien maintains this cannot be given, as has been said, a "Christian interpretation", but is "a heathen and unchristian fear – of an inscrutable power". Within the limits of human life, "Beowulf neither lived nor died in vain – brave men might say". It is the "end of Beowulf, and the hope of his people", but *not* the end of dragons.[24]

Further information on contemporary attitudes to Anglo-Saxon kingship can be gleaned by Tolkien's own extension to *The Battle of Maldon*, and in his commentary. Tolkien says he "utters" the famous words of Beorhtwold (spelling his name differently) from the Anglo-Saxon poem. However, he changes the emphasis somewhat in his own poem: *The Homecoming of Beorhtnoth Beorhthelm's Son* (written 1953, published 1975). Tolkien says that in a dream the words spoken by Torhthelm 'sum up' the "heroic code", probably "an ancient and honoured expression of heroic will", Tolkien says, he gives us the words from the *old* poem in modern English:

Will shall be the sterner, heart the bolder,
Spirit the greater as our strength lessens.

What does Tolkien tell us about the actual effect of the "heroic code" in practice, especially with regard to the king? We learn something of Anglo-Saxon ideas of the king's duty, even though the actual leader, the *dux bellorum* (like King Arthur) in *The Battle of Maldon* was the "duke of Essex", "duke" being a Norman title, in Anglo-Saxon terms, an *ealdor* or Alderman, and not King Æthelred II himself. The Vikings who, Tolkien says, *may* according to one version of the *Anglo-Saxon Chronicle* have been led by Olaf Tryggvason, destined to become King of Norway, had already ravaged Ipswich.

The Anglo-Saxon defenders looked to gain greater honour and glory by allowing the Vikings to cross. Tolkien maintains that this decision was an "act of pride and misplaced chivalry [that] proved fatal". The men of the duke's household, his *heorðwerod*, showed great loyalty, and deserved the much-prized *lof* and *dom*, the praise of their peers after their death. But what do we learn of the King's own man, taking full responsibility on the king's behalf? There are two views about this. The duke had to decide whether or not to accede to the proposition. He presumably knew, though the poet does not actually say so, that it was his duty to fight the marauding 'Danes' (in fact largely Norwegians) who would only pillage *again* if not defeated.[25]

Tolkien suggests that to invite the Vikings onto the mainland appears to have been motivated by "a defect of character in Beorhtnoth, and by his foolish desire for honour and glory, "in life and after death". The motive grows and drives "a man beyond the bleak heroic necessity to excess – to chivalry". What, then, *is* Tolkien's view of the duke's 'overweening pride'? It is more complex than simply a choice between 'pride' and 'practicality': it involves 'expectation'. Whose expectation, the *king's*, or is the whole problem rooted in the spirit of the age? Tolkien is abundantly clear about what he sees as the Anglo-Saxon view, as evidenced in the poem, of the duties of the King, of 'his man' the duke and of the members of his *heorðwerod*. That 'duty' was regarded as part and parcel of "the northern heroic spirit", the 'expectation' encapsulated in Beorhtwold's words, a 'spirit' that could be self-defeating. The duty of the serving soldier is to be loyal to the King, and to fight when required, until death if need be. As "personal pride was therefore in him at its lowest, and love and loyalty at their highest", such a hero unreservedly deserves his peers' praise.

There are heroic continuities in *Gawain and the Green Knight*, a poem employing alliterative verse, though its substance is of the medieval Romance tradition, exemplified by the earlier Chrétien de Troyes, and was probably written by a contemporary of Richard II. Tolkien says, "Gawain's conduct is more worthy because he is a subordinate. He is involved in the certain prospect of death simply . . . to secure the safety and dignity of his lord, King Arthur".[26] Compared with the duty of a subordinate, the duty of an Anglo-Saxon king is quite a different affair. It was, nevertheless, very much a matter of mutual responsibility between King and Man.

The same interdependence pertained even in medieval Iceland between the *goðar* – the chieftains – and the chieftains' *þingmen* – the farmer thingmen – on whom they relied in a similar way. "The personal relationships between chieftains and farmers constituted the core of chieftaincy".[27] In England, "historically", we read in *Edward the Confessor* (1992), "The first duty of the king was the leadership and protection of his people, especially in time of war . . . The preservation of the people came first".[28] Indeed, this notion of inter-dependence is a common Germanic theme found much earlier in Tacitus in *Germania* (AD 97-98), where the *comitatus* (the retinue) demonstrates the mutual "allegiance" shown by the chiefs and the companions. Tacitus says, "The chiefs fight for victory, the companions for their chief".[29]

Tolkien asserts that "The lord may indeed receive credit from the deeds of his knights, but he must not use their loyalty or imperil them simply for that purpose", for gaining self-glory, as they are mutually responsible for each other. Emphasis on greatness of spirit in the *old* poem is replaced in Tolkien's poem by "More proud the spirit as our power lessens". The meaning of *ofermod* is not overboldness but excess pride. Northern spirit is "never quite pure", as there are "different loyalties to serve". There is a mixture of "gold", heroic courage when the king preserves his people, and the "alloy . . . when the king wished for glory, or for a glorious death and courted disaster".[30]

Although the poet of *The Battle of Maldon* stresses duke Beorhtnoth's role as loyal defender of King Æthelred's land, perhaps even more than Tolkien does, it can still be said that the duke's *ofermod* causes him to fail in that duty too. The relation of Beorhtnoth to the King, a more sophisticated and more immediately historical situation than that in *Beowulf* (where the choice of action was made by the King himself), presents the image of primary authority and that of the vicegerent again, clearly a matter of concern to Tolkien.

Looking historically, Æthelred may have felt constrained, in view of the heroic code, to make the same choice, though because of the failure of the heroic policy of Beorhtnoth, Æthelred chose to pay Danegeld. Looking again at *Gawain and the Green Knight*, Gawain, a member of Arthur's *heorðwerod*, the Round table, is sent on a deadly errand, "to meet his match among men". We criticise Æthelred as we do Arthur; the question is asked, "Who ever heard tell of a king such courses taking"? The apparent choice for Æthelred's deputy, Beorhtnoth, between duty to his king and / or his men, *and* to *ofermod*, that is, an excess of pride, was a false one, pertaining only to his times. His apparent dilemma was, perhaps, due to the *Zeitgeist* – the northern heroic spirit of the Age.[31]

Tolkien's Ideal King: Middle-earth

In writing his "mythology *for England*",[32] Tolkien had, as Tom Shippey said, endeavoured to "root" his Story in authentic Anglo-Saxon tradition. Tolkien valued the "'Impression of depth'", provided by a literary fiction, and in his essay of 1953 on *Sir Gawain and the Green Knight*, he stated that the poem "belongs to that literary kind which has deep roots in the past, deeper even than its author is aware". Shippey suggests that he refers to literature like *Beowulf*.[33] This ignores that the Celtic-Romance elements in the Arthurian cycle are not present in Old English tradition. In his mythological Story, Tolkien's heroic kings and their societies have *their* "deep roots" in the distant past. In *The Lord of the Rings* for example, King Théoden and the Rohirrim are calqued on the Anglo-Saxons, though they "are not to be equated"[34] with them. Christopher Tolkien had said in *Lost Tales* that the mariner, Eriol, from Angeln, that part of Denmark from whence the English came, and his coming to Tol Eressëa was "brought into relation with the tradition" concerning Hengest and Horsa. Tolkien wished to 'root' his 'Story' in Anglo-Saxon tradition, with anything that he could find of it. Hengest appears in *Beowulf*. Christopher Tolkien clearly stated that his father's 'themes' were "especially in connection" with this.[35]

Tolkien's Story culminates in his ideal king, a type of Christ (like Williams and Lewis), whose qualities are seen in story, not in a discursive portrait of him. A sense of Christian vocation *is* inherent in *The Lord of the Rings*. Tolkien said in a letter of 2 December 1953 to Father Robert Murray, "*The Lord of the Rings* is of course a fundamentally religious and Catholic work".

Tolkien knew, he said, what Murray meant by "the order of Grace", and that his own "perception of beauty both in majesty and simplicity is founded" on Our Lady. Tolkien invented, or rather discovered, a mythology in which his Catholic beliefs have been "absorbed" without parodying Christianity.[36]

In a letter of 25 October 1958 to Deborah Webster, Tolkien said, "One critic (by letter) asserted that the invocations of Elbereth, and the character of Galadriel . . . were clearly related to Catholic devotion to Mary. Another saw in waybread (lembas) . . . a derivation from the Eucharist". He says that the fact that he is a Christian "can be deduced from [his] stories".[37] Tolkien tacitly accepts these attributions of transmuted Catholicism. We will, therefore, observe some Christian vocations in his story. Frodo surprisingly willingly, as Gandalf observed, accepted *his* vocation to bear the Ring, even though when the time came, he was unable to 'do what he came to do' and drop the Ring into the Fire of Mount Doom. Tolkien said in a letter of September 1963 to Eileen Elgar, "I do not think that Frodo's was a *moral* failure". Neither, according to the same letter, did Gandalf or Aragorn so regard it. It is, moreover, a statement of the corruption caused by the Ring.[38] Frodo certainly did not feel 'called' to be a king: he was sensitive to his position in the hierarchy. Sam Gamgee, one of Tolkien's 'Ordinary men', likewise did not hanker for such high office, nor did he expect to carry the Ring (except when he carried Frodo), but was content to continue to be a gardener.

Tolkien said in a letter of 7 June 1955 to W.H. Auden that he saw the value of Hobbits "in putting earth under the feet of romance, and in providing subjects for ennoblement and heroes more praiseworthy than the professionals: *nolo heroizari* [I do not wish to be a hero] is of course as good a start for a hero, as *nolo episcopari* for a bishop".[39] In a letter of "probably January or February" 1956 to Michael Straight, he said that his story which is 'hobbito-centric' is "primarily a study of the ennoblement (or sanctification) of the humble".[40] Gandalf was 'meant' to fulfil *his* mission and rule by his wisdom, though he said he did "not wish for mastery".[41] Galadriel was willing to rule by her example in renouncing the Ring when Frodo offered it to her, and said she would "remain Galadriel" and not become a terrible "Queen".[42] Aragorn had for many years accepted *his* long and difficult vocation. After "a hard life and a long" as a Ranger, protecting the enemies of Mordor, he said that his sword would be reforged and, symbolising the renewal of his vow to follow his calling, vowed firmly, "I will come to Minas Tirith",[43] to take up his destined kingship.

In a letter of 25 April 1954 to Naomi Mitchison, Tolkien says that his Story is "cast in terms of a good side, and a bad side . . . tyranny against kingship".[44] Aragorn's long struggle was, in particular, against his "hereditary foe", the Witch-King of Angmar, who had actually "obliterated" his ancestors in the North Kingdom.[45] In the antithesis between The Lord of the Nazgûl (formerly King of Angmar) and King Aragorn, we see perhaps a parallel, to which I have referred, with the semi-human Monster, Grendel, in *Beowulf* and the heroic King Beowulf, both pairs knowing a life-long enmity between good and evil forces. This virtually endless battle is seen symbolically in Aragorn's struggles, and with reasonable 'hope' of a right outcome. In *The Return of the King* (1955), Gandalf showed Aragorn a sapling of the White Tree of Númenor in the Court of the Fountain, the symbolic image that there was hope and life. Similarly, in Tolkien's last Story, *Smith of Wooton Major* (1967), it was Smith who "saw the King's Tree springing up".[46]

In the Story, the important position the characters all share, says Verlyn Flieger, "is that of the link, the connector or mediator between the 'real' or natural world and the world of Faërie – the supernatural world of myth and imagination". She says that the "ultimate refinement" of the function of Ælfwine as mediator is Smith, or rather his grandfather the Master Cook, who "is not even fully aware that he is an Elf-friend, nor is the reader . . . Nevertheless", she says, "We see the faery world through his eyes and experience its mystery through his perceiving consciousness". Smith wanders "in a myth he does not understand" and "witnesses a whole world to which he does not have the key; nor, in consequence, does the reader.[47] In Wooton Major, Smith's sight of the "King's Tree" is redolent of Gandalf showing Aragorn the young tree in Gondor. Aragorn saw, aware of a feeling of both the glory of light and the stillness of awe, "a sapling no more than three foot high". A "sapling of the line of Nimloth the fair", the White tree of Númenor, it was descended from the elder of the Two Trees of Valinor, both of which had been destroyed by Melkor and Ungoliant in the First Age. The Light of Valinor had thus been disastrously extinguished; the only remaining Light was in the Great Jewels, the Silmarils, which had been fashioned by the royal Noldorin Elf Fëanor. "The sign has been given",[48] said Aragorn. The White Tree in Gondor is symbolic of 'Hope', and of the continuity of the Kings of the line of Elendil, Kings of Gondor, their continuity indicated by the sign of the even longer line of the White Trees. It is, perhaps, also symbolic of Tolkien's own 'Hope' in the lasting value of kingship.

However, a sense of the numinous pervades the whole Story. It is through the mystical quality of Alf, the King of Faery, that we perceive something of the essence of Tolkien's Ideal King. Lewis had said in "Transposition" that "What is happening in the lower medium can be understood only if we know the higher medium".[49] It is through the metaphysical idea of the truly mythical King of Faery that we see a reflection of the sacramental quality that Tolkien imputes to the 'true' king in the 'real' world – the world created by God, the divine King. Later, Smith went to the water's edge and, "filled with wonder . . . heard elven voices singing". Their "grace . . . enchanted him", and he went on his "journey home". Smith was brought before "the Queen herself. She wore no crown and had no throne. She stood there in her majesty and her glory", the very epitome of the Glory of Royalty that Tolkien, like Williams and, obliquely like Lewis, admired. Smith saw that the

Queen was, in a sense, another 'ordinary person', as he recognised the dancer whose "grace" had enchanted him. Like Chesterton's mystic in *Orthodoxy*, Smith, kneeling before the Queen, likewise seemed to be "both in the World and in Faery".

Tolkien's theme of 'Renunciation' is exemplified when the Queen gave Smith, one of Tolkien's 'ordinary men', who she called "Starbrow", a message. If he met the King, he should say, "Let him choose", that is to say, whether or not to renounce the silver star that gave him entry into Faery. Smith *did* meet the old apprentice, Alf, the King of Faery in disguise, who encouraged Smith to relinquish the Star he had been given, a magic star. In accord with Tolkien's advocating freedom from "possessiveness" in *On Fairy-Stories*, Smith chose and renounced it willingly.[50] Not only does this show deference to the king, but also that Smith is not guilty of 'possessiveness', rather that he is willing to share, according to whatever the king wills for him.

The "great jewel like a radiant star " on Smiths's forehead,[51] is somewhat reminiscent of King Aragorn's "great jewel of green that shone from afar . . . his head was bare save for a star upon his forehead".[52] This jewel is symbolic of the 'Glory' of the 'true' King, the king who steadfastly fought to maintain good and defeat evil. It was the emblem, like the Saint-King Oswald's Cross, with which Aragorn went into battle against evil. The contrast between the good king and his evil counterpart is seen when the divine Image of Ilúvatar in King Aragorn is 'marred' in the tyrant ex-king of Angmar. Tom Bombadil had told the Hobbits that Men of Westernesse had forged the knives he chose for them. Foes of the Dark Lord, "they were overcome by the evil king of Carn Dûm in the land of Angmar",[53] thus explaining Aragorn's long and bitter enmity with the King of the Nazgûl.

Did Tolkien depict evil power as an absence of good or as threateningly present in the ambiguous Ringwraith? The King of the Nazgûl, Shippey suggests, "*looks* like a man, and carries a sword, but it is a 'pale' or insubstantial one; he bursts the Gate [of Gondor] not only by Grond [a battering ram] but by a projection of fear and dread . . . On the one hand he turns almost to distraction, a 'vast menace of despair', as also to an image of the unexistence of evil, a 'huge shadow' which Gandalf tries to send back to 'nothingness'". The Witch King "had a kingly crown", but no real head was visible under it, an echo from Death in *Paradise Lost*. The 'nothingness' – Tolkien's 'Shadow' – "can still have power and control . . . He calls himself Death".[54] The heroic King Théoden of Rohan, spiritually healed by Gandalf, was slain in battle by the Lord of the Nazgûl. Sauron's corrupting influence was seen in King Théoden's tardiness to take Gandalf's advice to fight both Saruman and Sauron, though Gandalf was able to free him, enabling him to fight with the men of Gondor against Sauron. Théoden's 'folk', the Men of Rohan, Sindarin Elvish for 'horse-country', called themselves the Rohirrim (horse-lord people) or the

Eorlingas (the sons of Eorl). "With one admitted exception, the Riders of Rohan resemble the Anglo-Saxons down to minute details". They were horse-lords, unlike the Anglo-Saxons in that respect. The Rohirrim resembled the 'ancient English' not so much in their "history" as in their "poetry or legend". When Aragorn, Gandalf, Legolas and Gimli approach the Golden Hall of "Meduseld" (a Beowulfian word for 'hall'), they do so "on the procedure for approaching kings" in *Beowulf*.

The names of *all* the kings from Théoden back to Brego, except two, are as Christopher Tolkien noted, "Old English words for 'king'". The founder of the line, Eorl the Young and the chieftains before his dynasty began were, in fact, called by Gothic names like Vidugavia, to create an impression of greater depth for the Rohirrim. Their function is to "suggest language behind language". There is a "dim tradition that the word Goths meant Horse-folk. The Battle of Pelennor Fields "closely follows the account, in Jordanes' *Gothic History* of the Battle of the Catalaunian Plains, in which also the civilisation of the West was preserved from the Easterlings, and in which the Gothic king Theodorid was trampled by his own victorious cavalry with much the same grief and glory as Tolkien's Théoden".[55]

Aragorn's own descent has deep roots, stemming from the Kings of Númenor and the Lords of Andúnië, whence came the faithful Elendil and his sons. Traceable through the mists of time to the Elven Kings and the Maiar (lesser angels) in the First Age of Middle-earth, we see in Aragorn the epitome of Tolkien's ideal sacral monarch, a Saint-King, God's vicegerent who, ruling with justice and love is a type of Christ. Tolkien deals with the difficulty of applying the concept of monarchy to the 'real' world by remaining in a fantasy world, where the 'true king', Aragorn, is a descendent of the Half Elven, the Peredhil, Elros and Elrond. Maybe he sees the 'fantasy' world's idea of monarchy as what he would call 'applicable' to the real world.

Tolkien shows in the King's Elven ancestry, as in the healing power of the king's touch, something of the *magic* quality he associates with the office of King, a possession of almost supernatural powers, and reminiscent of the Anglo-Saxon belief in the healing powers of an anointed king like Edward the Confessor.

In 'The Mirror of Galadriel', Sam had recognised magic in the magical woods of Lothlórien. He said, "If there's any magic about, it's right down deep". Sam told Frodo that he would "dearly love to see some Elf-magic". Galadriel, a Noldorin Elf, is about to let Sam see *her* almost supernatural powers in her mirror's visions. She says to him, "For this is what your folk would call magic, I believe; though I do not clearly understand what they mean", as they seem to use the same word "of the deceits of the Enemy"[56] – of Sauron. Elves represent, at two removes, the creative power of God. In his mythical world Tolkien uses Elven ancestry to emphasise Aragorn's position as Ilúvatar's vicegerent, who acts with His authority, like the Anglo-Saxon king in the 'real' world, whose kingship is underpinned by *his* descent, ostensibly from the gods, Woden or Saxneat. The King's ancestry from the

Elves suggests the sacred, virtually sacramental quality of his office. When the Kings of Númenor came to an end there was no equivalent to priesthood. There was, indeed, no discernible evidence of religion in Gondor except, as Tolkien said in the letter of 4 November 1954 to Robert Murray, that he imagined that although the Númenórians offered "no petitionary prayers to God", they *did* preserve "the vestige of thanksgiving",[57] an expression perhaps echoing Chesterton's observations in his *Autobiography*, "I hung on to the remains of religion by one thin thread of thanks".[58]

Faramir, Steward of Gondor, and his men "all turned and faced west in a moment of silence". This was to look towards "that which is beyond Elvenhome and will ever be", referring to the Blessed Realm of the Valar.[59] In the 1954 letter to Murray, Tolkien said there had been a Hallow on Mount Mindolluin, only approachable by the King, who had there "anciently offered thanks and praise on behalf of the people". But it had been forgotten, it was re-entered by Aragorn, symbolically, and there he found a sapling of the White Tree, descendant of Nimloth, and "replanted it in the Court of the Fountain". The worship of God "would be renewed" and "His Name (or title) more often heard", but there "would be no *temple* of the True God while Númenórian influence lasted".

In a letter of "c. 1963" to "a reader of *The Lord of the Rings*", Tolkien said, "A Númenórian King was *monarch*, with the power of unquestioned decision in debate; but he governed the realm with the frame of ancient law, of which he was administrator (and interpreter) but not the maker", and listened to his counsellors at "the Great Council".[60] Here, Aragorn is showing himself to be a true vicegerent of the archetypal King, Ilúvatar, in that he is undoubtedly Monarch, gives authoritative, righteous commands and acts according to His divine Law. At the same time Aragorn takes into account his counsellors as Ilúvatar involved the Valar, even in His creative work, if only to 'adorn' rather than create *ex nihilo*, as befits a vicegerent.

Aragorn is clearly seen to be Tolkien's Ideal King. Tolkien said, "I love England",[61] and would have given his allegiance (even with its democratic Government) to his country, to King George V and to the devoutly (even if not Roman Catholic) Christian King George VI and Queen Elizabeth II. Perhaps Tolkien, like Belloc, thought the monarch hopelessly compromised by the ruling class after 1688 – or maybe he thought in this matter as in others (literature, culture, etc.), everything was compromised much earlier. If so, his ideal monarch would, presumably, have been more powerful than either King George VI or Queen Elizabeth II.[62]

Through mythology, Tolkien celebrates the Kingship of Christ and the benign purposes of the divine Creator-King. The perfect image of God as Man is seen in Christ. In the Story, Aragorn is the ideal 'reflection' of Ilúvatar in Middle-earth. At Aragorn's coronation, significantly aligning the thrones of heaven with the thrones of earth, Gandalf says, like an archbishop as he crowns Aragorn, "Now come the days of the King, and may they be blessed while the thrones of the Valar endure!"[63]

The Development of Tolkien's Ideal of Kingship

Sam Gamgee, described by Tolkien in the letter of 1951 to Milton Waldman as the chief hero",[64] wished to learn the poem about the "mighty kings in Nargothrond and Gondolin".[65] Like Sam, we can 'look back' to "The Fall of Gondolin", the manuscript of which was, Christopher Tolkien says, the "original one of the tale, dating from 1916-17",[66] where we find the first impressions of Tolkien's ideal of kingship.

At the very beginning of his writing career, Tolkien depicted King Turgon of Gondolin as a shrewd and wise king, who kept his city completely hidden from the wiles of Morgoth; another Noldor, King Finrod, King of Nargothrond, who prophesied an 'intervention' of Ilúvatar, as a good and gracious King, both wise and just, and the King of the Teleri, King Thingol of Doriath, as a great and noble king. Thingol was married to the Maia (angel), Melian, who enclosed the realm with an enchanted barrier for its protection. A distant forbear of King Aragorn, she thus gave him angelic ancestry. Tolkien portrays these kings in his early mythology as not dissimilar to the Anglo-Saxon kings. The Elven Kings were good, heroic kings in a long struggle against Morgoth, even if at times capable of employing expediency.

As John Garth says in *Tolkien and the Great War* (2003), "How strange it is that J.R.R. Tolkien should have embarked upon his monumental mythology in the midst of the First World War, the crisis of disenchantment that shaped the modern era".[67] Tolkien, a Second Lieutenant fighting on the Somme, lost many (if not most) of the friends he had known at King Edward the Sixth School in Birmingham. Garth says that the Elves in "The Fall of Gondolin" are "tall, fierce, and grim". He points out that in a letter to Christopher Tolkien during the Second World War, Tolkien said that he realised that he (Christopher) desired to express his *"feeling* about good, evil, fair, foul in some way", and 'looking back', he added significantly, "In my case it generated Morgoth and the History of the Gnomes". Garth tells us that "Faerie had not entirely captured his [Tolkien's] heart as a child", and that "Tolkien declared much later: 'A real task for Fairy-stories was wakened by philology on the threshold of manhood, and quickened to full life "by war."'[68]

It is not surprising that the seemingly endless Wars of Beleriand in which the Elven Kings (the "Gnomes") and the Chieftains of the Men of the Three Houses of the Edain were involved, found heroes who fought relentlessly, in spite of *feeling* sure they were fighting a hopeless series of battles against the powerful Morgoth. Tolkien relates their plight as being like the Beowulfian "common tragedy of inevitable ruin".

He creates a vivid picture of ultimate despair, in which the "history of kings and warriors", here that of the Elven Kings and Edain warriors, is like that of the kings in *Beowulf*, where "all glory . . . ends in night".[69] Tolkien's Chieftains of the Edain develop into *Kings* as a reward for their constancy and their heroic efforts in these wars. Eärendil, one of their number, obtained aid from the Valar, which defeated Morgoth in the Last

Battle. The Valar rewarded the Edain with the island realm of Númenor, and with the divinely authorised gift of *kingship*, as Tolkien revealed it. The elevation from Chieftains to Kings was, indeed, a development for the Edain, but *not* exactly for Tolkien, whose notion of kingship was already present in the Elven Kings. As Christopher Tolkien said of Middle-earth, the "development was seldom by rejection" but more like the "growth of legends among peoples".[70]

This is also what happens in the development of Tolkien's idea of kings and their kingship. By tracing the history of his kings over the many years spanned by his mythology, it is possible to infer that he saw his idea of a *king* as largely already there *ab initio*. Tolkien maintained that he did not so much 'invent' his story, but rather that he actually 'discovered' it, that it was, in fact, there all the time, waiting to *be* discovered. It seems, therefore, that Tolkien's idea of *kings* and *kingship* are gradually *becoming* throughout his legendarium in a sense, as St. Augustine once put it, 'what they already *are*'. For example, the Vala Manwë develops in Tolkien's own estimations until he is, and is named, the fullness of what it means to be *King* of the Valar, Elves and Men. His attributes are, as Tolkien said in his story generally, 'discovered' by the author, as he had put it himself.

Thus, Tolkien *discovered* that Manwe is *not* just a Lord, but is a King. He has the authority – Ilúvatar's authority – to reign and rule. This, of course, invited the question: Is then Ilúvatar a King? Tolkien never actually *called* Him King. He does, however, name the chief of the Valar *King*. Tolkien's vision of *king* was there then from the first, his vision of Manwë *and* the almost immortal Elven kings, what may we conclude of Ilúvatar?

Tolkien said that the Arthurian myth "contains the Christian religion", and for reasons he would "not elaborate", he thought that was "fatal", and that "myth and fairy-story must, as all art, reflect and contain in solution elements of moral and religious truth (or error), but not explicit, not in the known form of the primary 'real' world".[71] In the light of this, I suggest that not only did Tolkien *unconsciously* model his mythological god, Ilúvatar, on Yahweh, but that, at the same time, he *instinctively* deliberately refrained from ever calling him *King*, though He was indeed just that. Tolkien desisted consciously to obviate any hint of parody or allegory, which would in his view have greatly weakened the power of his Myth *qua* Myth. In contrast to the Arthurian legends, Tolkien did not wish to let *his* myth 'contain' the Christian religion, though it *did* come 'near' to it at times, he set out to tell a good story rather than to preach.[72]

A development is found as Tolkien's creation myth itself grew, but very gradually, as Christopher Tolkien said, like the legends of peoples. He also said that the creation myth emerged from the first, "with solidity and completeness". In the "Music of the Ainur" in *Lost Tales*, written while Tolkien was working on the Oxford English Dictionary, Ilúvatar had propounded a theme to the Ainur, telling them that "Even now the world unfolds and its history begins".

As much as thirty later, in the last version of 'The Music' (the Ainulindalë), the "most significant difference", says Christopher Tolkien, is that "The Ainur's first sight of the World was in its actuality, not as a vision that was taken away from them and only given existence in the word of Ilúvatar: Eä! Let these things be",[73] indeed a gradual development. In *Lost Tales*, Tolkien developed the idea that Ilúvatar would devise that Men should "design their life beyond even the original Music of the Ainur",[74] thus covertly allowing the Christian virtue of Hope of eternity to emerge. In *The Silmarillion* (1977), a much later development appears, *viz.* that Tolkien explicitly includes the "gift of freedom", and the gift to "seek beyond the world". He now calls "Death" the "gift of Ilúvatar".[75] Tolkien develops the notion that Manwë's royalty infers, though he does not say this directly, that Ilúvatar, whose vicegerent he is, is also inherently essentially royal. Tolkien had 'discovered' that the Lord of the Valar, Manwë, was actually their King, and also that he had been created in the *thought* of Ilúvatar. As His vicegerent, he had inherited His quintessential Kingship, the Mystique of royalty of which Nicolson had spoken (though *he* had not supposed divine provenance for it).

As Manwë developed from being a Lord to a King, so, without any "rejection" of his present qualities, Tolkien deepened his delineation of this Vala. In the "Ainulindalë" in *The Lost Road*, he was not only described as being "not fain of his own honour, nor jealous of his power", but additionally, we hear that he "ruleth all to peace".[76] Melkor (Morgoth), however, in the early part of the legendarium rebelled against Ilúvatar and waged seemingly endless wars against the Elven kingdoms, without claiming the kingship of the Earth. Tolkien's vision of Morgoth as a tyrant develops, when Morgoth illicitly demands a kingship to which he is not entitled. Eventually, in the post-*Lord of the Rings* version of the 'Ainulindalë', Tolkien clinched the idea of Morgoth's intended tyranny, when he claims the Earth as his "own kingdom".[77]

Tolkien develops his vision of all the angelic beings, the Valar, as well as Manwë and Morgoth, from his creation myth onwards, as they go on 'becoming what they already are in Ilúvatar's *thought*. They are a joyous, collegiate society – a society created by Ilúvatar – and are a reflection of the angels around Yahweh and His Court. As early as the *Lost Tales* (edn. 1983), the Valar were asked by Ilúvatar to 'adorn' His Creation, but they were *not* asked to give it being, that is to say, they took no part in its actual creation, any more than did the angelic beings of the Old Testament. However, later, in *Morgoth's Ring*, Tolkien developed their role (though not actually radically changed it) when they *were* "engaged in a demiurgic labour",[78] but even then only to aid the construction of the earth, and not to create it. Tolkien's *final* assessment of their function was that they were "to exercise delegated authority in their spheres (of rule and government, *not* creation, making or re-making)".[79] The Valar granted the island of Númenor to the Edain – the second ones – the Elves being the Firstborn Children of Ilúvatar – as their reward in the wars against Morgoth. Tolkien developed – or rather deepened – his idea of kings with the Númenórian Kings' belief in and worship of Ilúvatar at the Hallow in their three annual festivals, reminiscent of both the ancient Hebrew and the Celtic festivals. Perhaps the most significant development, which did not cause any underlying changes in Tolkien's ideal of kingship, is found in his being 'freed' by the Celtic myths and the medieval Romance poets, including the poet of *Sir Gawain and the Green Knight*, which he edited with E. V. Gordon in 1925.

This emancipation is from the somewhat constricting influence of the pagan beliefs entrenched in the northern spirit of being heroic but hopeless. Tolkien says although the Christian poet of *Beowulf* tries to present *his* story as a purely pagan story of kingship, ideas about heaven "inadvertently escaped from Christian poetry".[80] This is perhaps what happened when Tolkien, inadvertently or otherwise, allowed King Finrod to foresee an 'intervention' by Ilúvatar, an 'inadvertence' that came close to 'parody'. However, by the time of *The Lord of the Rings*, much Celtic influence, and the heroism in Romance poetry had been brought to bear. Aragorn, while acting in keeping with the 'northern spirit of courage', without *certain* 'hope', heroically pursued the hobbits, and encouraged Gimli the Dwarf and Legolas the Elf to do likewise. Nevertheless, Aragorn, whose name Estel actually means 'hope', came to have the Christian hope of life, as he put it, "beyond the circles of the world".[81] Some at least of what Christopher Tolkien calls the "wholly different mode" [82] of *The Lord of the Rings* is, perhaps, due to what Tolkien said of *The Return of the King*, that it contains . . . much of what I personally have received from the study of things Celtic". Tolkien 'absorbed' the Christian virtue of 'hope' in his 'Story'.

Of the Christian aspects of Tolkien's Story, he said to Father Murray in a letter of 1953, "*The Lord of the Rings* is of course a fundamentally religious and Catholic work".[83] In spite of his natural assertion, it seems true to say that some of what he refers to as specifically Roman Catholic is, in fact, what we may call mainstream Christian, for example his references to the connection between Waybread, lembas, and the bread of the Eucharist. However, the prayers to Elbereth and the character of Galadriel and the Virgin Mary, are, perhaps, seen as belonging to the Roman Catholic Church.

Tolkien's Christian belief is also seen in King Aragorn's hope of life beyond the circles of the world, showing that his kingship ultimately derives from Ilúvatar. Although a pagan king in the mythology, Aragorn, as a type of Christ, remains sufficiently 'absorbed' in the Story as not to lessen the power of Tolkien's myth. In the light of God the divine King, His glory reflected in Man, His Vicegerent in Middle-earth, in what ways, then, do the respective ideals of kingship, divine and human, coalesce in the writings of the three central Inklings?

PART FOUR

Insinuated Republic – Constitutional Monarchy – King in Council

Chapter Twelve

The Inklings and the Place of Royalty

Conclusions

Majesty and grace are in the royal office
Monarchy in some form is universal
for it seems to be a necessity in government.
John Buchan, The King's Grace (1935), p.158.

The three central Inklings, Charles Williams, C.S. Lewis and J.R.R. Tolkien, present us with three partially coinciding views in their ideals of kingship. They had much in common in their ideas as mid-twentieth-century writers; they had a profound belief in *Christus Rex*, who reigned "from the tree",[1] as Pelikan put it. They could all draw on Frazer and Nicolson, classical, Anglo-Saxon, medieval and early-modern sources. For example, Tolkien seems less directly influenced by Dante than either Williams or Lewis when it comes to constitutional monarchy. In *De Monarchia*, I, iii, Dante had said, for instance, that "the being [is in existence] for the sake of the operation",[2] a being that includes the king and his function. Nevertheless, as is not surprising with such original thinkers, they do, in fact, manifest some telling differences in outlook, not least in how they regard the office of King.

Williams believes in the concept of a Monarchy that essentially engenders egalitarian qualities, where a Republic has "insinuated itself beneath the folds of a Monarchy",[3] as Walter Bagehot puts it. Lewis, on the other hand, asserts that "monarchy is the channel through which all the vital elements of citizenship"[4] trickle and, to obviate tyranny, the King's power needs limiting in a Constitutional Monarchy. However, Lewis is much less sympathetic than Williams to republican egalitarianism and more interested in civic responsibility than in civic rights. Tolkien, viewing the matter differently from both Williams and Lewis, and the most unreconstructed monarchist of them all, believes in the idea of the King in council, with his "unquestioned decision in debate".[5] It is helpful, in the cause of clarity, to draw parallels by comparing both their similarities of view and their differences of opinion, by considering them separately.

Divergences in the Inklings' Ideals of Kingship

Many of the differences between the three writers' ideals of kingship are not widely divergent, but rather of a more subtle nature, although some of the differences are, nevertheless, quite fundamental. Williams's king, like the Anglo-Saxons, leads and protects his people, and reminiscent of the *Rex Pacificus*, brings 'peace and plenty' to the realm, as, indeed, did King Solomon. Lewis, on the other hand, who fought in the Great War and taught Anglo-Saxon at Oxford, is keen to limit the king's power to prevent the risk of tyranny. Lewis wished to limit the power of the king, and reminds us of the Anglo-Saxons, who in their "coronation ceremony . . . put limits and conditions on the king", at the same time as rallying "loyalty to his person and to the office".[6] Tolkien, however, was influenced by wide Germanic attitudes to kingship. He looked to the continental background to *Beowulf* rather than to a narrowly Anglo-Saxon setting. Christopher Tolkien said that his father "developed certain original theories, especially in connection with the appearance of Hengest in the Old English poem, *Beowulf*".[7] These 'theories' included the northern "theory of courage", a belief that engendered winning the esteem of one's peers by offering "absolute resistance, perfect because without hope",[8] a theory reflected in King Aragorn. The stern outlook of the Anglo-Saxons was later modified through Celtic influence to include a more positive Christianised idea of 'hope', even "beyond the circles of the world". [9]

Although Tolkien, as a Christian, *believed* in *Christus Rex*, he did *not* present his ideal king, Aragorn, as having been actually 'modelled' on Him. Tolkien 'absorbed' Christ into his story, making Aragorn a type of Christ, while avoiding any kind of allegory or parody of Christianity. Lewis presented his lion-King, Aslan, and Maleldil in the science-fiction trilogy, as allegorically *representing* Christ. Williams 'models' his ideal king on Christ, King of love and King of glory, though he says that King Arthur cannot emulate His kingship, unless reconciled to God through the Grail. As vicegerents, Williams and Lewis's kings are not only 'reflections' of God, but rather they are either metaphorical, allegorical presentations or modelled on Him. On the Tolkien's mythological King of the Valar, Manwë, is the vicegerent of Ilúvatar, whose kingship is 'reflected' in King Aragorn, Tolkien's ideal king. Aragorn is a 'rightful king' in Middle-earth, whose kingship is itself appointed by the Valar, and is thus divinely authorised by, and reflective of, Ilúvatar Himself.

According to Lewis, obedience is due to God, the divine King and, by extension, to His vicegerent, the earthly king. This is because of God's declaration, 'I AM', referring to both His 'Absolute Being' and 'Absolute Beauty', and also to His creative activity and His claim to Sovereignty. Williams does *not* specifically emphasise obedience as such, but also does he look for co-inherence, a living-in-and-for each other, a Pauline idea that includes the king with his people. Tolkien, by contrast, presents a picture of a king, Aragorn II, who listens to his Great Council, somewhat like Richard II, and is then obeyed without question. Obedience is *not* discussed as a concept by Tolkien, but is implicit in his 'Story' where, for instance, Ilúvatar *is* obeyed by the Valar, with the exception of Morgoth. Creation itself received its 'Being' through obedience to Ilúvatar's royal command: "Eä! Let these things Be!"

All three writers abhor, as Nicolson said of the ancient Romans, the man who becomes a tyrant and who, as Aristotle said, "seized kingship, and perverted it for their own benefit".[10] Nevertheless, the Inklings' individual concepts of a tyrant are not identical. Williams, though he profoundly detests injustice, presents us with a so-called tyrant, whom King Arthur has to remove from the as yet untamed land of Logres. Williams's overstated 'tyrant' is King Cradlemas who, not even a 'barbarian', was merely the last "sinister representative of the Roman civilisation".[11]

Williams's Headless Emperor of P'o-Lu is certainly more unpleasant than Cradlemas, but though Williams describes his threat as 'spiritual' rather than physical, his evil qualities are rather understated and are, perhaps, mollified by Williams's belief that "the whole universe is known to be good".[12] Lewis's idea of a tyrant is of a person rather more wicked than merely 'sinister'. His White Witch in the *Narnia Chronicles* is ostensibly a queen, the self-styled Queen of Narnia, who attempts to dominate the land, entirely for her own evil pleasure, having already destroyed the world of Charn. She is, in fact, the deadly enemy of Aslan, whom she sacrificed, allegorically representing Christ. The Queen perverts the Aristotelian archetypal idea of rulership by claiming to be Queen without the support of public approbation. A tyrant (though not a king but a god), and the other side of the same coin, who features in *The Last Battle* (1956), is the demon god of Calormen, Tash, who, diametrically opposed to Christ, actually feeds on the sacrificial blood of his people, a real perversion of the laws of nature and morality.

Tolkien's tyrants are perhaps even *more* deadly than those of Williams, or even of Lewis, displaying seemingly limitless power that they employ ruthlessly to achieve their own selfish ends. His tyrants first appear among the Valar, those angels whom the mythological god, Ilúvatar, had invited to share the developing of His designs for the world to which He had already given Being, that is to say, had created *ex nihilo*. The supreme example of an evil tyrant in Tolkien's *Legendarium* is the Vala, Morgoth. As Christopher Tolkien says in his "Introduction" to *The Tale of the Children of Húrin* (2007), Melkor (Morgoth) had "become permanently incarnate, in form a gigantic and majestic, but terrible King in the north-west of Middle-earth".[13] In *The Lost Road* (1987), Morgoth, without any right whatsoever, "forged for himself a great crown of iron, and he called himself The King of the World".[14] In Tolkien's 'sub-created' world, the author is able to create instances of dreadful 'evil' – the result of which is *much more* than a mere absence of 'good'.

In *The Children of Húrin*, Morgoth epitomises the sheer extremity of his degraded mind in a conversation with Húrin.

I am the Elder King: Melkor, first and mightiest of all the Valar, who was before the world, and made it. [Tolkien's image of 'evil'] The shadow of my purpose lies upon Arda, and all that is in it bends slowly and surely to my will. But upon all whom you love my thought shall weigh as a cloud of Doom, and it shall bring them down into darkness and despair. Wherever they go, evil shall arise. Wherever they speak, their words shall bring ill counsel. Whatsoever they do shall turn against them. They shall die without hope, cursing both life and death.[15]

Morgoth's lieutenant, Sauron, even more *insidiously*, spread his evil into the whole of Middle-earth, as the evil 'Shadow' that is more difficult to overcome. Evil, as against an absence of 'good' is seen personified in the tyrant, the Witch-King of Angmar, who had been lured into Sauron's service by the deceitful offer of a Ring of Power. Supposing himself to be working for his own ends, he was in reality giving unremitting obedient service to his tyrannical master. Sauron had once been a Maia, a lesser angel who had become another would-be king of Middle-earth. Tolkien said more, in both senses, than Williams or Lewis on the subject of tyrants. The vividness of the Inklings' portrayal of *good* kings is, to an extent, in proportion to the intensity of the evil depicted in their tyrants, their 'perverted' kings. Williams was decidedly ambivalent concerning the use of physical force to remove a tyrant, whereas both Lewis and Tolkien had no hesitation in doing so, perhaps a reflection of the fact that they had both served as soldiers but, for reasons of health, Williams had not.

Williams's 'good' king is the legendary King Arthur, a Christian king who ruled justly in Logres before it became Britain. Williams's ideal expectations of a king are found in Arthur, though being presented as legendary, he seems more distant from the reader that the historical kings in the biographies of James I and Elizabeth I. Lewis's 'good' kings are found in his allegorical stories, and again feel somewhat removed from the reader's experience, though they are readily imagined. Tolkien's 'good' kings, on the other hand, in particular Aragorn, are presented ostensibly as actual history, and even though mythological, are *received* by the reader more sympathetically, and as immediate and (almost) familiar. Their 'history' takes place in what readers often say *feels* like recognisable surroundings. This may well be why Christopher Tolkien said that it is difficult to realise that the whole thing "exists only in the mind". To repeat, he told me he might have said this "in opposition to those who claim to find its origin in some known part of the physical world".

Lewis demonstrates a belief in *democratised* kingship, encapsulated in Ransom who, in *Perelandra*, 'enacts' Christ, and discovers that he *is* the miracle sent to rescue the King and Queen of that planet from an attack on its innocence. In accepting his individual responsibilities, he exemplifies *democratised* kingship, the idea expressed by the French Jesuit, Jean-Pierre de Caussade, that people can "all surrender themselves to his [God's] action", and that "every soul can aspire to a crown".[16] Neither Williams nor Tolkien maintain any such notion as *democratised* kingship.

Williams and Lewis accept the need for order in society, though they do not view the matter identically. This sense and concept of order goes beyond individual responsibility as found in Lewis's *democratised* kingship, and regards the whole society as responsible for the right use of individual functions that contribute to the good of the whole body politic. Williams finds order in his mythological Emperor of Byzantium who, Lewis said, "symbolises God", and who thus mirrors divine order. Williams symbolises order as the 'straight hazel stick', whether used for exact measurement or the harsh discipline of slaves. He sees order signifying the pattern for right kingship, as it enables the independent life of co-inherence. He sees a reflection of the divine King's perfection.

However, Lewis believes in the centrality of the concept of Hierarchy, God the heavenly King at the apex and the earthly king as His vicegerent, to both of whom obedience is due. This is, to Lewis, a matter of loving response to the divine King's love, not one of coercion. He speaks of "the reconciliation of order and freedom",[17] and the delight he sees in the order of "dancing a minuet".[18] Tolkien does not express a belief and comfort in hierarchy as such, though it is, in fact, implicit in his story, nor does he define an idea of order. However, he does, indeed, evince a profound *sense* of order, 'absorbed', as he puts it, in his 'Story'. There we find a 'sub-created' world, as he calls the fictional world he invented or, as he says, 'discovered', a world he made acting in what he saw as his most God-like capacity, that is, being creative.

There is a 'reflection' of the Creator-King's activity in Tolkien's secondary world, an ordered world which, as C.S. Lewis reminds us, is complete with its own myths, history, languages, palaeography, flora, fauna, geography, geology and theology, orders of beings, and "is a world full of creatures beyond count".[19] Tolkien's Creation myth of his possibly unique fictional world is arguably influenced by the medieval description of the angels singing continuously around the throne of God, since Tolkien knew the medieval concept of the Music of the Spheres. Boethius spoke of the harmonising of beings that helped to "produce the plenitude of creation".[20] Tolkien's mythological god, Ilúvatar, likewise brought *his* world into 'being' through imagery of themes of music, similarly creating an ordered world.

Tolkien came very close to the parody he wished to avoid, when King Finrod prophesied that Ilúvatar would one day intervene and come into the world in person (as the ancient Hebrews believed that Yahweh would do on their behalf) to prevent the evil wiles of Morgoth from thwarting His purposes of joy for His creatures. Tolkien came no nearer than this to a direct expression of his Christian beliefs about the Incarnation of *Christus Rex*. As he said, it was "surely not parody".

Lewis, on the other hand, in a direct contrast, apart from his overtly Christian theological writings, manifested an Anselmian view of salvation that he allegorically represented in *The Lion, the Witch and the Wardrobe* in the sacrifice of the Lion King, Aslan, where He Substituted Himself for the traitor, Edmund, whose price of redemption had to be paid to the Emperor-over-Sea, who represents God the Father. Likewise, if the mythological planet in *Perelandra* should fall to Professor Weston, the Unman's temptations to disobey Maleldil, representing Christ, "this world also would hereafter be redeemed", and there would be "some act of even more appalling love, some glory of yet deeper humility",[21] indicating another act of Substitution.

Williams, in a somewhat similar approach to Lewis's, believes that the highest level of Christian dogma is that of "Exchange between men and God in the single Person".[22] Lewis said of Williams's idea of Atonement that it can be "summed up" in three propositions. First, there is "Substitution". Second, we can "Bear each other's burdens", and thirdly, Williams speaks of "Exchanges". Williams did, in fact, devote a whole chapter in *He Came down from Heaven* (1938) to "The Practice of Substituted Love".[23] *Christus Rex* 'saved' His people. Williams's earthly king is there to 'serve' his people, as befits a Christian king, rather than be served by them. In the *Arthuriad*, Williams had broached the question: is "the king made for the kingdom, or the kingdom made for the king"?[24] His answer is encapsulated in his quotation from Dante that he places significantly at the beginning of the *Arthuriad*: "The proper operation (working or function) is not in existence for the sake of the being, but the being for the sake of the operation" (*De Monarchia*, I, iii). The king is clearly there to serve.

The King's reconciliation is found in the image of the grail. Williams believes that it will prove efficacious in reconciling King Arthur and "King Pelles in Broceliande, / the holder of the Hallows",[25] the spear of Longinus, with which Christ was wounded, the nails used in the Crucifixion and above all, the grail, all of which are found at the sacred Carbonek in the care of the wounded King. In "Notes on the Arthurian Myth" in *The Image of the City* (1958), Williams, referring to the wounded King, said of the dolorous blow, itself an image of the Fall, that it "has to work itself out through the King",[26] that is, the King must be reconciled to God through the grail. Lewis believes the king is there not so much to 'serve' as to '*pre-serve*' his people from the Fall and its disastrous effects, as did Ransom in *Perelandra*, by enacting Christ, and epitomising *democratised* kingship, as I said, in the acceptance of his individual responsibilities. He actually *becomes* the Fisher-King, the wounded King, reminiscent of Logres and the Pendragon, and takes a meal of bread and wine, with distinctly Eucharistic overtones, reminding us of Williams's emphasis on the Grail. The focus, in Lewis's idea, of the King's function is of spiritual preservation, rather than a mere political protection of his subjects. For example, in *The Last Battle* (1956), Lewis had no qualm about letting all the Narnians die, but is keen to encourage them, led by the High King, Peter, to take the ultimate step, trusting the royal and divine Lion, Aslan, and walk through the mysterious door into the paradisal world of eternity. Tolkien makes no direct mention of the king serving the people or of preserving them from perdition, and does not refer to the Fisher-King, the wounded King. He *does* however, see his ideal king, Aragorn, as having (almost Christian) hope to go beyond "the circles of the world"[27] into the joy he trusts Ilúvatar purposes for Man.

Nevertheless, Tolkien's primary concern for the King is that in Middle-earth he will persistently and heroically struggle against omnipresent evil, and courageously defend his people (both Men and Hobbits) against the ubiquitous snares of the would-be King, Sauron, and *lead and protect* them in a land of peace and plenty, where the King's justice prevails. We see in this ideal a convergence of the Davidic Kings in the Old Testament, and the Homeric Kings, in their mutual idea of a Shepherd-king.

Coinciding Concepts of Kingship

Williams, Lewis and Tolkien were Christian writers who believed in the idea of a Christian king, whether this was directly stated or, as Tolkien puts it, a belief that inevitably gets "taken up" in his Story.[28] All three Inklings see their king as God's vicegerent. Approached from individual angles, Williams models his ideal king on Christ, (even though King Arthur cannot actually emulate Him), and regards the king as God's Vicegerent, his 'anointed one', like King David.

The Inklings all believed that glory pertains to the King whether he is found in actual history, in an allegory or yet in a mythological Story set in a secondary world. Williams believed that the king reflects the Glory that Yahweh radiated when he "entered the sanctuary".[29] He saw Christ's glory mirrored in the earthly king, as is apparent in his biographies of James I and Elizabeth I, and in the legendary King Arthur, *after* he was anointed and crowned.

Lewis, on the other hand, spoke of Joy rather than directly of glory. He told, however, of the Creator-King's Absolute Beauty. Furthermore, in *Out of the Silent Planet*, his imagery depicts "planets of unbelievable majesty", planets observed by Ransom journeying to Malacandra, and "celestial sapphires, rubies, emeralds and pin-pricks of burning gold",[30] evoking an atmosphere suggestive of both the glory of Creation, and the splendour of royalty. Lewis referred in *Letters to an American Lady* to the "glories and dangers and responsibilities" attaching to monarchy, when he described the coronation of Queen Elizabeth II.[31] In *The Book of Lost Tales*, Tolkien talks of both glory and splendour. When the Ainur "bowed" to Ilúvatar, an action redolent of 'majesty', Ilúvatar "unfolded a history" to them, a history unequalled in its "glory and splendour".[32] The glory of which Tolkien spoke is, of course, the *heavenly* glory that belongs to the divine King, Ilúvatar, and also to the majestic Ainur.

Tolkien's idea of earthly glory is seen when Sauron, the would-be King of Middle-earth, fell, and the messenger sings, "Sing and be glad, all ye children of the West, for your King shall come gain", the song echoing Psalms 33 and 24, inviting the "King of Glory" traditionally interpreted with Christocentricism, as Christ, to come in.[33] Tolkien's emphasis here is of the glory that directly reflects divine glory, where Williams and Lewis both stress the glory of earthly kings, or the glories of creation as *perceived* by Man. Akin to glory is 'Holiness'. Lewis found a cool morning innocence" in George MacDonald's *Phantastes*, and "a new quality: holiness".[34] Lewis said in a letter of 1st July 1930 to his friend Arthur Greeves, "The light of holiness shines through William Morris's romanticism".[35] Lewis linked the idea of holiness with the Kingdom of God. Lewis said in a letter to his American friend, Sheldon Vanauken, "Seek ye first the Kingdom of God . . . Your part is through what you are already doing . . . the increasing effort after holiness".[36]

Tolkien does not actually use the word *King*, or God, for Ilúvatar his mythological god, nor parallel royal words, such as *reign* or *rule*, but in the cosmology uses the word *king* in a negative sense for Morgoth (also called Melko), and for Manwë in a positive sense. However, in his Creation myth, Tolkien's distinctive model for kingship is found in God as the Creator. He presents us with a perfect paradigm of God's kingship, compatible with Judaeo-Christian belief. Williams does not refer directly to the idea of hierarchy. However, he saw King Arthur as the Pendragon, the Chief and leader in the battles. He did not refer to his position in a hierarchy, but rather as a king who would serve his people in a spirit of co-inherence. Lewis, on the other hand, was keen to promote the importance he saw in hierarchy, where God is at the pinnacle, and the king at the apex of earthly society.

Tolkien does not actually *discuss* the idea of hierarchy as such; but he does indeed fully accept Ilúvatar in his Story and God in the 'real' world as supreme, and the king on earth, as His vicegerent, to stand at the top of society, with 'unquestioned decision' in debate, as we have seen. Like Yahweh in the Judaeo-Christian tradition, Ilúvatar gave the world its design and created it *ex nihilo*, that is to say, gave it actual 'Being'. The Valar were invited to help, as demiurges, to complete the working out of the plans for Arda, but they did *not* play any part in giving it Being. There is in these comparisons a remarkable resemblance between the scholars' theory of Yahweh as divine King in the Old Testament, and Tolkien's theory of his mythological divine King, Ilúvatar. Williams had seen King Arthur as God's Vicegerent, emphasising the importance of having been, like King David, anointed. Lewis saw the earthly king as having allegiance to God, as it were to the High King, and thus His vicegerent with His authority to rule and reign.

Williams does, indeed, regard the office of the king as holy and his monarchy as sacred in that he is Christ's vicegerent. For instance, he sees

King Arthur's kingship as actually "willed" by God.[37] As he said of King Inkamasi, the king unites within himself his "own individual being and the mysterious night of his *holy* and awful office" (my italics).[38] Nevertheless, he does not actually discuss the notion of holiness as such. Williams is less Eurocentric than Lewis or Tolkien, since he explores *African* kingship, here influenced, perhaps, by Frazer and Rider Haggard.

Tolkien likewise does not discuss the idea of holiness in so many words. He does, however, 'absorb' the idea in his Story. For example, he depicts the Númenórian kings as priest-kings who function in that capacity at their festivals at the shrine called the Hallow, an open-air shrine like that of the ancient Hebrews. The festivals that take place at the Hallow are also reminiscent of the ancient Celtic shrine for the New Year festival, *Samain*, also in an agrarian society. The shrines of the ancient Hebrews had been on High Places for the worship of Yahweh. Similarly, the Hallow was on a 'High Place', made 'holy' for the worship of Eru Ilúvatar.

Lewis sees the earthly king as God's vicegerent, in that the king has allegiance to God, as it were to the High King. However, Tolkien specifically names the King of the Valar, Manwë, as Ilúvatar's Vicegerent. As such, the King is the Judge who brings justice to the realm.

Epilogue
The Inklings and the Wider World of Fantasy

Having explored the writings of Williams, Lewis and Tolkien, we have discovered that their concepts of kingship were largely similar though, as we have seen, their individual ideas showed some differences of extent and emphasis. Their respective backgrounds and circumstances all contributed to their personal outlooks and the tenacity of their devotion to their ideals of kingship. Their 'attachment' to monarchy perhaps varied with their individual geographical and conceptual distances from central London, an emphasis on London that begins with Williams, increases in Lewis and is paramount in Tolkien.

All three Inklings' engagement with conceptualising the ideal of kingship was, to an extent, a response to the perceived crisis of European faith and order, religious and political, after the First World War. This was not uncommon for the era, Eliot had, for instance, built an imaginative structure emanating from the Europe-wide situation in *The Waste Land*. There had, of course, been *other* 'imaginative structures', in writings that the Inklings, as widely-read men would have been familiar with.

Lewis was fully aware that a number of the naturalistic ideas expressed in some contemporary literature were taking 'root' in the popular mind, having engaged with many of these 'imaginative structures'. Lewis had encountered such works of 'fantasy', where he became cognisant of this dangerous risk as an actuality, works of 'imagination' such as Olaf Stapledon's *Last and First Men*, with its godless picture of the universe, set in several different eras, such as Haldane's *Possible Worlds*, where people would 'evolve' and move from planet to planet, and Wells's *Time machine*, with its horrific prognosis for human kind. Lewis's friend Owen Barfield had suggested that we needed to distinguish between what were merely 'sweet delusions' and the 'more perdurable productions of the Romantic spirit', achieved by Coleridge's distinction between *'fancy'* and *'imagination'*. Tolkien had said of *fancy* (or *fantasy*) that its peculiar quality of 'joy' can be experienced as a sudden 'glimpse' of the underlying reality or truth, as in a 'secondary world', where what the author relates is 'true'. Williams's novels, on the other hand, though he does not directly speak of 'fantasy', have frequently been referred to as 'spiritual thrillers' where, for example, 'death' could be overcome by the use of pseudo-scientific techniques. The word 'spirituality' has inherent dangers, as G.K Chesterton pointed out, when he asserted that it is all too easy for a man to think that as he passes from the 'ape', he is necessarily going to the angel, although he could just as well pass to the 'devil'. Lewis took up the challenge to his Christian beliefs by 'smuggling into people's minds' ideas to 'baptise their imaginations', by writing science-fiction (itself a type of fantasy) with a Christian ethos.

For hundreds of years before the Inklings tales of a decidedly fantastic nature had existed, such as *Beowulf*, about which Tolkien had written and lectured, *Sir Gawain and the Green Knight*, which he and E.V. Gordon had edited, Malory's *Le Morte D'Arthur*, which had fired Williams's imagination to write his *Arthuriad*. Tennyson, who had "learned much from the Romantics, was not of their number", as Sir Maurice Bowra said in *The Romantic Imagination*,[1] had called *his* re-telling of the 'tale' an 'idyll', whereas Terence White's 'sequence' of Arthurian novels, *The Once and Future King*, first published in 1958, was a *fantasy* novel with an 'anti-war', or pacifist, message. All three Inklings had themselves been affected by Arthuriana, if with somewhat differing reactions, as has been said. Historians today are still trying to discover just how much Arthurian matter is history, and how much is, in fact, actually *fantasy*. In *The Discarded Image*, Lewis had spoken of a time when 'the very words *story* and *history* had not yet been desynonymised'.

David Lindsay's *Voyage to Arcturus* (1920) with its inherent Calvinism, is a 'spiritual adventure' story, as Lewis put it. However, the world of the genre known generally as fantasy has been in existence from only comparatively modern times, a little over a hundred years, when we include the writings of one of Lewis's heroes, George MacDonald, with his enchanted secondary world in *Phantastes* (1858). The achievements of the Inklings in their 'imaginative' writing is only adequately described as 'phenomenal', quite literally. The enormous success of Tolkien's *The Hobbit*, *The Lord of the Rings* and *The Silmarillion* are astonishing. They are even now very popular with readers, and have been portrayed on BBC radio and watched as films, which have become the scene of many a visit to the film-set of Hobbiton, in what is (almost) a 'fantastic pilgrimage'. Lewis's *The Chronicles of Narnia* and his science-fiction trilogy are still as popular as ever, both with children and adults, who find there something of real spiritual depth. The continuing popularity of Lewis's imagined worlds can be seen with the recent film adaptations. The writings of Williams are experiencing something of a resurgence of popularity, especially his 'spiritual thrillers', with their underlying Christian values. Tolkien is considered the doyen of writers of fantasy. As with Lewis, readers are finding in Tolkien's mythology a profound spiritual meaning to their lives. Tolkien said he was writing about the struggle between 'Good' and 'Evil', and that his main theme was, in fact, 'death', which he explored through comparisons of the different destinies of Dwarves, Elves and Men. There are today many imitators of this type of fiction, writers who mostly seem to find a challenge to write large-scale stories of at least trilogy length. We find, *inter alia*, William Horwood's *The Duncton Chronicles* (1980). Richard Adams's fantasy novel *Watership Down* (1972), relates a tale of animals that inhabit their own cultural and religious structures. Stephen Donaldson, in *Lord Foul's Bane* (1977) and *The Chronicles of Thomas Covenant* (1981), attempts to break the mould of the Tolkienian idea of fantasy. The fantasy stories have tended to become longer, while there seems to be no sign of *any* diminution in the output of the authors who followed in the wake of the Inklings.

The Inklings' own lasting contribution to *fantasy* literature, both brilliantly imaginative and inventively original, was itself written to general very high acclaim by its readers. In Williams, Lewis and Tolkien's 'Stories' we have not only found the central place given to the figure of the king, but also discovered their highest 'Ideals of Kingship'.

Notes

Notes Part One

Prologue

1. I am using this expression in the sense of the term in Continental Philosophy.
2. Williams, C., 1958, "The Cross" in *The Image of the City*, 131-132.
3. Williams, 1912, *The Silver Stair*, 68.
4. That is to say 'inherent' in the three authors' texts, and also 'contextual' in the popular belief of the time.
5. Havard, R.E. & Stephenson in the first *Socratic Digest*, 1942-3.
6. Lewis, 1944, *Socratic Digest*, Number 2.
7. Green & Hooper, 1974, 233.
8. Hooper, 1997, 607.
9. Robinson, 1962, 13, 46.
10. Lewis, 1964b, edn. 1998, 19, 76.
11. Lewis, 1947b, edn. 1998, 5-7, 11.
12. Lewis, 1947a, 17-18, 27.
13. Lewis, 1947b, ed. 1998, 15.
14. Anscombe, 1948, *Socratic Digest*, No.4, Bodleian Library, shelf mark: Per 267e. 20; pp.7-9.
15. Lewis, 1947a, 19.
16. Price, 1948, *Socratic Digest* No. 5, 45.
17. Lewis, 1948a, *Socratic Digest*, No. 5, 48, 50.
18. Immanent, OED.
19. Williams, 1958, 131.
20. Op. cit. 132.
21. Op. cit. 133-134.
22. Williams, 1958, 104, 135.
23. Op. cit. 127-9.
24. Op. cit. 96.
25. Williams, 1958, 96-7.
26. Cavaliero, G., 1983, *Poet of Theology*, 26.
27. Marx, 1843-4.
28. Nicolson, H., 1952, *King George V: His Life and Reign*, 120.
29. Bagehot, W., 1867, edn. 1963, *The English Constitution*, 82, 86, 94, 96, 100.
30. Williams, C., 1934, *James I*, 145.
31. Tolkien, J.R.R., 1981, *The Letters of J.R.R. Tolkien*, 324.

32. Saul, 1999 & 2003, 51.
33. Lewis, edn. 2000b, *Essay Collection and Other Short Pieces*, 140.
34. Lewis, edn. 2000b, 140-141.
35. Tolkien, 1964a, edn. 1975, 49.
36. Shippey, 1982, edn. 1992, 46.
37. Op. cit. 46.
38. My emphasis.
39. Tolkien, 1981, 145.
40. Medcalf, S., 1999, 43.
41. Lewis, 2000b, 213.
42. Lewis, 1964b, 75-6.
43. Lewis, 1964b, 77, 79.
44. Observations made by Stephen Medcalf.

Chapter One

1. Pelikan , 1999, 26.
2. Johnson, ed. Hooke, m1958, 214.
3. This idea was given to me by the Rt. Revd. John Ford, Bishop of Plymouth in a conversation.
4. Chaney, 1970, edn. 1999, 70.
5. Hadfield, A.M., 1959, *An Introduction to Charles Williams*, vii, 11-13, 16, 18, 22, 26, 29.
6. Op. cit. 77, 136-137.
7. Barlow, 1970, edn. 1997, 179.
8. Johnson, ed. Hooke, 1958, 207.
9. Smith, ed. Hooke, 1958, 70.
10. Johnson, ed. Hooke, 1958, 207-208.
11. Bury and Meiggs, 1972, 52.
12. Nicolson, 1962, 13.
13. Frazer, 1905, 253-254.
14. Smith, ed. Hooke, 23.
15. Nicolson, 1962, 64.
16. Burn, A.R., 1965, *The Pelican History of Greece*, 98.
17. Figgis, 1896, & 1970, 4.
18. Buchan, J., 1921, *The Path of the King*, 309-310.
19. Buchan, J., 1935, *The King's Grace*, 158, 160.
20. Williams, C., 1939, *The Descent of the Dove*, 86.
21. Eaton, 1986, *Kingship and the Psalms*, 176-177.
22. Johnson, ed. Hooke, 1958, 206.
23. Widengren, ed. Hooke, 1958, 196.
24. Pelikan, J., 1985 & 1999, 27.
25. Saul, ed. Goodman & Gillespie, 1999 & 2003, 37.
26. Hadfield, A.M., 1983, *Charles Williams: An Exploration of his Life and Work*, 32.
27. Hadfield, 1983, 14-15.
28. Williams & Lewis, 1948, 5-6.
29. Guest, 1906, edn. 1997, 190.
30. Williams, 1958, 179.
31. Williams, 1958, 180.
32. Williams & Lewis, 1948, 37.

33. Op. cit. 82-84.
34. Tennyson, 1969, 4, 7, 9.
35. Williams, 1958, 187.
36. Williams & Lewis, 79.
37. An unpublished letter of Charles Williams, kindly lent by Grevel Lindop.
38. Williams & Lewis, 1948b, 79fn.
39. Williams & Lewis, 1948, 79.
40. Rousseau, edn. 1968, 82.
41. Plato, C. 375 BC, *The Republic*, 45.
42. Williams, 1958, 82.
43. Williams, 1943, 40.
44. Hadfield, 1983, 32.
45. Lewis, 1948b, 97.
46. Taliesin (one 's'), 6th Century, d. 1988, 30.
47. Russell, 1946, edn. 1961, 535.
48. Williams, 1958, 137.
49. Op. cit. 105.

Chapter Two

1. Williams, 1944, edn. 1991, 107.
2. Williams, 1931a, & posthumously 1948, 96.
3. Williams, 1917, 22.
4. Lewis, 1942, issued 1960, 73 & 78.
5. Williams, 1917, 112-113.
6. Rousseau, 1762, ed.1968, 49.
7. Williams, 1958, xlvi.
8. Op. cit. 149.
9. Hadfield, 1983, 32.
10. Op. cit. 112.
11. Cavaliero, 1983, 13.
12. Williams, 1938, 83, 87-8, 92.
13. Op. cit. 93-4, 96-8, 100.
14. Op. cit. 101.
15. Williams, 1938, 101, 103-4.
16. Op. cit. 107-8, 112-113, 120.
17. Hadfield, 1959, 33.
18. Williams, 1912, 51.
19. Hadfield, 1983, 18.
20. Henderson, 1995, 150.
21. Williams, 1912, 75.
22. Henderson, 1995, 150-151.
23. Williams, 1912, 81.
24. Hadfield, 1959, 33.
25. Williams, 1958, 137.
26. Beasley-Murray, 1962, 987.
27. Williams, 1912, 8-9, 46, 83, 89,
28. Williams, 1912, 68.
29. Cavaliero, G., 1983, 26, 29, 32-3, 151.
30. Williams, 1912, 46.

31. Williams, 1912, 86.
32. Williams, 1912, 87.
33. Williams, 1912, 72.
34. Williams, edn. 1991, 103-4.
35. Williams, edn. 1991, 103-4.
36. ed. Guest, C. 13th century, 1906, edn. 1997, 197.
37. Williams, 1991, 104, 107.
38. Lewis, 1948b, 104-105, 107.
39. Anne Ridler in Williams, 1958, xxxii.

Chapter Three

1. Conquest, 1957, 42-5.
2. Op. cit. 44-5.
3. Medcalf, S., Unpublished comments made in the margin of p.45 of the Conquest essay.
4. Conquest, 1957, 46, 48-50.
5. Op. cit. 50-51.
6. Op. cit. 54-55.
7. Conquest, 1957, 54-5.
8. Pitt, 1957, 331-332.
9. Op. cit. 333.
10. Williams, 1958, 176.
11. Pitt, 1957, 333.
12. Williams, edn. 1991, 36.
13. Op. cit. 54-55.
14. Lewis, 1948b, 133-134.
15. Williams, edn. 1991, 53-54.
16. King, 1990, 73.
17. Williams, edn. 1991, 54.
18. King, 1990, 73.
19. Williams, edn. 1991, 55.
20. King, 1990, 74.
21. Williams, edn. 1991, 55.
22. King, 1990, 74.
23. Op. cit. 81.
24. Lewis, 1948b, 109-110.
25. King, 1990, 82.
26. Ridler, A. in Williams, 1958, xxxvi.
27. Pitt, 1957, 333.
28. Lewis, 1948b, 139-140.
29. Pitt, 1957, 334.
30. Lewis, 1948b, 142.
31. Lewis, 1948b, 139.
32. Williams, edn. 1991, 269, 284.
33. Williams, 1937b, 26-8, 155, 161.
34. Spacks, 1957, 336-7.
35. Ridler in Williams, 1958, xxx.
36. Williams, edn. 1991, 280-281.
37. Williams, edn. 1991, 107, 269.
38. Lewis, 1948b, 99.

39. Dronke, ed. & tr. 1949, 47-48.
40. Cavaliero, 1983, 101.
41. Williams, 1958, lii.
42. Lewis, 1948b, 99.
43. Williams, edn. 1991, 105.
44. Op. cit. 39.
45. Lewis, 1948b, 115-116. Lewis, 1948b, 116.
46. Lewis, 1948b, 116.
47. Williams, edn. 1991, 40.
48. Ridler quoting Patmore in Williams, 1958, xxxviii.
49. Op. cit. xxxii.
50. Op. cit. xxv.
51. Op. Cit. xxxiii.
52. Op. cit. opp. lviii.
53. Op. cit. xliii.
54. Cavaliero, 1983, 9, 15.
55. Hadfield, 1983, 219.
56. King, 1990, 55 & 71.
57. Op. cit. 64.
58. Op. cit. 128, 139.
59. King, 1990, 65.
60. Williams, 1958, 87.
61. Williams, edn. 1991, 119.
62. King, 1990, 64.
63. Williams, 1912, 23.
64. Cavaliero, 1983, 133.
65. Henderson, 1995, 140-141.
66. Ridler in Williams, 1958, xvi.
67. Hadfield, 1983, 151.
68. Lewis, 1948b, 141-142.
69. Williams, edn. 1991, 104, 107.
70. Sayers in Williams, 1934, edn. 1951, xiii.
71. *Chambers Dictionary of Etymology*, ed. Barnhart, R.K., 1988, reprinted 2003. Chambers Harrap, Edinburgh, p. 610.
72. Williams, edn. 1991, 69.
73. Cavaliero, 1983, 125.

Chapter Four

1. Williams, 1912. 68, 75.
2. Lewis, 1948b, 104.
3. King, 1990, 19.
4. Lewis, 1948b, 100.
5. Williams,1945, 5.
6. Williams, 1958, 178.
7. Hadfield, 1983, 118-119.
8. Williams, 1927, 'Victorian Narrative Verse' in *The Image of the City*, edn. 1958, 1.
9. Williams, 1934, reprinted 1951, 4-5.
10. Op. cit. 33.

11. Williams, 1934, 55.
12. Williams, 1937a, 36-37, 91, 167.
13. Williams, 1937a, 216.
14. Williams, 1936b, 10.
15. OP. cit. 14-15, 25.
16. Op. cit. 54-55.
17. Williams, 1936b, 57, 60-62, 73-74.
18. Williams, edn. 1991, 35-36.
19. Williams, 1937a, 1, 34-35.
20. Op. cit. 51.
21. Op. cit. 59.
22. Williams, 1937a, 65.
23. Figgis, 1896 & 1970, 6.
24. Churchill, W., 1675, *Diva Britannici*, Rare Books, University of Exeter.
25. Williams, 1934, 8, 18, 170, 192.
26. Nicolson, H.,1962, *Monarchy*, 13.
27. Op. cit. 138-9, 145, 196.
28. Williams, 1934, 139, 141,
29. Op. cit. 130, 227, 253.
30. Op. cit, 142, 218, 254.
31. Stephen Medcalf mentioned the notion of the Tory and Whig prayers.
32. Cranmer, 1549, 194-5.
33. Williams, 1934, 140.
34. Cavaliero, 1983, 33 & 36.
35. Williams, 1936a, 12, 38, 50, 138.
36. Op. cit. 49, 89, 93.
37. The idea of being a 'ritualist' came from Dr Brian Horne in a conversation.
38. Williams, 1941, edn. 1959, 33, 42, 77-80.
39. Williams , 1936a, 57, 112, 135-6.
40. Op. cit. 44, 63, 82.
41. Williams, 1931 / 1948, 12, 59-61.
42. Williams, 1931a, 1948, 61, 63-4.
43. Williams, 1931a, 1948, 66-7, 89, 104, 107.
44. Williams, 1912, 83.
45. Williams, c., 1931a, 1948, 182.
46. Op. cit. 183.
47. Williams, 1931a, 1948, 184-5.
48. Op. cit. 185, 207.
49. Op. cit. 207-8, 210, 212.
50. Williams, 1948, 84.
51. Williams, 1958, 132.
52. Williams, edn. 1991, 36.
53. Williams, 1948, 79.
54. Williams, edn. 1991, 269.
55. Williams, edn. 1991, 107.
56. Williams, 1948, 28.
57. Williams, edn. 1991, 177.
58. Op. cit. 56.
59. Williams, 1943, 40.

60. Williams, 1934, 139, 227.
61. Williams, 1931a, edn. 1948, 185.
62. Williams, 1958, 175.
63. Dodds in Williams, edn. 1991, 280.
64. Acton, 1887, in Creighton, 1904, Vol.1, Ch. 13.
65. Williams, edn. 1991, 57 & 280.
66. King, 1990, 44.
67. Williams, edn. 1991, 35.
68. Lewis, 1948b, 120.
69. Hadfield, 1983, 27.
70. Nicolson, 1962, 318.
71. Nicolson, 1952, 145.
72. Bradford, 1989, 279-280.
73. My emphasis, Crellin, 1996, 509.
74. Williams, 1937, in an unpublished letter to Anne Ridler, née Bradby.
75. Williams, 1958. 188.
76. Hadfield, 1983, 192.
77. Lewis, 1948b, 186.
78. Williams, 1933, *Reason and Beauty in the Poetic Mind*, 9.
79. Williams, 1932, *The English Poetic Mind*, 3.
80. Cavaliero, 1983, *Charles Williams: Poet of Theology*, 9-10.
81. Pelikan., 1999, *Jesus through the Centuries*, 26.
82. Williams, 1931a & 1948, 185.
83. Williams, 1937, in an unpublished letter to Anne Ridler, née Bradby.
84. Williams, ed. Dodds, Ll.D., 1991, *Arthurian Poets*, 284.
85. Op. cit. 30.
86. Williams, 1945, 5.
87. Lewis, 1948b, 104.
88. Ridler, in Williams, 1958, xxx.
89. Williams, ed. Dodds, 1991, *Arthurian Poets*, 107.
90. Figgis, 1896 & 1970, 4.
91. Rousseau, J.-J., 1762, edn. 1968, 34, 64, 82.
92. Berlin, I., 1958, published 1969, "Two Concepts of Liberty" in *Four Essays on Liberty*, 165.
93. Berlin, 1969, 167.
94. Ridler in Williams, 1958, xvi.
95. Hadfield, 1983, 151.
96. Bradford, S., 1989, *George VI*, 279.

Notes to Part Two

Chapter Five

1. Hooper, 1996, 3.
2. Hooper, W., 1996, edn. 1997, *C.S. Lewis: A Companion and Guide*, 3-5, 8-9.
3. Lewis, 2000b, 139.
4. Pelikan, 1999, 26.
5. Lewis, C.S., 1979, a letter of 1931, in *They Stand Together*, 428.
6. Lewis, 1948b, "Williams and the Arthuriad" in *Arthurian Torso*, 123.
7. Lewis, 1947, 1st. edn. of *Miracles*, 159.

8. Lewis, 1943, *Perelandra*, 145.
9. De Caussade, 1741, edn. 1966 & 1981, *L'Abandon à la Providence Divine*, 45.
10. Lewis, 1938, *Out of the Silent Planet*, 28.
11. Downing, D.C., 1992, *Planets in Peril*, 29.
12. Lewis, 2000, *Letters, Volume 1*, 911.
13. Lewis, 1967, edn. 1971, *Letters to an American Lady*, 18.
14. Widengren, ed. Hooke, 1958, 169-170.
15. Barlow, 1970, edn. 1997, 61.
16. Stenton, F.M., 1943, 35.
17. Lewis, 1947, edn. 1998, *Miracles* (revised), 7.
18. Barlow, 1970, edn. 1997, 179.
19. Lewis, 1967, 18.
20. Downing, 1992, 15.
21. Lewis, 1955, 22fn.
22. Barfield, 1989, 111.
23. Op. cit. 107.
24. Lewis, 1955, 23-24.
25. Ibid.
26. Nicolson, 1962, 17.
27. Hooper, W., 1996 & 1997, *C.S. Lewis: A Companion and Guide*, 597-598.
28. Lewis, 1955, 45.
29. Downing, 1992, 16.
30. Lewis. 1938, 11.
31. Lewis, 1979, 135.
32. Lewis, 1955, 64, 188, 190.
33. Lewis, 1943b, 48.
34. Hooper, 1996, 148.
35. Butler, 1903, edn. 1936, 131.
36. Lewis,1969, 1950 Preface, 4-5.
37. Duriez, 2002, 61.
38. Lewis, 1936, edn. 1958, 45.
39. Lewis, 1979, 445fn.
40. Lewis, 1933, 3rd edn. 1977, 9, 11-12.
41. Lewis, 1955, 217, 218-9, 223.
42. Lewis, 1979, 239.
43. Green & Hooper, 1974, 90.
44. Lewis, 1969, 135, 152,177.
45. Hooper, 1996, 157.
46. Lewis, 1955, 215, 217.
47. Lewis, 1955, 217, 218-9, 223.
48. Lewis, 1938, 25.
49. Downing, 1992, 13, 28.
50. Lewis, C.S., Bodleian Library, (Modern Papers), Oxford, Undated MS, Dep. D. 241, 1.
51. Eliot, T.S., 1928, edn. 1970, 7.
52. Op. cit. 111.
53. Nicolson, 1962, 280.
54. Eliot, 1928, 35.
55. Hooper, 1996, 559.
56. Lewis, 1955, 208-9.

57. Downing, 1992, 35-6, 46.
58. Barfield, 1999, 41.
59. Downing, 1992, 31.
60. Downing, 1992, 29, 44.
61. Lewis, edn. 2000a, 911.
62. MacDonald, G., 1883, 3rd printing of 1912, printed 2000, 14, 98-99.
63. Vanauken, S., quoting Lewis, 1977 & 1978, 206.
64. Downing, 1992, 39.
65. MacDonald, 1872, reissue 1964, edn. 1996, 236.
66. Lewis, 1955, 210.
67. Chesterton, 1925, 9, 18.

Chapter Six

1. Lewis, 1955, 218.
2. Lewis, 1955, 210.
3. Hooper, 1996, 182-3.
4. Duriez, 2002, 165.
5. Lewis, 1933, issued 1977, 218.
6. Lewis, 1979, 369.
7. Lewis, C.S., Bodleian Library, (Modern Papers), Oxford, Undated MS, Dep. d. 241, p.62. Information given by the Marion E. Wade Center, Wheaton College, Illinois, USA; and by Walter Hooper.
8. Downing, 1992, 27-8.
9. Lewis, 1966, 261.
10. Downing, 1992, 40-41.
11. Hooper, 1996, 207.
12. Lewis, 1938, edn. 2000, 68, 95, 122-4.
13. Op. cit. 125-6, 143.
14. Lewis, 1947a, (first edition), 159.
15. Chesterton, 1925, reprinted 1953, 181.
16. Chesterton, 1909, edn. 2002, 164.
17. Lewis, 1951, edn. 1998, 43.
18. Lewis, 1954, 187.
19. Lewis, 1938, edn. 2000, 148.
20. Tolkien, 1954a, 137.
21. Lewis, 1943a, edn. 2000, 148.
22. Lewis, 1938, edn. 2000, 69.
23. Lewis, 1942, 78.
24. Lewis, 1938, edn. 2000, 144.
25. Lewis, 1938, edn. 2000, 105, 124, 140, 142, 144,
26. Lewis, 1938, edn. 2000, 81, 84.
27. Lewis, 1955, 190.
28. Chesterton, 1909, edn. 2002, 198-9.
29. Lewis, 1938, edn. 2000, 77.

Chapter Seven

1. Op. cit. 68, 73, 123.
2. Hooper, 1996, 281.

3. Lewis, 1940, edn. 1957, 133, 137-8.

4. Lewis, 1943a, edn. 2000, 217.

5. Lewis, 1955, 221-2.

6. Lewis, 1952, 49.

7. Lewis, 1933, edn. 1977, 228.

8. Lewis, 1943a, edn. 2000, 132.

9. Rousseau, 1762, edn. 1968, 64.

10. Lewis, 1938, edn. 2000, 68.

11. Lewis, 1940, issued in Fontana 1957, 138.

12. Lewis, 1940, issued in Fontana 1947, 138 & 141.

13. Lewis, 1940, issued in Fontana 1957, 109, 111, 115.

14. Lewis, 1933, issued 1977, 228-9.

15. Lewis, 1966, 261.

16. Downing, 1992, 64.

17. Lewis, 1942, 73.

18. Mascall, 1949, edn. 1966, 3.

19. Lewis does not say which work of Montaigne's he is referring to, I suggest perhaps it was 'Apologies'. Lewis, 1942, 74-6.

20. Op. cit. 76-79.

21. Downing, 1992, 73.

22. Lewis, 1942, v.

23. Williams, 1958, 129-130.

24. Lewis, 1961b, issued in Fontana 1967, 52-3.

25. Lewis, 1947a, 1st Edition, 150.

26. Downing, 1992, 72.

27. Williams, 1958, 128.

28. Lewis, 1942, 74-5.

29. Lewis, 1956, edn. 1978, 54, 63, 136.

30. Op. Cit. 210, 235, 284.

31. Hooper, 1996, edn. 1997, 252.

32. Lewis, 1956, edn. 1978, 302, 305, 320.

33. Lewis, 1956, edn. 1978, 305-6, 316-7.

34. Medcalf, 1991, 136.

35. Lewis, 1947a, (first edition), 150.

36. Lewis, 2000b, 139.

37. Lewis, 1943a, edn. 2000, *Perelandra*, 79.

38. Plato, revised 1987, xxxv.

39. Lewis, 1943a, edn. 2000, *Perelandra*, 20.

40. Lewis, 1966, 283.

41. Lewis, 1943a, edn. 2000, *Perelandra*, 42, 59.

42. Chesterton, 1909, edn. 2002, 211.

43. Lewis, 1943a, edn. 2000, *Perelandra*, 59-60.

44. Morris, 1858, 1907, edn. 1973, 26.

45. Lewis, 1943a, edn. 2000, *Perelandra*, 63.

46. Tolkien, 1981, 192.

47. Lewis, 1943a, edn. 2000, *Perelandra*, 65.

48. Golding, 1955, 191.

49. Kinkead-Weekes & Gregor, 1967, edn. 1985, 124.

50. Lewis, 1942, 84.

51. Downing, 1992, 102, 104.
52. Lewis, 1938, edn. 2000, 11.
53. Lewis, 1955, 214,
54. Lewis, 1943a, edn. 2000, 66.
55. Lewis, 1964b, edn. 1998, 24-25.
56. Lewis, 1943a, edn. 2000, 46.
57. Lewis, 1942, 71.
58. Lewis, 1943a, edn. 2000, 61, 68.
59. Traherne, T., 1673-1717, edn. 2002, xvi, 4-5.
60. Lewis, 1943a, edn. 2000, 21, 148-9.
61. Chesterton, 1909, edn. 2002, 87-9.
62. Lewis, 1943a, edn. 2000, 71.
63. Lewis, edn. 2000b, 312-313.
64. Hooper, 1996, edn. 1997, 593.
65. Chesterton, 1909, edn. 2002, 104-5.
66. Stoppard, 1972, revised edn. 1986, 43-45, 75.
67. Hunter, 2000, 19, 63-4, 71, 73-4.
68. De Caussade, 1741, edn. 1966 & 1981, 16.
69. Lewis, 1943a, edn. 2000, 77.
70. Manlove, 1975, edn. 1987, 129.
71. Manlove, 1975, edn. 1987, 129.
72. Op. cit. 130-131, 136.
73. Lewis, 1943a, edn. 2000, 118, 213-4.
74. Lewis, 1943, edn. 2000, 211 & 216.
75. Williams, 1931a, published 1948, 208, 215.
76. Knight, 1990, 162-3.
77. Williams, 1931a, published 1948, 198.
78. Middleton & Rowley, edn. 1998, 21, 88, 88fn, 132.
79. Manlove, 1975, edn. 1978, 148-149.
80. Lewis, 1943a, edn. 2000, 67.
81. De Caussade, 1741, edn. 1966 & 1981, 26, 38, 70.
82. Lewis, 1967, printed in GB 1969, 18.
83. De Caussade, 1741, edn. 1966 & 1981, 45.
84. Lewis, 1943a, edn. 2000, 134.
85. Orwell, 1949, edn. 1987, published 1989, 268, 276, 297, 300.

Chapter Eight

1. Lewis, 1943a, edn. 2000, 141, 145,
2. Op. cit. 154.
3. Lewis, 1942, 90.
4. Lewis, 1943a, edn. 2000, *Perelandra*, 95.
5. Chesterton, 1908, Introduction by Medcalf, edn. 1996, x.
6. Lewis, 1943a, edn. 2000, 115, 133.
7. Brockbank, 1962, 9.
8. Lacey, Alan, *The Oxford Companion to Philosophy*, OUP (1995) ed. Drabbe, M.
9. Lewis, 1964, Canto edition 1994, reprinted 2000, 17-18.
10. Lewis, 1943a, edn. 2000, 92, 94-5, 122.
11. Chesterton, 1909, edn. 2002, 220.
12. Mann, 1947, edited & translated 1968, 477.

13. Downing, 1992, 39.
14. Mann, Th., 1933-4, *Reden und Aufsätze (4)*, p. 744, information given me in a conversation with Roland Spahr, editor and publisher of Mann's writings, at S. Fischer Verlag, Frankfurt-am-Main.
15. Lewis, 1943a, edn. 2000, 10.
16. Mann, 1933-4, *Reden und Aufsätze*, 744.
17. MacDonald, 1883, third reprinting of 1912, ed., reproduced 2000, 96.
18. Lewis, 1943a, edn. 2000, 130-1.
19. Chesterton, 1909, edn. 2002, 201.
20. Lewis, 1961a, 9, 38.
21. Lewis, 1952, 150-152.
22. Lewis, 1943, 58-59.
23. Golding, 1956, paperback, 1962, 193-195.
24. Op. cit. 197.
25. Hynes, Golding quote, edn. 1985, 129.
26. Chesterton, 1925, reprinted 1993, 243.
27. Lewis, 1943a, edn. 2000, 147, 157-8, 172, 174, 185-6.
28. Williams, 1931b, edn. 1952, 201-2.
29. Duriez and Porter, 2001, 186.
30. Widengren, ed. Hooke, 1958, 196.
31. Lewis, 1942, 119, 121.
32. Lewis, edn. 2000b, 340.
33. Lewis, 1945, edn. 2000, 151, 322.
34. Op. cit. 35.
35. Duriez, 2002, 14.
36. Op. cit. 198.
37. Lewis, 1943b, issued in Fount paperbacks 1978, 46-7.
38. Lewis, 1945, edn. 2000, 62.
39. Lorris, G. de, c.1225, edn. 1994, 3.
40. Lewis, 1945, edn. 2000, 65, 143, 149.
41. Op. cit. 157-8.
42. Matthews, 1994, 139.
43. Williams, 1948, 17. Williams's spelling of Melchizedeck.
44. Lewis, 1945, edn. 2000, 158.
45. MacDonald, 1872, Puffin Books 1964, edn. 1996, 234.
46. De Caussade, 1741, 1996, ed. & tr. 1981, 26.
47. Lewis, edn. 2000b, 332-337.
48. Lewis, edn. 2000b, 335, 337, 339.
49. Lewis, 1952, 183.
50. Lewis, 1945, edn. 2000, 190-1.
51. Op. cit. 322-3.
52. Lewis, 1943, edn. 2000, 111, 157.
53. The square brackets are Hooper's, and probably denote an illegible word by wear or damage.
54. Hooper, 1996, 581.
55. Lewis, 1967, 18.
56. De Caussade, 1741, edn. 1966 & 1981, 45.
57. Barfield, 1989, 107.
58. Lewis, 1943b, 48.

59. Hooper, 1996, 148.
60. Lewis, 1969, 1950 Preface, 4-5.
61. Duriez, 2002, 239.
62. Lewis, 1969, 135.
63. Lewis, 1955, 215-218, 223.
64. Op. cit. 218.
65. Lewis, 1955, 210.
66. Lewis, 1936, Paperback 1958, 45.
67. Lewis, 1933, third edition 1977, 11-12.
68. Lewis, Bodleian Library, (Modern Papers), Oxford, Undated MS, Dep. D.241, p. 62.
69. Lewis, Bodleian Library, Undated MS, Dep. D. 241, p.1.
70. Hooper, 1996, 559.
71. Downing, 1992, 29.
72. Lewis,1938, 144.
73. Lewis, 1942,73.
74. Lewis, 1943, 149.
75. Lewis, 1943a, edn. 1987, 145.
76. Lewis, 1943a, edn. 2000, 144.
77. Williams, 1937, in an unpublished letter to Anne Ridler, née Bradby.
78. Lewis, 1956, published by Puffin 1964, 143, 163, 165.

Notes to Part Three

Chapter Nine

1. Tolkien, J.R.R., ed. Carpenter, H. & Tolkien, C., 1981, 37, 55, 218.
2. Carpenter, H., 1977, *J.R.R. Tolkien: A Biography*, 10-11, 13.
3. Tolkien, J.R.R., ed. Carpenter, H. & Tolkien, C., 1981, 215.
4. Tolkien, 1964b, edn. 2001, 21 & 37.
5. Pelikan, 1999, 26.
6. Tolkien, J.R.R., 1966, Forword to *The Lord of the Rings*, 7.
7. Tolkien, 1977, *The Silmarillion*, 20.
8. Tolkien, 1981, *The Letters of J.R.R. Tolkien*, 342.
9. Saul, N., 1999 & 2003, ed. Goodman & Gillespie, *Richard II: The Art of Kingship*, 52, 62, 76, 82.
10. Carpenter, H., 1977, *J.R.R. Tolkien: A Biography*, 128.
11. Lewis, 1948b, 104.
12. Smith, S. in *Myth, Ritual and Kingship*, ed. Hooke, S.H., 1958, 23.
13. Tolkien, J.R.R., 1977 ed. Tolkien, C., *The Silmarillion*, 26, 40.
14. Tolkien, 1981, 178.
15. Nicolson, 1962, 64.
16. Tolkien, J.R.R., 1983, ed. Tolkien, C., *The Book of Lost Tales*, Part One, 53.
17. Johnson, ed. Hooke, 1958, 214.
18. Shippey, 1982, ed. 1992, 180-181.
19. Widengren, ed. Hooke, 1958, 159, 162.
20. Tolkien, J.R.R., ed. Tolkien, C., 1993, *Morgoth's Ring*, 328
21. Tolkien, 1993, 321, 356.
22. Kilby, C., 1976, edn. In UK 1997, *Tolkien and the Silmarillion*, 59.
23. Tolkien, 1993, 12, 330.

24. Johnson, ed. Hooke, 1958, 206-08.
25. Barlow, 1970, edn. 1997, 179.
26. Chaney, 1970 & 1999, 257-259.
27. Cambridge Guide to Literature in English, Ousby, I, 1993, 1998, p. 1044.
28. Eaton, J., 1976, edn. 1986, *Kingship and the Psalms*, 29, 97-98.
29. Shippey, T., 1982, edn. 1992, 272.
30. Lewis, The Discarded Image, 1964, 179.
31. Tolkien, J.R.R., ed. Tolkien, C., 1983, *The Book of Lost Tales*, Part One, 23.
32. Tolkien, J.R.R., 1936, *Beowulf – The Monsters and the Critics*, 20-23, 39-40.
33. Tolkien, 1954, "The Two Towers" in *The Lord of the Rings*, 22.
34. Tolkien, 1936, 27.
35. Stenton, 1943, 35.
36. Tolkien, 1955, rev. 1966, 136.
37. Tolkien, 1981, 144.
38. Tolkien, 1993, 328, 335, 356.
39. Carpenter, 1977, 92.
40. Tolkien, 1993, 356.
41. Tolkien, 1993, 356.
42. Tolkien, 1981, 267.
43. Tolkien, 1964b, 1988, edn. 2001, viii.
44. Medcalf, 1999, 36.
45. Shippey, 1982, edn. 1992, 47.
46. Tolkien, 1964a, edn. 1975, 17, 41, 49, 70-1.
47. Brown, R.E., 1977 & 1993, *The Birth of the Messiah*, 26.
48. Lewis, 1947b, edn. 1998, 68.
49. Shippey, 1982, edn. 1992, 274.
50. Tolkien, edn. 1981, 333.
51. Tolkien, 1983, 3 & 7.
52. The term "rigorous obliqueness" was suggested by Stephen Medcalf.
53. Tolkien, C., 1983, 4.
54. Tolkien, C., 1983, 4.
55. Lewis, 1964, 179.
56. Tolkien, 1983, 1, 3-4.
57. Stephen Medcalf had told me that this was said in a conversation that he had with Christopher Tolkien.
58. Observation made in a talk in the *Tolkien Teaching Pack*.
59. Tolkien, C., in a letter to me of 17th March, 2005.
60. Carpenter, H., 1977, *J.R.R. Tolkien: A Biography*, 224.
61. Tolkien, 1964a, edn. 1975, 68.
62. Tolkien, op. cit. 17, 41, 49, 68, 70.
63. Lewis, edn. 2000b, 520.
64. Stephen Medcalf mentioned this exception in a conversation with me.
65. Tolkien, 1981, 264-5,
66. Tolkien, 1954 & 1966, *The Fellowship of the Ring*, 41.
67. Tolkien, 1981, 161.
68. Chesterton, 1909, edn. 2002, 50.
69. Tolkien, 1964a, edn. 1975, 120, 123.
70. Tolkien, 1955, revised 1966, *The Return of the* King, 250.
71. Tolkien, 1955, revised 1966, 245.

72. Tolkien, 1964a, edn. 1975, *Tree and Leaf*, 51, 72.
73. Tolkien, 1983, *The Book of Lost Tales, 1*, 56.
74. Tolkien, 1977, *The Silmarillion*, 19-20.

Chapter Ten

1. Tolkien, 1983, 8 & 9.
2. Tolkien, 1977, *The Silmarillion*, 26.
3. Tolkien, 1983, 45, 49, 52-3.
4. Eden, edn. 2003, 183-5.
5. Lewis, 1964; 2000, 222.
6. Tolkien, 1964; 1975, 42-3.
7. Tolkien, 1977, 15.
8. Tolkien, 1983, 53-4.
9. Kilby, 1976, edn. In UK 1977, 59.
10. Tolkien, 1983, 62.
11. Op. cit. 62.
12. Tolkien, 1993, *Morgoth's Ring*, 303-4, 330, 387.
13. Tolkien, 1983, *The Book of Lost Tales, 1*, 59.
14. Tolkien, 1983, 59-60, 63.
15. Tolkien, 1977, 41-2.
16. Tolkien, 1986, *The Shaping of Middle-Earth*, 76, 78, 166.
17. Tolkien, 1986, 262-3.
18. Tolkien, 1987, edn. 1991, *The Lost Road and Other Writings*, 9, 63-4.
19. Tolkien, 1987, edn. 1991, 155-6.
20. Tolkien, 1987, edn. 1991, 156-7, 164.
21. Tolkien, J.R.R., edn. Tolkien, C., 1987, *The Lost Road and Other Writings*, 155.
22. Tolkien, 1987 & 1991, 159, 162-3.
23. Tolkien, 1993, 20.
24. Tolkien, 1987, edn. 1991,
25. Tolkien, J.R.R., edn. Tolkien, C., 1983, 8.
26. Tolkien, 1981, *The* Letters *of J.R.R.* Tolkien, 143, 160.
27. Tolkien, 1981, 172.
28. Tolkien, 1993, 47-8, 51.
29. Tolkien, 1993, 8-9, 11-12.
30. Op. cit. 12, 14.
31. Tolkien, 1977, 18.
32. Tolkien, 1993, 25.
33. Op. cit. 13.
34. Op. cit. 13-14.
35. Tolkien, 1977, 20.
36. Tolkien, 1993, 14.
37. Tolkien, 1977, 20.
38. Tolkien, 1983, 55, 67.
39. Tolkien, 1993, 14-15.
40. Tolkien, 1987, edn. 1991, 64, 163.
41. Tolkien, 1977, 25.
42. Tolkien, 1993, 143, 145.
43. Tolkien, 1977, 21, 25 & 40.

44. Tolkien, 1981,
45. Op. cit. 146, 267.
46. Day, edn. 1998, 78.
47. Clifford, edn. 1990, 1, 030.
48. Eaton, 1976, edn. 1986, 36-7.
49. Tolkien, C., in a letter to me, 17 March, 2005.
50. Bright, 1960, revised edn 1972, 149-150.
51. Op. cit. 147, 149-150.
52. Nicolson, 1962, 17.
53. Bright, 1960, revised edn, 164, 215, 222.
54. Bright, 1960, revised edition 1972, 221-222, 258, 287.
55. Op. cit. 163, 287.
56. Op. cit. 220-222.
57. Mowinckel, 1962, 34.
58. Eaton, 1976, 2nd edn. 1986, 97-8, 172.
59. Op. cit. 29, 120.
60. Goulder, 1982, 86, 89, 123ff.
61. Salvesen, edn. 1998, 133-4, 136-7.
62. Day, edn. Day, 1998, 84.
63. Bright, 1960, revised edition 1972, 153.
64. Clifford, edn. 1990, 1,030.
65. Gillingham, edn. 1998, 222-3.
66. Barton, edn. 1998, 375-8.
67. Day, edn. 1998, 84, 86.
68. Rowland. edn. 1998, 475.
69. Clifford, edn. 1990, 1,030.
70. Tolkien, 1983, 53.
71. Tolkien, 1977, 15, 20.
72. Anderson, edn. 1962, 167.
73. Bright, 1960, revised edition 1972, 450.
74. Stalker, edn. 1962, 233.
75. Flieger, 1983, revised 2002, 53-5.
76. Tolkien, 1981, 284.
77. Davies, edn. 1962,
78. Tolkien, 1983, 49.
79. Tolkien, 1993, 320, 328.
80. Irwin, edn. 1962, 405.
81. An idea suggested by Stephen Medcalf.
82. Chesterton, 1929, 49.
83. Barker, 2004, 17, 25, 37.
84. Barker, 2003, 157.
85. Tolkien, 1977, 15.
86. Hooke, edn. 1962, 180.
87. Tolkien, 1993, 321, 335.
88. Tolkien, 1993. 356.
89. Turner, edn. 1962, 1051-2.
90. Tolkien, 1981, 206.
91. Tolkien, 1980, 166, 223.
92. Bright. 1960, revised edition 1972, 223.

93. Scott, edn. 1962, 40.
94. Hooke, edn. 1962, 178.
95. James, S., 1999, *The Atlantic Celts*, 40.
96. Carpenter, H., 1977, *J.R.R. Tolkien: A Biography*, 223-4.
97. Cunliffe, B., 1997, *The Ancient Celts*, 188-9.
98. Tolkien, 1980, 166.
99. Tolkien, 1977, 261.
100. Shippey, T., 1982, edn. 1992, 180-1.
101. Bright, in *Peake*, edn. 1962, 490.
102. Tolkien, 1981, 160.

Chapter Eleven

1. Tolkien, C. in Tolkien, J.R.R., 1983, 23.
2. Bede, 731, tr., & Intro. 1955, revised 1965, 55-6.
3. Shippey, T., 1982, edn. 1992, 268-9.
4. Tolkien, C. in Tolkien, J.R.R., 1983, 23.
5. Tolkien, C. in Tolkien, J.R.R., 1983, 23.
6. Tolkien, 1982, edn. 1998, 27-8, 33.
7. Tolkien, 1982, edn. 1998, 27-8, 33.
8. Tolkien, 1982, edn. 1998, 3, 33, 63-6.
9. Tolkien, 1936, 'The Monsters and the Critics', 13, 20, 22-3, 27.
10. Tolkien, 1936, 27-8, 31.
11. Tolkien, 1936, 20-3, 39-40, 43, 45.
12. Tolkien, 1954b, revised 1966, 22.
13. Tolkien, 1936, 24.
14. Shippey, 1982, edn. 1992, 184.
15. Tolkien, 1936,
16. Tolkien, 1936, 17-18, 29, 37.
17. Tolkien, 1954a, revised 1966, 137.
18. Tolkien, 1936, 29, 31-3.
19. Tolkien, 1936, 34-6.
20. Tolkien, 1936, 39, 41-42.
21. Op. cit. 43.
22. Anon, edn. Alexander, M., 1973, Penguin Books, London, 151.
23. Op. cit. 39, 41, 42, 44, 45.
24. Tolkien, 1936, 45, 51.
25. Tolkien, 1964a, edn. 1975, *Tree and Leaf*, 149-152.
26. Tolkien, 1964a, edn. 1975, 169-171, 173-4.
27. Sigurdsson, edn. 1992, 213.
28. Barlow, 1970, edn. 1992, 162.
29. Tacitus, P.C., AD 97-98, *Germania*, 112.
30. Tolkien, 1964a, edn. 1975, 166, 169, 172-5.
31. Tolkien, 1964a, edn. 1975, 30, 174.
32. Carpenter, 1977, 89.
33. Shippey, 1982, edn. 1992, 203, 272-3.
34. Op. cit. 112.
35. Tolkien, C. in Tolkien, J.R.R., 1983, 23.
36. Tolkien, 1981, 172.
37. Tolkien, 1981, 288.

38. Op. cit. 326-7.
39. Tolkien, 1981, 215.
40. Op. cit. 237.
41. Tolkien, 1954b, revised 1966, 190.
42. Tolkien, 1954a, 381.
43. Op. cit. 262.
44. Tolkien, 1981, 178.
45. Kocher, 1972, 134.
46. Tolkien, 1964a, edn. 1975,123.
47. Flieger, edn. 2000, 185, 195-6.
48. Tolkien, 1955, revised 1966, 249-250.
49. Lewis, edn. 2000b, 271.
50. Tolkien, 1964a, edn. 1975, 59, 126, 129-131, 134, 136,
51. Op. cit. 135, 143.
52. Tolkien, 1955, revised 1966, 244.
53. Tolkien, 1954a, revised 1966, 157.
54. Shippey, 1982, edn. 1992, 193.
55. Shippey, 1982, edn. 1992, 14, 106,112, 115, 314.
56. Tolkien, 1954a, revised 1966, 376-7.
57. Tolkien, 1981, 206.
58. Chesterton, 1936, 94.
59. Tolkien, 1945b, revised 1966, 284-285.
60. Tolkien, 1981, 324.
61. Op. cit. 65.
62. An idea suggested by Stephen Medcalf.
63. Tolkien, 1955, revised 1966, 246.
64. Tolkien, J.R.R., ed. Carpenter, H. & Tolkien, C., 1981, 161.
65. Tolkien, J.R.R., ed. Tolkien, C., 1983, *The Book of Lost Tales: Part One*, 4.
66. Tolkien, J.R.R., ed. Tolkien, C., 1984, *The Book of Lost Tales: Part Two*, 146.
67. Garth, J., 2003, *Tolkien and the Great War*, xiii.
68. Op. cit. 38-39.
69. Tolkien, 1936, *Beowulf: The Monsters and the Critics*, 23.
70. Tolkien, J.R.R., ed. Tolkien, C., 1983, 8
71. Tolkien, J.R.R., ed. Carpenter, H. & Tolkien, C., 1981, 144.
72. He told Oubouter this, adding that an author's beliefs would come through
    their 'Story'.
73. Tolkien, 1983, 62.
74. Tolkien, 1983, 59.
75. Tolkien, 1977, 41-42.
76. Tolkien, 1987, edn. 1991, 162.
77. Tolkien, J.R.R., ed. Tolkien, C., 14.
78. Tolkien, 1993, 330.
79. Tolkien, 1981, *The Letters*, 146.
80. Tolkien, 1936, *Beowulf: The Monsters and the Critics*, 44.
81. Tolkien, 1955, 344.
82. Tolkien, J.R.R., ed. Tolkien, C., 1983, 4.
83. Tolkien, 1981, 172.

Notes to Part Four

Chapter Twelve

1. Pelikan, J., 1985 & 1999, *Jesus through the Centuries*, 26.
2. Williams, C., 1943, *The Figure of Beatrice: A Study in Dante*, 40.
3. Bagehot, W., 1867, edn. 1963, *The English Constitution*, 94.
4. Lewis, 2000b, 139.
5. Tolkien, 1981, 324.
6. Barlow, 1970, edn. 1997, 61.
7. Tolkien, J.R.R., ed. Tolkien, C., 1983, 23.
8. Tolkien, 1936, 20-21.
9. Tolkien, 1955, revised 1966, 344.
10. Smith, ed. Hooke, 1958, 23.
11. Lewis, 1948b, 104.
12. Ridler in Williams, 1958, *The Image*, xxx.
13. Tolkien, J.R.R., ed. Tolkien, C., 2007, "Introduction" to *The Tale of the Children of Húrin*, 15.
14. Tolkien, 1987 & 1991, *The Lost Road*, 233.
15. Tolkien, J.R.R., ed. Tolkien, C., 2007, *The Tale of the Children of Húrin*, 64.
16. De Caussade, 1741, 1966, edn. 1981, 45.
17. Downing, 1992, 73.
18. Lewis, 1961b, issued in Fontana 1967, 53.
19. Lewis, edn. 2000b, 520.
20. Eden, edn. 2003, 183-5.
21. Lewis, 1943, edn. 2000, 149.
22. Hadfield, 1983, 112.
23. Lewis, 1948, 123.
24. Williams, edn. Dodds, 1991, 36.
25. Williams, edn. Dodds, 1991, 107.
26. Williams, edn. Ridler, 1958, 176.
27. Tolkien, 1955, 344.
28. Tolkien, 1981, 267.
29. Johnson, edn. Hooke, 1958, 214.
30. Lewis, 1938, 28.
31. Lewis, 167, edn. 1971, 18.
32. Tolkien, J.R.R., ed. Tolkien, C., 1983, 53.
33. Shippey, 1982, edn. 1992, 180-181.
34. Downing, 1992, 29.
35. Lewis, edn. 2000a, 911.
36. Vanauken, 1977 & 1987, *A Severe Mercy: With Eighteen Letters by C.S. Lewis*, 206.
37. Williams, ed. Dodds, 1991, 104.
38. Williams, 1931a, edn. 1948, 185.

Epilogue

1. Bowra, M., *The Romantic Imagination*, OUP, Oxford, 1950, 197.

Bibliography

Primary Sources

Lewis, C.S., 1933, first edn. Fount, 1977, *The Pilgrim's Regress*, Fount / Harper Collins, Glasgow.

Lewis, C.S., 1936, paperback 1958, *The Allegory of Love*, OUP, Oxford.

Lewis, C.S., 1938, edn. 2000, *Out of the Silent Planet*, Harper Collins, London.

Lewis, C.S., 1940, Fontana 1957, *The Problem of Pain*, G. Bles, London, Fontana Books, Collins, London & Glasgow.

Lewis, C.S., 1942, issued 1960, *A Preface to Paradise Lost*, OUP, Oxford.

Lewis, C.S., 1942-3, *Socratic* Digest, Number One, Oxonian Press, Oxford. In the Bodleian Library.

Lewis, C.S., 1943, 1946, edn. 1978, *The Abolition of Man*, OUP, London, G. Bles, London, Fount / Collins, Glasgow.

Lewis, C.S., 1943, edn. 2000, *Perelandra*, The Bodley Head, London, Voyager / Harper Collins, London.

Lewis, C.S., 1944, *Socratic Digest*, Number 2, Oxonian Press, Oxford. In the Bodleian Library.

Lewis, C.S., 1945, edn. 2000, *That Hideous Strength*, Bodley Head and Harper Collins, London.

Lewis, C.S., 1947a, (first edn.), *Miracles*, G. Bles, London.

Lewis, C.S., 1947b, edn. 1998, *Miracles*, Fount / Harper Collins, London.

Lewis, C.S., 1948a, *Socratic Digest*, Number 5, Oxonian Press, Oxford.

Lewis, C.S., (with Williams, C.,) 1948b, *Arthurian Torso*, Oxford University Press, London.

Lewis, C.S., 1950, edn. 1998, *The Lion, the Witch and the Wardrobe*, G. Bles, & Harper Collins, London.

Lewis, C.S., 1951, edn. 1970, *Prince Caspian*, Macmillan Publishing Company, New York.

Lewis, C.S., 1952, issued in Fontana, 1955, *Mere Christianity*, Fontana Books, Collins, London & Glasgow.

Lewis, C.S., 1953, Puffin 1965, *The Silver Chair*, G. Bles & Puffin / Penguin Books, Harmondsworth.

Lewis, C.S., 1954, Puffin 1965, *The Horse and His Boy*, G. Bles & Puffin / Penguin Books, Harmondsworth.

Lewis, C.S., 1955, *Surprised. by Joy*, G. Bles, London.

Lewis, C.S., 1956, edn. 1978, *Till We Have Faces: A Myth Retold*, G. Bles, Fount / William Collins Sons & Co. Ltd., Glasgow.

Lewis, C.S., 1961, by Fontana 1967, repr. Fount 1977, *Reflections on the Psalms*, Fount / Harper Collins, London & Glasgow.

Lewis, C.S., 1961, *A Grief Observed*, Faber and Faber, London

Lewis, C.S., 1964a, edn. Canto 1994, repr. 2000, *The Discarded. Image*, Cambridge University Press, Cambridge.

Lewis, C.S., 1964b, G. Bles, edn. 1998, *Prayer: Letters to Malcolm*, Fount / Harper Collins, London.

Lewis, C.S., edn. with a Memoir, Lewis, W.H., 1966, *The Letters of C.S. Lewis*, G. Bles, London; Harcourt Brace Jovanovich, New York.

Lewis, C.S., 1967, first edn. Great Britain 1969, ed. C.S. Kilby, 1971, *Letters to an American Lady*, Hodder & Stoughton, London.

Lewis, C.S., 1969, ed. W. Hooper, 1950 Preface, *C.S. Lewis: Narrative Poems*, G. Bles, London.

Lewis, C.S., ed. W. Hooper, 1979, *They Stand Together: The Letters of C.S. Lewis to Arthur Greeves (1914-1963)*, Collins, London.

Lewis, C.S., ed. W. Hooper, 1991, edn. 1993, *The Diaries - All My Road Before Me*, Fount / Harper Collins, London.

Lewis, C.S., ed. W. Hooper, 2000a, *Collected. Letters, Vol. 1, 1905-1931*, Harper Collins, London.

Lewis, C.S., ed. L. Walmsley, 2000b, *C.S. Lewis: Essay Collection and Other Short Pieces*, Harper Collins, London.

Lewis, C.S., Undated. MS (untitled), the Bodleian Library (Modern Papers), Dep. d. 241.

Tolkien, J.R.R., 1936, 'Beowulf: *The Monsters and the Critics*', The British Academy, Volume XXII, OUP, London.

Tolkien, J.R.R., 1954a, edn. 1966, *The Fellowship of the Ring*, George, Allen & Unwin, London.

Tolkien, J.R.R., 1954b, edn. 1966, *The Two Towers*, George, Allen & Unwin Ltd., London.

Tolkien, J.R.R., 1955, edn.. 1966, *The Return of the King*, George, Allen & Unwin, London.

Tolkien, J.R.R., 1964a, edn. 1975, *Tree and Leaf*, George Allen & Unwin Ltd, London.

Tolkien, J.R.R., 1964b, 1975, 1988, ed. with Intro, C. Tolkien 2001, *Tree and Leaf* (incl. 'Mythopoeia'), Harper Collins, London.

Tolkien, J.R.R., ed. C. Tolkien 1977, *The Silmarillion*, George, Allen & Unwin, London.

Tolkien, J.R.R., ed. C. Tolkien 1980, *Unfinished. Tales of Númenor and Middle-Earth*, George, Allen & Unwin, London.

Tolkien, J.R.R., ed. H. Carpenter, Assist. C. Tolkien 1981, *The Letters of J.R.R. Tolkien*, George, Allen & Unwin, London.

Tolkien, J.R.R., ed. A. Bliss, 1982, edn. 1998, *Finn and Hengest: The Fragment and the Episode*, George, Allen & Unwin, Harper Collins, London.

Tolkien, J.R.R., ed. C. Tolkien 1983, *The Book of Lost Tales: Part One*, George, Allen & Unwin, London.

Tolkien, J.R.R., ed. C. Tolkien 1984, *The Book of Lost Tales: Part Two*, George, Allen & Unwin, London.

Tolkien Teaching Pack, 1995, Harper Collins, London.

Tolkien, J.R.R., ed. C. Tolkien 1986, *The Shaping of Middle-Earth*, Unwin, Hyman Ltd., London.

Tolkien, J.R.R., ed. C. Tolkien 1987 & 1991, *The Lost Road and Other Writings*, Unwin Hyman Ltd, & Harper Collins, London.

Tolkien, J.R.R., ed. C. Tolkien 1993, *Morgoth's Ring*, Harper Collins, London.

Tolkien, J.R.R., ed. C. Tolkien 2007, *The Tale of the Children of Húrin*, Harper Collins, London.

Williams, C., 1912, *The Silver Stair*, Herbert & Daniel, London. British Library, 011649 e 11.

Williams, C., 1917, *Poems of Conformity*, Milford, H., OUP, London. Given to the Library of the University of Sussex.

Williams, C., 1931a & posthumously in 1948, *Shadows of Ecstasy*, Faber & Faber, London.

Williams, C., 1931b, edn. 1952, *The Place of the Lion*, Faber & Faber, London.

Williams, 1932, *The English Poetic Mind*, OUP, Oxford.

Williams, 1933, *Reason and Beauty in the Poetic Mind*, OUP, Oxford.,

Williams, C., 1934, *James I*, A. Baker, Ltd. London.

Williams, C., 1936a, *Queen Elizabeth I*, Duckworth, London.

Williams, C., 1936b, *Thomas Cranmer of Canterbury*, OUP, Oxford.

Williams, C., 1937a, *Henry VII*, Arthur Barker, London.

Williams, C., 1937b, repr. 2001, *Descent into Hell*, W.B. Eerdmans, Grand Rapids, Michigan.

Williams, C., 1938, *He Came Down From Heaven*, Wm. Heinemann Ltd., London.

Williams, C., 1939, *The Descent of the Dove*, The Religious Book Club, London.

Williams, C., 1941, edn. 1959, *Witchcraft*, Meridian Books. Inc. New York.

Williams, C., 1943, *The Figure of Beatrice: A Study in Dante*, Faber & Faber, London.

Williams, C., 1944, ed. A.R King Jr., 2002, *To Michal from Serge*, The Kent State University Press, Kent & London.

Williams, C., 1945, *The House of the Octopus*, Edinburgh House Press, London.

Williams, C., (and Lewis, C.S.), 1948, *Arthurian Torso*, OUP, London.

Williams, ed. A. Ridler, 1958, *The Image of the City*, OUP, London.

Williams, C., ed. D. Dodds, Ll., 1991, *Arthurian Poets: Charles Williams*, Boydell Press, Woodbridge; & D.S. Brewer, Cambridge.

Secondary Sources

Anderson, G.W., in *Peake's Commentary on the Bible*, 1962, ed. M. Black, & H.H. Rowley, Nelson & Sons Ltd., London.

Anscombe, G.E.M., 1948, *Socratic Digest*, No. 4, (Double Number), the Bodleian Library, Shelf mark: Per 267e 20, Oxonian Press, Oxford.

Bagehot, W., 1867, edn. 1963, Intro. R.H.S. Crossman, *The English Constitution*, Fontana / Collins, Glasgow.

Barfield, O., ed. G.B. Tennyson, 1989, *Owen Barfield on C.S. Lewis*, Middletown, Connecticut: Wesleyan University Press, Hanover, USA & London.

Barfield, O., ed. G.B. Tennyson, 1999, *A Barfield Reader*, Wesleyan University Press, Hanover, USA & London.

Barker, M., 2003, *The Great High Priest: The Temple Roots of Christian Liturgy*, T. & T. Clark, London.

Barker, M., 2004, *Temple Theology: An Introduction*, SPCK, London.

Barlow, F., 1970, edn. 1997, *Edward the Confessor*, Yale University Press, New Haven and London.

Barton, J., ed. J. Day, 1998, *King and Messiah in Israel and the Ancient Near East*, University of Sheffield Academic Press, Sheffield.

Beasley-Murray, G.R., ed. M. Black, & H.H. Rowley, 1962, *Peake's Commentary on the Bible*, Nelson & Sons Ltd., London.

Bede, 731, tr. & Intro, 1955, edn. 1965, Sherley-Price, L., *A History of the English Church and People*, Penguin Books, Harmondsworth.

Berlin, I., 1958, 'Two Concepts of Liberty', Publ. 1969, *Four Essays on Liberty*, Oxford University Press, Oxford.

Bradford, S., 1989, *George VI*, Penguin Group, London.

Bright, J., 1960, edn. 1972, *A History of Israel*, SCM Press, London.

Bright, J., ed. Black, M. & Rowley, H.H., 1962, *Peake's Commentary on the Bible*, Nelson & Sons, London.

Brockbank, J.P., 1962, *Marlowe: Dr. Faustus*, Edward Arnold (Publ.) Ltd., London.

Buchan, J. 1921, *The Path of the King*, Hodder & Stoughton, London.

Buchan, J., 1935, *The King's Grace*, University of London Press, London.

Bury, J.B. & Meiggs, R., 1975, *A History of Greece*, 4th edn., Macmillan, London.

Butler, S., Publ. posthumously 1903, edn. 1936, *The Way of All Flesh*, OUP, London.

Carpenter, H., 1977, *J.R.R. Tolkien: A Biography*, George, Allen & Unwin, London.

Cavaliero, G., 1983, *Charles Williams: Poet of Theology*, W.B. Eerdmans, Publishing Co., Grand Rapids, Michigan.

Chaney, W.A., 1970, edn. 1999, *The Cult of Kingship in Anglo-Saxon England: The Transition from Paganism to Christianity*, Manchester University Press, Manchester.

Chesterton, G.K., ed. & Intro. S. Medcalf, 1908, edn. 1996, *The Man Who Was Thursday*, OUP, Oxford & New York.

Chesterton, G.K., 1909, ed. C.M. Kibler, 2002, *Orthodoxy*, Reformation Press, Lenoir, N. Carolina.

Chesterton, G.K., 1925, repr. 1993, *The Everlasting Man*, Ignatius Press, San Francisco.

Chesterton, G.K., ed. J.P. de Fonseka, 1929, *GKC as MC: Being a collection of Thirty-Seven Introductions*, Methuen, London. 33.

Chesterton, G.K., Intro, A. Burgess, 1936, *Autobiography*, Hutchinson, London.

Churchill, W., 1675, *Diva Britannici*, Rare Books, University of Exeter.

Clifford, R.J., ed. P.E. Fink,, 1990, *The New Dictionary of Sacramental Worship*, Gill and Macmillan Ltd., Dublin.

Conquest, R., January, 1957, *The Art of the Enemy*, Essays in Criticism, Vol. VII, No.1, Blackwell, Oxford.

Cranmer, T., 1549, repr., *The First Prayer-Book of King Edward VI*, Griffith, Farran Browne & Co. Ltd, London.

Creighton, M., 1904, *Life and Letters of Mandell Creighton*, Vol. 1, quoting Lord Acton. Longmans, Green, London.

Crellin, V., 1966, *Tongues of Men*, Hutchinson Educational, London.

Davies, W.D., ed. M. Black, & H.H. Rowley., 1962, *Peake's Commentary on the Bible*, Nelson & Sons, London.

Day, J., ed. J. Day, 1998, *King and Messiah in Israel and the Ancient Near East*, University of Sheffield Academic Press, Sheffield.

De Caussade, J-P., 1741, 1966, tr. & ed. K. Muggeridge, 1981, *The Sacrament of the Present Moment*, William Collins Sons & Co Ltd., Glasgow, London.

Downing, D.C., 1992, *Planets in Peril: A Critical Study of C.S. Lewis's Ransom Trilogy*, The University of Massachusetts Press, Massachusetts.

Dronke, U., ed. & tr. & Commentary, 1949, *The Poetic Edda*, Codex Regius MS, 13th Century, Oxford University Press, Oxford.

Duriez, C. & D. Porter, 2001, *The Inklings Handbook*, Azure, London.

Duriez, C., 2002, *The C.S. Lewis Encyclopedia*, Azure, London.

Eaton, J.H., 1976, second edn. 1986, *Kingship and the Psalms*, SCM Press, & JSOT Press, University of Sheffield, Sheffield.

Eden, B.L., ed. Chance, J., 2003, *Tolkien the Medievalist*, Routledge, London.

Eliot, T.S., 1928, ed. V. Eliot, 1970, *For Lancelot Andrewes: Essays on Style and Order*, Faber & Faber, London.

Figgis, J.N., 1896, edn. 1970, *The Divine Right of Kings*, P. Smith, Gloucester, MA.

Flieger, V., 1983, edn. 2002, *Splintered. Light: Logos and Language in Tolkien's World*, The Kent State University Press, Ohio.

Flieger, V., ed. V. Flieger, & C. F. Hostetter, 2000, *Tolkien's Legendarium: Essays on 'The History of Middle-Earth'*, Greenwood Press, Westport, Connecticut, London.

Frazer, J.G., 1905, *Lectures on the early History of the Kingship*, Macmillan, London.

Garth, J., 2003, *Tolkien and the Great War*, Harper Collins, London.

Gillingham, S.E., ed. J. Day, 1998, *King and Messiah in Israel and the Ancient Near East*, University of Sheffield Academic Press, Sheffield.

Golding, W., 1955, *The Inheritors*, Faber & Faber, London.

Golding, W., 1956, edn. 1962, *Pincher Martin*, Faber & Faber, London.

Goodman, A., ed. A. Goodman, & J.L. Gillespie, 1999, *Richard II – The Art of Kingship*, Oxford University Press, Oxford.

Goulder, M.D., 1982, *The Psalms of the Sons of Korah*, University of Sheffield Academic Press, Sheffield.

Goulder, M.D., 1996, *The Psalms of Asaph and the Pentateuch*, University of Sheffield Academic Press, Sheffield.

Green, R.L. & W. Hooper, 1974, *C.S. Lewis: A Biography*, William Collins Sons Co Ltd, London and Glasgow.

Guest, C.E.G., transl. 1906, edn. 1997, *The Mabinogion*, Dover Publications, Inc., Mineola, New York.

Hadfield, A.M., 1959, *An Introduction to Charles Williams,* Robert Hale Ltd., London.

Hadfield, A.M., 1983, *Charles Williams: An Exploration of His Life and Work*, OUP, London.

Henderson, K.L., ed. Horne, B., 1995, *Charles Williams: A Celebration*, Gracewing Fowler Wright Books, Leominster.

Herbert, G., 1633, edn. 1986, in *The Temple*, New English Hymnal, The Canterbury Press, Norwich.

Hooke, S.H., ed. M. Black, & H.H. Rowley, 1962, *Peake's Commentary on the Bible*, Nelson & Sons, London.

W. Hooper, 1996, edn. 1997, *C.S. Lewis: A Companion and Guide*, Fount / Harper Collins, London.

Hunter, J., 2000, *Tom Stoppard*, Faber & Faber, London.

Hynes, S., ed. N. Page, 1985, *William Golding: Novels, 1954-67*, Macmillan, Houndmills & London.

Irwin, W.A., ed. M. Black, & H.H. Rowley, 1962, *Peake's Commentary on the Bible*, Nelson & Sons, London.

James, S., 1999, *The Atlantic Celts*, British Museum Press, London.

Johnson, A.R., ed. S.H. Hooke, 1958, *Myth, Ritual, and Kingship*, Oxford University Press, London.

Kelly, J.N.D., 1958, repr. 1980, *Early Christian Doctrines*, Adam & Charles Black, London.

Kilby, C., 1976, edn. in UK 1977, *Tolkien and the Silmarillion*, Lion Publishing, Berkhamsted, Herts.

King, R.A., Jr., 1990, *The Pattern in the Web*, The Kent State University Press, Ohio.

Kinkead-Weekes, M. & I. Gregor, 1967 & 1985, ed. N. Page, *William Golding: Novels, 1954-67*, Macmillan Publishers Ltd., Basingstoke & London.

Knight, G., 1990, *The Magical World of the Inklings*, Shaftesbury, Element Books, Longmead.

Kocher, P.H., 1972, *Master of Middle-Earth: The Achievement of J.R.R. Tolkien*, Thames and Hudson, London.

Lorris, G. de, C.1225, edn. 1994, tr. & Intro, F. Horgan, *The Romance of the Rose*, OUP, Oxford.

MacDonald, G., 1872, reissue 1964, edn. 1996, *The Princess and the Goblin*, Puffin Group, London.

MacDonald, G., 1883, third printing of 1912 edn., reproduced. 2000, *The Princess and Curdie*, Chatto and Windus, London, Blackie & Son, London, Classic Editions, Johannesen, Whitehorn, California.

Manlove, C.N., 1975, edn. 1987, *Modern Fantasy*, Cambridge University Press, Cambridge.

Mann, Th., 1933-34, *Reden und Aufsätze (4), Tagbuchblätter aus den Jahren 1933-1934*. S. Fischer Verlag, Frankfurt-am-Main.

Mann, Th., 1947, ed. H.T. Lowe-Porter, tr. 1968, *Doktor Faustus*, Penguin Group, London, in Association with Martin Secker and Warburg.

Marx, K., Feb. 1844, 'Introduction' in *A Contribution to a Critique of Hegel's Philosophy of Right*, Deutsch-Französische Jahrbucher, Paris.

Marsh, J., 1962, ed. M. Black, & H.H. Rowley, *Peake's Commentary on the Bible*, Nelson & Sons, London.

Mascall, E.L., 1949, edn. 1966, *Existence and Analogy*, Darton, Longman & Todd Ltd., London.

Matthews, J., 1994, *King Arthur and the Grail Quest*, Blandford, Cassel, London.

Medcalf, S., ed. P.J. Schakel, & C.A. Huttar, 1991, 'Language and Self-Consciousness: The Making and Breaking of C.S. Lewis's Personae', *Word and Story in C.S. Lewis*, University of Missouri Press, Columbia and London.

Medcalf, S., 1999, 'The Language Learned. of Elves: Owen Barfield, 'The Hobbit' and 'The Lord of the Rings'' in *Seven*, Vol. 16, Wheaton College, USA.

Medcalf, S., "A light lunch for the soul" in *The Times Literary Supplement*, 1 October 2004.

Middleton, M. & W. Rowley, ed. & Intro. N.W. Bawcutt, 1998, *The Changeling*, Manchester University Press, Manchester & New York.

Morris, W., 1858, ed. & Intro. Faulkener, P., published. 1907 & 1973, *William Morris: Early Romances in Prose and Verse*, J.M. Dent and Sons, London.

Mowinckel, S., 1962, *The Psalms in Israel's Worship*, Basil Blackwell, Oxford.

Nicolson, H., 1952, *King George V - His Life and Reign*, Constable & Co. Ltd., London.

Nicolson, H., 1962, *Monarchy*, Weidenfeld and Nicolson, London.

Orwell, G., 1949, edn. 1987, published. 1989, *1984*, Penguin Group, London.

Pelikan, J., 1985 & 1999, *Jesus Through the Centuries*, Yale University Press, New Haven & London.

Pitt, V., July 1957, 'The Art of the Enemy', *Essays in Criticism*, Vol. VII, No. 3, Blackwell, Oxford.

Plato, tr. & Intro. H.D.P. Lee, rev. edn. 1987, *The Republic*, Penguin Group, London.

Price, H.H. 1948, *Socratic Digest*, Number 5, Oxonian Press, Oxford

Robinson, J.A.T., 1962, *Honest to God*, SCM, London.

Rousseau, J-J, 1762, edn. 1968, tr. & Intro. C. Cranston, *The Social Contract*, Penguin Group, London.

Rowland, C., ed. J. Day, 1998, *King and Messiah in Israel and the Ancient Near East*, University of Sheffield Academic Press, Sheffield.

Russell, B., 1946, edn. 1961, *History of Western Philosophy*, Routledge, London.

Salvesen, A., ed. Day, J., 1998, *King and Messiah in Israel and the Ancient Near East*, University of Sheffield Academic Press, Sheffield.

Saul, N., ed. A. Goodman & J.L Gillespie, 1999, *Richard II – The Art of Kingship*, Oxford University Press, Oxford.

Sayers, D., 'Introduction' to C. Williams, *James I*, 1934, repr. 1951, A. Baker, Ltd., London.

Scott, R.R.Y., ed. M. Black & H.H. Rowley, 1962, *Peake's Commentary on the Bible*, Nelson & Sons, London.

Shippey, T., 1982, edn. 1992, *The Road to Middle-Earth*, Grafton, Harper Collins, London.

Shorter Oxford English Dictionary, the, OUP, Oxford & New York.

Sigurdsson, J.V., ed. G. Pálson, 1992, *From Sagas to Society*, Hisarlik Press, Enfield Lock, Middlesex.

Smith, S., ed. S.H. Hooke, 1958, *Myth, Ritual, and Kingship*, Oxford University Press, London.

Spacks, P.M., July 1957, 'The Art of the Enemy', *Essays in Criticism*, Vol. VII, No. 3, Blackwell, Oxford.

Stalker, D.M.G., ed. M. Black, & H.H. Rowley, 1962, *Peake's Commentary on the Bible*, Nelson & Sons Ltd., London.

Stenton, F.M., 1943, reissued 1998, *Anglo-Saxon England*, OUP, Oxford & New York.

Stoppard, T., 1972, revised. edn. 1986, *Jumpers*, Faber & Faber, London.

Tacitus, P.C., AD 97-98, published. 1948, *Germania*, Penguin Classics, Middlesex.

Taliesin, (6th century) edn. 1988, tr. & ed. Pennar, M., *Taliesin Poems*, Llanerch Enterprises, Lampeter.

Tennyson, A., ed. & Introduction, C. Andrews, 1969, *Idylls of the King*, Airmont Publishing Co. Inc., New York.

Traherne, T, c.1673-1717, selected. & Intro. Inge, D., 2002, *Thomas Traherne: Poetry and Prose*, SPCK, London.

Turner, N., ed. M. Black, & H.H. Rowley, 1962, *Peake's Commentary on the Bible*, Nelson & Sons, London.

Vanauken, S., 1977 & 1978, quoting Lewis's letter to Vanauken, S., *A Severe Mercy*, Harper San Francisco, New York.

Widengren, G., ed. S.H. Hooke, 1958, *Myth, Ritual, and Kingship*, Oxford University Press, London.

Wood, R.C., 2003, *The Gospel According to Tolkien: Visions of the Kingdom in Middle-Earth*, Westminster John Knox Press, Louisville, Kentucky.

Index